WAKE UP, YOU'RE LIBERAL!
TED RALL

CONTENTS

FOREWORD

GEORGE S. McGOVERN

The late Speaker of the U.S. House of Representatives, Sam Rayburn, was not prone to offering compliments, but he once told a friend and colleague of mine, Frank Thompson of New Jersey: "I like that guy McGovern. He tells it like it is." Since compliments to me from Texas are scarce, I'm still hanging on to those words of forty-six years ago.

So I begin this introduction of a superb book by asserting that I like Ted Rall because he tells it like it is. That is a trait I have long admired in James Carville—President Bill Clinton's brilliant political strategist. The same goes for Bill Moyers, Molly Ivins, Bill Grieder, Ellen Goodman, Lewis Lapham, Victor Navasky, Jim Hightower, Julian Bond, Robert Kuttner, and the magnificent Paul Krugman of the *New York Times*.

Where would we be without these precious few golden voices that serve to keep us in touch with reality and common sense? Tomorrow I am sure I will recall others that should be on this honor roll of journalistic saints.

At the funeral of President Theodore Roosevelt, Gifford Pinchot, the great conservationist and naturalist, said of TR: "He was hated by those who should have hated him and loved by those who should have loved him." The same could have been said of the Hebrew prophets and of the matchless Teacher of Galilee who gave us the Sermon on the Mount.

I don't lay claim to these virtues, but I recognize them when I see them, and I see them plainly in the author of this challenging book. I'm going to send it to Senator John Kerry, another war hero and a great and good man who now appears to be the Democratic frontrunner. This talented candidate will be even better if he reads and absorbs this modern-day "Common Sense." Tom Paine would be proud of Ted Rall, just as I am.

I can only say to you, the reader: Digest every page and become a more enlightened American on the road ahead for this great land we all love.

Senator George S. McGovern, Democratic Party presidential nominee in 1972, is the first United Nations global ambassador on hunger.

CREDO

I believe these things:

Each human being is morally obligated to work as hard as possible to make life as good as possible for himself and his fellow human beings, not in that order.

The burden of the effort to improve life should fall most heavily on those in the best position to do so, beginning with the wealthy, powerful, educated, healthy, grandfathered, and otherwise privileged. This is unfair, yet necessary. If not on them, whom?

We are mortal. Time is the one thing that we have no right to waste. Also: forming a committee to study a problem that common sense makes obvious to almost everyone is a stalling tactic. Anyone who does this is stealing time from life. People who have, therefore, are guilty of a kind of murder.

Any society that can afford it should guarantee its citizens the basic essentials of life: food, housing and medical care. Despite occasional arguments to the contrary, the United States of America is such a society.

Radical problems require radical solutions.

Existing systems are usually adequate to handle modest problems.

Most problems are modest.

Politics is the process of arguing about what is right. Law is the result of politics.

We judge other people's actions based on whether we can imagine ourselves behaving similarly under analogous circumstances. "If I found myself in that guy's position, is there any way I would do what he did?" we ask before passing judgment. Not only do we have the right to pass judgment, we have the obligation to do so.

Not everyone means well.

The United States of America is a grand experiment whose laws and rhetoric are unsurpassed by any in history. All too often, we fail to live up to our ideals. The gap between what we say and what we do—not jealousy, or reverse nationalism, or religion—is the root cause of anti-Americanism around the world.

As citizens of the wealthiest and most powerful nation to have ever existed in the history of our species, there is no excuse for our short-comings. We Americans can accomplish anything we decide to do. When we fail, it is almost always because we have never truly tried.

Our binary political system logically leads to binary thinking, that there are two sides—no more, no fewer—to any issue. A nation whose population exceeds 290 million people has more than two sides for most issues, and should have more than two major politi-cal parties to represent those views.

The two-party system is so deeply entrenched that we should not expect to see it disappear any time soon.

As bad as a two party system is, a de facto single party system is infi-nitely worse.

The American people are fundamentally good, but are more often than not misled by thugs and charlatans.

We Americans are rich and strong, but that doesn't make us any better than citizens of other countries. We are lucky, not special.

Any country that pays women less than men, that executes chil-dren, and whose landscape is dotted with racially segregated hous-ing has a long way to go before telling other countries what to do.

It is true that, in the United States, most poor people live better than many middle-class people do in the third world. So what? That fact doesn't vindicate neglecting the relative poverty in our midst.

Because revolution tends to be anarchic, destructive, and ineffectual, reforming existing systems is usually the wiser course of action.

Sometimes the powers that be are so entrenched and so goddamned stubborn that they refuse to allow significant reforms to occur. At such times, revolution is essential.

Powerful and wealthy people give up some of what they have under two circumstances: when it's taken by force or when violence threatens to take away everything.

There is no reason why someone who mines coal or flips hamburgers or sweeps garbage doesn't earn as much money as a CEO who sits at a desk.

Anyone who is concerned about what kind of sex people have or who they have it with needs to shut the fuck up.

We need a separation between church and state because the state is stupid enough as it is.

It's up to politicians to make citizens interested in voting; citizens are not, nor should they be, required to vote. Nonetheless, citizens do not have the right to ignore current events or to choose to remain uninformed. Citizenship is hard work.

Human behavior is partly explainable by Rall's Theorem, which states the following: The louder someone volunteers, without being asked, that they possess a certain habit or character trait, the more likely it is that they are the exact *opposite* of what they say. For example, the person who suddenly describes herself as a good tipper—without having been asked about it—is not only not an exceptionally generous diner, but is in fact known for being cheap. Rall's Theorem especially applies to public figures. The more that a politician claims to care about the people, or balancing the budget, or defending the country from its enemies, the more likely it is that he is a corrupt, money-wasting traitor. The corollary to the theorem is that the opposite is also true: the less someone throws around an adjective of self-description, the less they think about its subject and the more likely it is to actually apply to them.

A permanent legislature assumes, by definition, that the best solution to any given problem is a new law. Because legislators are judged based on the number and prominence of new laws that they cause to be enacted, lawmaking bodies continue to burden us with new rules past the point at which they are necessary. There should be another body whose sole function is to evaluate existing laws, in order to determine which should be done away with.

Nothing lasts forever.

I reserve the right to change my mind.

WAKE UP, YOU'RE LIBERAL!

chapter 1
WHAT'S
LEFT
MY NAME IS TED AND I'M A DEMOCRAT

> Liberalism is dead, so dead that Democrats have all become
> moderate Republicans, and the heavy hand of Big Government
> is now limp and damp and trembly.
> —Garrison Keillor in *Time*, April 2, 1996

Where are the Democrats?

That question, born of despair for most Americans who pose it and of mere curiosity for the rest, has been floating over this troubled nation since 2002, when the Republican Party consolidated control of all three branches of our federal government. It's also been the agonized cry of wounded liberals for the last four decades. Why don't Democratic politicians fight as hard for their constituents and the issues they care about as their Republican counterparts do for theirs? Why has it been so long since we've seen a major Democratic legislative victory—while the Republicans rack them up one after another? Why do Democratic campaign managers shy away from the vicious tactics that work so well when the GOP deploys similar attacks against them? Why do Democratic presidents consistently bend over backwards to accommodate Americans who voted against them—such as when they appoint Republicans to their cabinets—while Republican presidents rarely make similar concessions?

In short: why are Democrats such pussies?

Several theories come close to explaining the current state of Democratic impotence. Although Dems feed alongside them at the corporate trough, the Republicans' closer alliance with big business puts significantly more money for campaign advertising at their disposal. Ironically—it was originally a progressive idea—the latest round of campaign finance reform slashed "soft money" contributions that mostly went to Democrats, thereby intensifying an already large disparity of political wealth between parties.

Incompetence exacerbates impotence. Traditional Democratic constituencies—poor people, minorities, the young—aren't nearly as likely to show up at the polls as registered Republicans; when they do, they're less likely to vote along party lines. Democrats, as Will Rogers famously observed, don't belong to an organized political party; right-wingers from Genghis Khan to Adolf Hitler have always seemed (and been) a hell of a lot better at getting things done than their counterparts on the left. The repeatedly debunked myth of the liberal media aside, the GOP employs dominant media corporations like Fox News and Clear Channel Communications as powerful party propaganda organs. The Democrats are left to make do with PBS and National Public Radio, outfits with anemic ratings that divide their time between begging for donations and bending over so far backwards to seem fair that they wind up parroting the official conservative line.

Finally, there's the pussy thing. Were you shocked when I used that word? If so, I'm sorry.

No. I'm not.

I recently unleashed the "P" word upon a public forum at a packed house at an appearance in Charlottesville, Virginia, around the time that the United States was preparing to invade Iraq. I used it to make a point about George W. Bush's hypocrisy. When he had had his chance to serve his country in Vietnam, I pointed out, Bush hid out in the Texas Air National Guard and then ran away, first going Absent Without Leave (AWOL) and ultimately being absent so long (1972–74) that he qualifies as a deserter. Such a goddamned pussy, I went on, had one hell of a nerve asking young men and women to fight and die for his war in Iraq.

I still wish that I could have come up with a more eloquent term than that uglyish epithet, but I was so angry, so furious at the carnage that Bush was about to unleash, that I just couldn't think of one at the time. Hypocrite, coward: they just didn't go far enough. I pride myself on talking like an ordinary person. Talking the way most people talk helps you to be an ordinary person. On the other hand, honest talk sometimes leads you to the gutter. Then, as Senator John Kerry learned when he accurately commented that Bush had "fucked up" Iraq, there's a price to pay.

A gasp rose from the audience, followed by wild cheering. I wasn't the only person present who thought that a little cursing suited the desperation of the occasion. Afterward, however, a half dozen earnest-looking women—I'd draw their eyes as perfect little circles—politely confronted me. "We really wish you hadn't used that word," their spokesperson scolded me. Her face scrunched up: " . . . Pussy. It's a terribly sexist term used by those who oppress women."

Jesus fucking Christ.

"Aw, come on," I replied defensively. "You *know* I was talking about Bush, not gender politics." Caught by surprise and unable to formulate an articulate defense, however, I said I was sorry if I'd offended anyone. I wasn't there to make women feel bad. Hell, I imagine that *my* genitals would be pretty angry if someone compared them to a despicable worm like George Bush.

I make mistakes all the time; when I do, I apologize. There's strength in admitting when you're wrong. I've thought about what happened in Charlottesville since then, however, and ultimately decided that I shouldn't have let those upright, uptight Virginians get me down. Bush *is* a pussy, and there was no more effective way to convey that sentiment, no more accurate way to describe the kind of guy who dispatches thousands of young men and women to die on his behalf after he refused to take the same risk himself, than the use of a word lifted from an eighth-grade locker room. (Comparisons with Bill Clinton don't wash here. Clinton dodged the Vietnam draft by taking a college deferment, but he opposed the war. He carried antiwar signs at demonstrations. Bush, however, favored the Vietnam War that he worked so hard to avoid fighting.)

Pussy was the wrong word to use but it was the right thing to say, and dammit, I said it. As for the sexist origins of the word—something of which I'm not entirely convinced, incidentally—who would want to live in a world purged of politically incorrect verbiage? Are there better ways to convey the verbs *to welch* or *to gyp*?

The reaction of Charlottesville's tiny political correctness squad and my susceptibility to being cowed into an inappropriate apology serves as an apt parable about the perils of make-everyone-happy liberalism. For it's not just the Democrats—as in Democratic politicians—who wallow in pussification. Liberal-minded activist groups and individual Democrats do it as well. It's easier to focus on the Democratic Party because they're falling down on the job, but few of their left-wing ideological allies are covering themselves with glory either. While lefties sit around ripping out each other's lungs over insipid semantics, the Right is taking over the world.

WHAT IT MEANS TO BE LEFT
To keep things as simple as possible, the contemporary, postmodern American Left includes mainline liberals, Greens, socialists, and adherents of such political special-interest movements as environmentalism, gay rights, feminism, and animal rights, as well as those who oppose unfettered

MAJOR LEGISLATIVE ACCOMPLISHMENTS SINCE 1980

Democrats	Republicans
The Family Medical Leave Act requires employers to give workers unpaid time off to have a baby	Supply-side economic policies revamped the social, economic, and political structure of the United States to reward individual initiative at the expense of New Deal and Great Society–era social safety net programs
	Flattening income tax rates slashed taxes for extremely wealthy individuals and businesses and increased them for the poor and working class
	Cutting social programs made hundreds of thousands of people homeless, millions more poorer and more miserable
	North American Free Trade Agreement (proposed by Republicans, signed by President Clinton) reduced tariffs, increased corporate profits, and cost hundreds of thousands of American
	Welfare reform (proposed by Republicans, signed by President Clinton) eradicated the proposition, given since FDR, that government should help the weak and downtrodden
	GATT/World Trade Organization (proposed by Republicans, signed by President Clinton) abrogated American sovereignty to increase the ability of international corporations to earn greater profits

"free trade." Like it or not, though numerous minority parties espouse progressive principles, the Democratic Party is the only organization with sufficient mainstream clout to bring these ideas to the forefront of our national debate. Most leftists recognize political reality by seeking to reform, or working within, the Democratic Party structure.

By all rights, this liberal voting bloc—people who care about people and the things around them more than they care about entries in a ledger— ought to enjoy majority status on both a national and local level in virtually every state. In most Americans' minds, after all, the difference between the two biggest parties is best summed up by an explanation my mother composed for me when I was nine years old. As we walked from house to house passing out McGovern for President pamphlets in Kettering, Ohio, the predominantly Republican suburb of Dayton where I grew up, my mom delineated the main difference between the parties of Lincoln and Jackson.

"The Republicans," she explained, recapping the great political realignment of 1932 in eighteen words as she marched up to our neighbor's screen door that brilliant fall evening, "are the party of big business and the rich. The Democrats are for us regular people."

That was more than thirty years ago. A lot has changed since 1972. The Democratic Party has repeatedly sold out its core values. It has frequently failed to look out for ordinary Americans. But the notion that average folks need a party to defend their interests against corporations and the rich remains the party's guiding principle. Perhaps more importantly, most people still belive that the Dems still care about them. That can be a self-fulfilling conceit.

THE DEFEATED DEMOCRATIC MAJORITY

About 80 percent of the American people are "regular" citizens who earn less than $100,000 a year. When you consider how hard demographic and economic trends have been on these typical citizens in recent years—as Juliet Schor showed in her classic work *The Overworked American*, they're working an average of fifty-two hours a week at 1.3 jobs, yet earning significantly less than their less-productive parents—one would think that they would prove receptive to a political party that promises to defend them against rapacious employers, tries to soak the rich so that most people's taxes can be reduced, and attempts to do something about the rising cost of healthcare.

And they are. That's why, throughout the twentieth century, most registered voters have been Democrats.

The future, some say, looks bright for Democrats. In their book *The Emerging Democratic Majority*, John Judis and Ruy Teixeira predict that current demographic trends—they foresee an increasing proportion of African-Americans and Hispanics in the general population (resulting in relatively fewer whites) and an increasing number of people who work in the postindustrial, high-education businesses that tend to foster a liberal culture—will provide Democrats with an overwhelming electoral advantage by 2008. But predictions are a tricky business. I remember reading a booklet that came with a box of Cracker Jacks I bought at a Cincinnati Reds game when I was a kid. "The Future," it was called. By 1980, it promised, cars would fly, or at least hover. Imagine my disappointment when 1980 brought Chrysler's hideous K Car, which could barely drive. Prophecies, particularly optimistic ones, have a way of not working out. (On the other hand, early-sixties demographers turned out to have been correct about a job shortage they predicted would plague Generation Xers in the wake of the Baby Boom generation.) Demographics may save the Democrats or they may not. Doing nothing, however, would be an absurd way to react to the current crisis of liberalism. Far too much is at stake to sit around hoping for things to improve.

What's certain is that the political party that most closely reflects the economic values and beliefs of the overwhelming majority of Americans is doing badly at the polls. Which is downright weird.

Whether or not the Democratic Party eventually recaptures its New Deal–era dominance, no one should dispute that the American Left has been in big trouble for a long time. That's bad news for America, not just liberals. A party that represents the interests of the majority of voters should usually—not always, since minority rights are an important motivator in representative democracy, but usually—dictate a country's national agenda. Our current situation, in which Republicans, whose domestic and foreign policy agendas are carefully tailored to benefit a narrow socioeconomic segment of wealthy individuals and large corporations, win nearly every major policy debate, is unfair. More to the point, it's dangerous.

Any nation in which the interests of the few repeatedly trump the interests of the majority lives under a form of apartheid. Long-term one-party rule, especially when that party represents a relatively small portion of the population, is democracy in name only, a cynical variation on the dictatorship-lite that has caused internal strife in countries ranging from Mexico to South Korea. It's dangerous for the same reasons that totalitarian states are intrinsically unstable, albeit under a thin veneer of control. It normally takes a while to become evident, but oppressed majorities inevitably discover that they're getting the shaft. After failing to achieve change within the existing system, they conclude that replacing it entirely offers their only real chance for what they believe to be improvement. That validates the anger of would-be insurgents, creating a snowball effect. Channeling their rage into violence shows revolutionaries that they're stronger than they had previously assumed, which provides them with the aggressive self-confidence they require to destroy all of the traces of the ancien régime—even those institutions that had functioned fairly well. Many minority regimes, like the former white minority government of South Africa, resort to oppressive tactics to maintain control, which disgusts and radicalizes former political moderates.

Alienation, followed by the violent convulsion of revolution, has frequently been the outcome of extended minority rule. Leftists are often tempted to romanticize revolution, but they should remember that the Terror followed the Rights of Man by merely a year and ultimately led to Napoleon's dictatorship. Revolutionaries rarely rule; revolutionary principles rarely become law. Once you shake things up, the uncertainty principle goes into overdrive. If possible, it's better to reform than to revolt.

True, Republicans frequently receive more votes than Democrats. But theirs remains the rule of a majority by a minority. This is because Republicans can't win elections without the support that they receive from self-identified Democrats. Cross-party drift cuts both ways—Bill Clinton, boosted by a booming economy and challenged by a feeble Republican nominee, attracted the votes of 13 percent of Republicans in 1996—but it more frequently impacts Democrats, as in 2000 when George W. Bush got the votes of 91 percent of Republicans and Al Gore just 86 percent of Democrats. If those who voted voted in every election and voted for the same party for which they were registered, Republican victories would be limited to a minority of seats in conservative states and districts.

Why people vote contrary to their economic self-interest remains one of this phenomenon's associated mysteries but there's no denying that passions stirred by "values" issues like abortion, civil rights, and the death penalty often trump pocketbook politics. There are obviously a number of other reasons—issues of perception, susceptibility to television advertising, the winner-take-all principle wherein voters prefer to vote for those perceived to be likely winners—that contribute to a minority party achieving national electoral dominance. Nonetheless, dissecting the reasons that working people sabotage their own fiscal futures by supporting a party that tries to keep them poor, figuring out how to educate them, and motivating them to act on their newfound knowledge are essential if we hope to end the current hegemony of the Right.

Despite the party's intrinsic demographic advantage, there hasn't been a real Democrat in the White House since Lyndon Johnson. We've had Democratic presidents for just twelve of the thirty-six years since LBJ and his famous scar went back to Texas. And neither Jimmy Carter nor Bill Clinton were liberals—certainly not in the vein of Roosevelt and Johnson, the kind of guys who promulgated big-vision social programs and enacted historic legislation reshaping the fundamental structure of American society. Our two most recent Democratic presidents were centrist caretakers whose conservatism on major defense and economic matters far outweighed their occasional nods to the Left on social issues.

ATTACK OF THE DIXIECRATS

Carter's post-presidential career as a jet-setting peace advocate sometimes obscures the fact that on foreign policy he was a proto-Reaganite. His 1978 federal budget package initiated the giant defense spending spree that Republicans maintained throughout the eighties. Carter governed like a right-wing Cold Warrior, refusing to send a U.S. team to the 1980 Moscow Olympics after the Soviet invasion of Afghanistan. He precipitated the Tehran embassy hostage crisis by welcoming the Shah of Iran after he was deposed by Islamic revolutionaries. Carter, younger liberals may have forgotten, enacted our current system of selective service registration for a future military draft.

Clinton was but a smidgen better. He ran as an architect of the centrist Democratic Leadership Council's "New Democrat" strategy, but used his first days as president to push for allowing gay and lesbian servicepeople to serve openly in the military—a traditionally liberal position. (In his characteristic toe-dipping way, however, Clinton wasn't willing to go to the mat for gay troops. He ultimately settled on a lame "don't ask, don't tell" policy as a perfect compromise—one that displeased everyone equally and left the underlying question to be resolved by some future successor.) The relatively minor controversy over homosexual soldiers, coupled with a "Republican Revolution" that led to the 1995 "co-presidency" with GOP Speaker of the

House Newt Gingrich, convinced him to revert to the conservative Southern Democrat approach that had gotten him elected originally. Throughout the remainder of his presidency, Clinton would never again expend significant political capital on a liberal stance.

Admittedly Clinton nominated a lot of women and minority judges, but his highly symbolic approach to affirmative action, which mainly benefited graduates of Ivy League law schools, didn't come close to a systemic solution to the vexing problem of discrimination. The great legislative achievements of the Clinton years, the benchmark events that changed the way future generations of Americans would work and live, included a Republican-authored welfare reform act that effectively unwound Johnson's Great Society, and the North American Free Trade Agreement with Canada and Mexico, a pro-business tariff arrangement fiercely opposed by labor unions. (Republican presidents dating back to Nixon had failed to get NAFTA through Congress.) Soon after Clinton left office in 2001, the incoming Bush administration jettisoned most of his midlevel female and minority political appointees. Bush's cabinet remained as ethnically diverse as Clinton's, but the resulting ideological shift overshadowed whatever symbolic value a few dark-skinned faces on CNN offered the disenfranchised residents of American slums. They too could become National Security Advisor, African-Americans learned—as long as they opposed civil rights.

Carter and Clinton were essentially Dixiecrats, liberal Republicans who ran for office under the Democratic banner because it was the best way to win.

Both major parties have, since 1968, limited themselves to ideological territory that midcentury Americans would have considered traditionally conservative. Of course, there have been sporadic skirmishes over such issues as the minimum wage, the tax structure, and defense spending. But the two parties agree on a myriad of basic assumptions that cause those scuffles to occur on Republican home turf.

For example, Democrats have proposed, and occasionally obtained, increases in the minimum wage. But even when polls showed that voters favored a big wage hike, actual increases have always fallen far short of keeping up with inflation. Democrats have never fought hard for a meaningful increase. Though they disagree on the details, the two "sides" have worked together to create a flatter, less progressive federal income-tax scale. And both parties agree that defense spending ought to remain staggeringly robust—the only disagreement between them concerns the size of the annual *increases*. Some analysts say, and I agree with them, that the parties agree on so many issues primarily because they're both financed by corporate donations. Many corporate chief executives hedge their bets, making equal contributions to the Democratic and Republican candidates for the same exact office! But the majority of voters don't care about the reasons that the parties are so similar. They merely know that it's so, and many turn away from electoral politics as a result.

Running as a third-party candidate in 2000, consumer activist Ralph Nader campaigned as an alternative to two political parties that Americans from left to right had come to see as virtually indistinguishable. With the exception of their positions on such inane faux "values" issues as a proposed constitutional amendment to ban the burning of the American flag and the fight over whether or not Christian prayers should be recited at public high school football games, Nader argued, the D's and R's agreed about almost everything else.

"The two parties are humming along on parallel tracks, moving to the marching orders of the corporate paymasters," Nader argued. The Green Party standard-bearer hammered away at that point in appearance after appearance during the 2000 race. There was no meaningful difference between the Democrats and the Republicans, Nader went on, but not because the two parties had melded into one. If anything, the Republican Party had moved steadily right since 1980. Rather than holding their ground, the Democrats had chased them across America's ideological fifty-yard line, abandoning traditional liberalism in favor of a "kinder and gentler" (the first President Bush's words) form of Republicanism that essentially differed only in its degree of tolerance for ethnic minorities and gays. Whereas Republicans represented what had formerly been considered the party's far right wing, Democrats assumed positions previously identified with the lib-eralish Rockefeller Republicans. The Left no longer enjoyed mainstream representation.

RISE OF THE REPUBLICRATS

The stances of the two supposed adversaries had merged so closely by 2000 that, on numerous important issues, Americans of every political stripe, left to right, found themselves ideologically disenfranchised. A substantial per-centage of voters, mostly conservative, adamantly oppose abortion. But while the Republican Party platform remains nominally pro-life, in prac-tice the GOP recognizes the reality of a pro-choice electorate. Because a strong and pronounced pro-life legislative initiative might cost the GOP too many pro-choice "swing voters," the party leadership is committed to a strategy of incremental attacks on Roe v. Wade: removing federal funding for medical facilities that conduct abortions, pushing for judicial rulings that permit pro-life picketers to intimidate pregnant patients, mandatory waiting periods for teens seeking the procedure. This approach may eventually wind up leading to the end of abortion as we know it, but from the standpoint of the individual abortion foes who bemoan the murder of millions of unborn babies each year, the party remains pro-life in name only. Time, after all, is something the fetuses they're hoping to save from gruesome deaths do not have. And Democrats are overtly pro-choice. Pro-lifers who would like to use the issue as a political litmus test have nowhere to turn; no major party truly supports their position.

Free trade is another example of majority disenfranchisement. Polls repeatedly show that most Americans, liberal as well as conservative, oppose unfettered free trade. (Liberals think such agreements hurt the environment and exploit foreign labor; conservatives worry about lost American manufacturing jobs and diminished national sovereignty.) But the two parties are so beholden to campaign contributions given by transnational corporations that they're both aggressively *pro*–free trade. (The 2004 presidential campaign saw some anti-NAFTA rhetoric driving the Democratic primary, but few expect the next Democratic president to renounce the agreement entirely.) A voter who fiercely opposes abortion must choose between Democrats whose stance he despises or Republicans who sometimes claim to agree with him but in reality are decades away from proposing an abortion-banning constitutional amendment. Similarly, a citizen who wants America to pull out of NAFTA—and that's most of us—must select between two parties, both of which proudly proclaim themselves in favor of the trade deal with Canada and Mexico. How can a country claim to be a true democracy when it offers voters no choice on issues that conjure so much passion?

Ralph Nader's argument that Democrats and Republicans were equally wed to the interests of rapacious corporations at the expense of the majority of citizens was hugely popular with millions of people who nonetheless voted against him—because they didn't believe that he could win and didn't want to "waste their vote." Nevertheless, Nader did draw so many votes that he denied former Vice President Al Gore, the Democratic candidate, the decisive victory he otherwise would have enjoyed over his inexperienced and inarticulate Republican opponent. (Nader carried nearly 100,000 votes in the key state of Florida, which Bush officially won by 537.) It was a bittersweet triumph. Nader had validated his assertion that Americans were unsatisfied with the monoparty system—imagine the returns he would have seen had people believed he could win!—while inadvertently contributing to the installation of one of the most regressive regimes in U.S. history.

After the Supreme Court voted to award the disputed presidential election to George W. Bush, reporters asked the Green Party candidate whether he regretted his previous assertion that it made no difference which candidate or party ultimately prevailed.

"The same decision makers under Clinton-Gore are operating under Bush-Cheney," Nader replied in February 2001, as the blood was still drying on the floor. "On the most basic issues of cordoning power from people as voters, consumers and taxpayers, they're very similar. Look at the massive mergers that went on during Clinton-Gore. GATT, NAFTA, corporate crime, corporate welfare—the same."

BUSH'S POWER GRAB

Until September 11, 2001, few intelligent observers of the American political scene would have disagreed with Nader. The terrorist attacks on Washington, New York, and Pennsylvania, however, set the stage for a wholesale political realignment nearly as dramatic as that of 1932, when Franklin D. Roosevelt's New Deal platform convinced Depression-shattered whites and African-Americans to abandon the party of Lincoln once and for all to form a left-of-center coalition of and for the disadvantaged.

The immediate effect of September 11 was two-fold: first, to complete the neutering of a Democratic Party already emasculated by losing control of the White House and House of Representatives; second, to provide an excuse for the right wing of the Republican Party to promulgate measures previously considered too extreme and therefore unpalatable for the American electorate. What began with a military response—an invasion of Afghanistan that toppled the Taliban regime—soon evolved into a series of legal and political maneuvers designed to intimidate opponents and concentrate power in Bush's executive branch. Confused, disorganized and unsure of themselves, Democrats stood by as Bush steamrolled radical agenda items through Congress, many of which had been developed by right-wing think tanks during the nineties.

Bush's decision to subject Taliban prisoners of war to trial by military tribunal, and then to deny them the basic protections accorded captured fighters by the Geneva Conventions, signaled that victims of his new War on Terrorism would be given no quarter. It also sent the message that the United States, already accused of unilateralism for its refusal to adhere to such agreements as the Kyoto Protocol on greenhouse emissions and the global ban on the deployment of antipersonnel mines in warfare, was unconcerned about international opinion. Because it incorporated neither the Central Intelligence Agency nor the Federal Bureau of Investigation, the creation of a new cabinet-level Department of Homeland Security did little to increase security or reduce the threat of future terrorist attacks. Instead, the Orwellian-sounding bureaucracy was created as an oblique means of enforcement for a new USA-Patriot Act that abolished or abridged the civil liberties of those who opposed the government on a wide variety of issues. Bush went so far as to issue a secret executive order granting himself the power to declare anyone, anywhere, an "enemy combatant" who could then be legally assassinated by U.S. government agencies. No evidence or justification would be needed to whack these pour souls; no warrant would be necessary to carry out the hits. Bush had assumed the powers of an absolute monarch.

Hollywood celebrities long accustomed to speaking their mind on political issues (they often lobby Congress about specific bills) found themselves demonized by right-wing media outlets as "unpatriotic," "un-American," and "treasonous" if they disagreed with Bush about such matters as whether or not to go to war against Iraq. Bill Maher, the libertarian talk host and comedian, had his *Politically Incorrect* TV show canceled by ABC after a remark he made about long-distance missile attacks was misinterpreted as calling U.S. troops serving in Afghanistan cowards. (Maher was, in fact, a Bush supporter and proponent of the war.) All across the board, whether the opponents of Bush's regime were actors, pundits, or politicians, the word was out: it was open season on the Left. Speaking out had become dangerous to one's career.

In my personal experience, the change in tone was subtle yet dramatic. Prior to September 11, some readers who took issue with something I'd said, written, or drawn in a public forum sent me hate mail. They'd let loose with scathing insults; some told me they hoped that I would die in excruciating pain, but that was about as far as it went. After GOP efforts to politicize the attacks, the tenor of hate mail became much more vicious. Threats began coming in that targeted my means of employment as much as my perceived flaws of opinion or personality. "I'll tell all of my friends to

REPUBLICANS STAND UP FOR THE FIRST AMENDMENT

It was heartwarming, even during the dark months after September 11, to see GOP leaders standing tall for the values that made America what it is today. Resisting the temptation to grandstand for reactionary audiences of flag-waving right-wingers, conservatives defended the Bill of Rights for, if they had done anything less, the terrorists would have won.
  Well, not exactly.

"How dare Senator Daschle criticize President Bush while we are fighting our war on terrorism, especially when we have troops in the field?"
—Senate Minority Leader Trent Lott,
Republican of Mississippi

"[Daschle's] divisive comments have the effect of giving aid and comfort to our enemies by allowing them to exploit divisions in our country."
—Representative Tom Davis,
Republican of Virginia

"[Critics'] tactics only aid terrorists—for they erode our national unity and diminish our resolve. They give ammunition to America's enemies and pause to America's friends."
—Attorney General John Ashcroft

"Should such a cartoonist be punished, arrested? Shot at dawn? Mr. Ted Rall should have been fired immediately by those with professional authority over him, or in contractual relations with him. Such action in defense of the decent judgment of this people in regard to 9/11 would be more than sufficient to keep such as Mr. Rall from subverting our national resolve. But it is worth remembering that when serious and sustained attempts to undermine public opinion on a matter genuinely essential to national life cannot be resisted by other means, governmental action may be necessary."
—Alan Keyes, former Republican presidential
candidate, reacting to one of my editorial cartoons

write to the publications that carry your work to demand that they stop carrying you," they'd say. "I'm going to organize a boycott. I'll make sure you never work again." This was new. Blackballing, unfashionable since the end of the McCarthyism of the 1950s, was back. Right-wing World Wide Web diarists who called themselves "warbloggers" (after the wars on terrorism, Afghanistan, and Iraq) rallied each other, egging one another on to deluge the employers of left-of-center pundits with missives demanding that such "offensive" commentators be fired. "The First Amendment gives you the right to write what you want," one such warblogger argued loftily, "but it doesn't give you the right to have it published. I'm not censoring you." Such sophistry—okay, so the guy was asking *someone else* to censor me—became commonplace during the dissident clampdown of 2001. With few Democratic leaders speaking out against it, a poisonous atmosphere of rightist repression became increasingly pervasive.

The loyal Democratic opposition beat its final retreat six months after the attacks, in the spring of 2002. Senate Majority Leader Tom Daschle issued a broadside asking why the administration had not, despite occupying Afghanistan since October, located Osama bin Laden, Mullah Mohammad Omar, or any other high-ranking al Qaeda or Taliban officials said to be directly or indirectly responsible for September 11. (Although it is widely assumed that bin Laden planned the attacks, to date no evidence has ever been presented linking him or any other al Qaeda official to the attacks. The media's tacit acceptance of an assertion that has never been reliably "sourced"—most newspaper editors require reporters to find at least two reliable sources for everything they print—is yet another magnificent tribute to the success of the Republican propaganda machine.)

Under normal circumstances, even in time of war, cross-party criticism is common, expected, and, one might say in a democracy, desirable. Daschle's comments, given Bush's failure to deliver on his cocky "wanted dead or alive" rhetoric about Osama bin Laden and other targets of the "war on terror," were nothing more than garden-variety political opportunism, the kind of caterwauling that goes on in Washington every day—or used to. It was neither admirable nor unusual. But Bush officials and Republican strategists saw in September 11 a golden opportunity to exploit the nation's grief and fear, to ram through an extremist agenda that wouldn't pass muster in a saner political climate. They understood something else as well: they could use post–September 11 patriotism as a bludgeon against any political opponent who might dare to question them.

That word, *dare*, went around a lot as Bush used September 11 to accrue and consolidate unprecedented levels of presidential power. How *dare* you question the president during a time of war? How *dare* you risk demoralizing our troops by opposing the war?

"Disgusting," spat House Majority Whip Tom DeLay, who had recently assumed the role of chief GOP hatchet man when he led his party's anti-recount forces in Florida. Thomas Davis, a Virginian who headed the House Republican campaign committee, accused Daschle of "giving aid and comfort to our enemies." "How *dare* Senator Daschle criticize President Bush while we are fighting our war on terrorism, especially when we have troops in the field?" barked Senate Minority Leader Trent Lott. A year earlier, one might have asked how Davis *dared* to impugn an important senator's right to speak out on an important matter of public policy. Now Daschle was being told in no uncertain terms to shut the hell up or risk being branded a traitor. Regrettably for his country and constituents, that's pretty much what he did.

The "war on terrorism," like previous campaigns against drugs and poverty, has no end in sight. Bush has called it "a different kind of war," one that will continue into the foreseeable future and will take the form of assassinations abroad and mass round-ups here in the United States. Our government admits that it won't tell its citizens what it's doing; it claims that it requires total obeisance—and secrecy from the citizens whose taxes pay its salaries—in order to prevent future attacks. "United We Stand" and "Support Our Troops and President Bush," read ubiquitous billboards and bumper stickers. Conformity equals patriotism equals loyalty. Criticism of the commander in chief, who appeared in an Air Force flight uniform on the aircraft carrier U.S.S. *Abraham Lincoln* under a "Mission Accomplished" banner, became tantamount to treason. Few Democrats spoke up to oppose him on any subject. Most went along with the Republicans on everything, even voting for two internationally condemned invasions, hoping that a recessionary economy would eventually convince voters to give them a chance.

Terrified that the disloyalty smear would stick, cowed Democrats ran milquetoast campaigns for the House and Senate during the midterm elections. If they looked like watered-down Republicans in 2000, in 2002 Democratic candidates looked like generation copies of Republicans. Mimicking the right proved to be a disastrous strategy; for the first time in memory an opposition party not only failed to make substantial gains but lost control of the Senate along with the House. Thanks to their 5-to-4 Supreme Court majority, the Republican Party simultaneously controlled the judicial, executive, and legislative branches of government.

Why did this disaster occur?

"Across the country, from California to New York, bland and compromised Democratic candidates were unable to motivate their own base, let alone attract the independents required to win close races," wrote pundit Joe Conason for *Salon.com* after the grim results were tallied. "There were moments during the midterm campaign when it seemed that the Democrats were nothing greater than the prescription drugs party. But that issue isn't enough to nationalize a midterm election, and certainly not enough to persuade voters uneasy about war and the economy. Those voters were listening for a powerful Democratic message about global security, the faltering economy, employment, education and healthcare. All they heard was 'prescription drugs [for seniors].'"

Meanwhile the Republicans reveled in their self-proclaimed role as the Official Party of the War on Terrorism™, which they used as a political bullwhip to flog hapless liberals. The war's main target, however, wasn't foreign Islamists. It was American liberalism.

Neoconservative Bushism is a revolutionary, radical ideological movement whose adherents believe that they possess a popular mandate to unravel what remains of pluralistic liberalism. They seek to replace the United States we studied in civics class with their new vision of a militarist, expansionist empire whose international aims brook no malcontents in "the homeland," as our nation is known in their neo-Nazi terminology. The first test of this radical approach was an unprovoked, preemptive war against Iraq despite low initial support on the homefront (a CBS News poll taken October 7, 2002, finding that just 30 percent of the public favored military action, called Americans "cool to the [Bush] doctrine of preemption") and fierce anger abroad, even while the occupation of Afghanistan was quietly disintegrating into a Vietnam-style quagmire. Agencies such as the Federal Bureau of Investigation, Central Intelligence Agency, National Security Agency, and Department of Homeland Security were given broad new powers to spy on Americans, search their homes without warrants, and subject them to arrest for indeterminate lengths of time, without being required to charge them with a crime or allow them access to a lawyer. Leftists who remembered Nixonian abuses of surveillance agencies during Watergate couldn't help but wonder whether they, rather than Islamist terror organizations, which continued to operate with impunity, were Bush's real targets.

The administration didn't limit its newfound political clout to initiatives tied to terrorism. Bush asked for, and Congress granted, a record $1.8 trillion in tax cuts—most of the windfall going to Americans earning more than $330,000 a year—during a time of recession and rising deficits. The federal budget, which at the start of Bush's term had been projected to enjoy a $4 trillion surplus over the next decade, faced a $6 trillion *deficit* less than a year after his inauguration. Roughly $10 trillion—more than six times the total Reagan deficit—had been squandered on tax cuts for a tiny coterie of extremely wealthy people, two dubious wars, and an extensive domestic surveillance bureaucracy. Despite their enormous size, the tax cuts failed to stimulate the economy as advertised; at this writing, the economy has lost more than three million jobs between 2001 and 2004 (a massive problem that a single anemic quarter of economic growth, in late 2003, did not begin to overcome). And the wars didn't make us safer. If anything, Middle East experts agree, the invasions of Afghanistan and Iraq increased the likelihood of future terrorist attacks against American targets.

Everything the Bush administration did contradicted basic American values. None of it worked, at least not the way that they claimed. But that didn't matter, because Democrats and their erstwhile allies in the media sat on their hands. In the absence of meaningful opposition, nothing could stop Bush's Republicans.

A February 2003 letter to the *Bremerton Sun*, a newspaper in Washington state, summed up the situation. "Bush is the most powerful man in the world right now," wrote Jon Volden. "He controls all branches of the government and commands our military. Plus he has fanatical support from a vast array of media sources including scores of AM commentators and the Fox cable news network. Unfortunately, what Bush wants, Bush gets. The media will see to that. For whatever reason, fortune has aligned all the power of our country with Bush, and he is going to use it to wage war in our names and no power on earth can stop him."

A MONOIDEOLOGICAL AMERICA

Something is very wrong when a single ideology, regardless of what that dogma is, dominates a society. That is doubly true in the case of the United States, a nation whose Constitution and history of peaceful transferals of power serve as shining examples to emerging democracies around the world. As our national debate narrows, our democracy fades. Other countries start to consider that other forms of government may suit them better after all.

The problem isn't that the Democrats have moved so far to the right, though they have. The problem isn't that they've lost their will to fight, though they have. The problem is that two major political parties for a country as large and diverse as the United States aren't nearly enough to begin with. When one of those parties ceases to be viable, a major crisis is at hand. Can a nation of 290 million people truly call itself a democracy when it has only one party capable of winning elections, getting bills passed into law, and setting its ideological tone? Can it claim to represent its people when only some of its citizens are eligible to vote, a fraction of those are registered and fewer than those actually cast a ballot?

Make no mistake, as George W. Bush likes to say: this isn't about the Democrats. If the present situation was reversed, if *Democrats* controlled all three branches of government with no immediate prospects of Republicans seizing power, if conservative ideas were so marginalized among elected representatives and in the media that they couldn't be seriously debated, much less put into action, if a substantial, rightist percent of the American public was so alienated by decades of repeated losses that it had stopped bothering to vote, if Republicans were Republicans in name only and expended their energies on passing Democratic initiatives, this book would need to be written just the same. A two-party system without a right, after all, would be no more a democracy than one without a left.

Parliamentary democracies such as those of Europe offer their citizens the choice among a wide selection of political parties from the extreme ends of the left and right; the chance that even a small splinter faction might rise to power as part of a coalition tends to energize the marginal edges of the electorate. This results in voter turnouts of more than 65 percent (see sidebar). Here in the United States, our unusual two-party system (most democratic republics prefer the multiparty parliamentary form of government) already excludes ideological extremes. We have the illusion of choice. Socialists who favor forced redistribution of wealth can vote for the Revolutionary Communist Party, and racist black-helicopter types can join the Michigan Militia, but neither the far left nor the far right has the slightest chance of winning so much as a local election. Go ahead and shrug "who cares?" but, as Weimar Germany learned after banning the Nazi Party and Pakistan is experiencing after driving its Islamist parties underground, a society ignores its own extremists at its peril. Pro-lifers determined to end what they perceive as the mass genocide of unborn children conclude that they have no choice but to resort to murdering physicians who perform abortions. Timothy McVeigh, alienated from a mainstream political system that wouldn't publish his letters to the editor, helped blow up the Murrah Federal Building in Oklahoma City. Whether or not extremist opinions are valid is beside the point; such factions are and always will be among us. Cutting them out of the body politic is a prescription for unrest.

Disaffection is the root cause of terrorism; a political system that allows no legitimate outlet for those with grievances to express themselves drives those not vested in the system to pursue the eradication of that system. Anything, they start to believe, is better than this. Most political scientists agree that Americans are becoming increasingly alienated from a monoideological system that appears to reflect the interests and priorities of an ever-shrinking percentage of the American public. This widespread lack of interest manifests itself most plainly in our nation's low voter turnout.

It's bad enough that there are only two major parties to begin with. If I had my way, Americans would have as many options at the voting booth as they do at the supermarket, where you can pick from any of a dozen brands of clear dishwashing liquid and a hundred brands of cereal. But historical precedent indicates that we probably won't be moving to a system of proportional representation any time soon. We've got what we've got, such as it is—or, more precisely, such as it was until recently.

Eliminating one of the major parties as a serious contender for power, whether it's the Democrats or the Republicans, risks pushing voter participation below its already abysmal present-day "norm." Without the Democrats, without a Left, American voters who used to say "Why bother? They're both the same anyway," don't need to ask the question in the first place.

Something is very wrong when half of registered voters, and only a quarter of eligible voters, bother to turn out for national elections. (Turnouts are often as low as an abysmal 10 percent for local races.) These numbers suggest that it's not just discouraged lefties who are staying home; self-identified conservatives, either feeling confident that their ideals won't be effectively challenged by the Left or, more likely, that politics don't much matter to them, are also voting with their feet. Polls taken by the *Washington Post* since 1964 show that only half of Americans respect their political leaders or trust them to do the right thing at any given time: a record low. Business

VOTER TURNOUT BY NATION

Rank	Country	Average Voter Participation (1945–1998)
1	Italy	92.5
2	Cambodia	90.5
3	Seychelles	90.1
4	Iceland	89.5
5	Indonesia	88.3
6	New Zealand	86.2
7	Uzbekistan	86.2
8	Albania	85.3
9	Austria	85.1
10	Belgium	84.9
11	Czech Republic	84.8
12	Netherlands	84.8
13	Australia	84.4
14	Denmark	83.6
15	Sweden	83.3
16	Mauritius	82.8
17	Portugal	82.4
18	Mongolia	82.3
19	Tuvalu	81.9
20	Western Samoa	81.9
21	Andorra	81.3
22	Germany	80.6
23	Slovenia	80.6
24	Aruba	80.4
25	Namibia	80.4
26	Greece	80.3
27	Guyana	80.3
28	Israel	80.0
29	Kuwait*	79.6
30	Norway	79.5
31	San Marino	79.1
32	Finland	79.0
33	Suriname	77.7
34	Malta	77.6
35	Bulgaria	77.5
36	Romania	77.2
37	Spain	77.0
38	Maldives	76.0
39	Comoros Islands	75.7

VOTER TURNOUT (CONT.)

Rank	Country	Average Voter Participation (1945–1998)
40	Cape Verde Islands	75.6
41	Ireland	74.9
42	United Kingdom	74.9
43	Republic of Korea	74.8
44	Monaco	73.8
45	Croatia	73.5
46	Turkey	73.5
47	St. Vincent and the Grenadines	72.4
48	Venezuela	72.2
49	Belize	72.1
50	Dominica	71.3
51	Argentina	70.6
52	Cyprus	70.4
53	Uruguay	70.3
54	Vannatu	70.2
55	Taiwan, Republic of China	70.1
56	Philippines	69.6
57	Togo	69.3
58	Papua New Guinea	69.1
59	Federal Republic of Yugoslavia	69.1
60	Japan	69.0
61	Dominican Republic	68.7
62	Costa Rica	68.4
63	Canada	68.4
64	Iran	67.6
65	France	67.3
66	Liechtenstein	67.3
67	Trinidad and Tobago	66.2
68	Ukraine	66.1
69	Madagascar	66.1
70	Grenada	64.8
71	Lesotho	64.3
72	Kazakhstan	64.3
73	Algeria	64.2
74	Hungary	64.1
75	Luxembourg	64.1
76	Nepal	63.7
77	Barbados	63.5
78	Bahamas	63.2
79	Latvia	63.1

VOTER TURNOUT (CONT.)

Rank	Country	Average Voter Participation (1945–1998)
80	Kiribati	62.4
81	Nicaragua	62.0
82	Singapore	62.0
83	Bolivia	61.4
84	Georgia	60.6
85	India	60.6
86	Moldova	60.5
87	Sri Lanka	60.5
88	Lebanon	60.2
89	Benin	60.1
90	Lithuania	60.1
91	St. Lucia	59.9
92	Fiji	59.9
93	Sao Tomé and Principe	59.6
94	Solomon Islands	59.0
95	Malaysia	59.0
96	Zimbabwe	58.8
97	Jamaica	58.5
98	Tunisia	58.4
99	St. Kitts and Nevis	58.1
100	Morocco	57.6
101	Cameroon	56.3
102	Paraguay	56.0
103	Bangladesh	56.0
104	Estonia	56.0
105	Gambia	55.8
106	Honduras	55.3
107	Russia	55.0
108	Panama	53.4
109	Poland	52.3
110	Uganda	50.6
111	Antigua and Barbuda	50.2
112	Burma/Myanmar	50.0
113	Switzerland	49.3
114	**United States of America**	**48.3**
115	Mexico	48.1
116	Peru	48.0
117	Brazil	47.9
118	Nigeria	47.6
119	Thailand	47.4

VOTER TURNOUT (CONT.)

Rank	Country	Average Voter Participation (1945–1998)
120	Sierra Leone	46.8
121	Botswana	46.5
122	Chile	45.9
123	Senegal	45.6
124	Ecuador	44.7
125	El Salvador	44.3
126	Haiti	42.9
127	Ghana	42.4
128	Pakistan	41.8
129	Zambia	40.5
130	Burkina Faso	38.3
131	Nauru	37.3
132	Yemen	36.8
133	Colombia	36.2
134	Niger	35.6
135	Sudan	32.0
136	Jordan	29.9
137	Guatemala	29.8
138	Djibouti	28.0
139	Egypt	24.6
140	Mali	21.7

*Kuwait prohibits women from voting.
Source: International Institute for Democracy and Electoral Assistance

leaders do slightly better than politicians, but when it comes to trust, Americans increasingly look to figures in their local communities—mayors, the heads of charities, etc.—over inside-the-Beltway Washingtonians they perceive as uncaring and out of touch. Americans of all political stripes believe that, whether or not they're personally affected by the machinations in the nation's capital, there's nothing they can do about them.

Both big parties, and by extension their fellow travelers among the activist groups on the left and right, have been tainted by the Watergate and Monica Lewinsky scandals. Both parties have suffered as their presidents were exposed as liars and hypocrites before facing the ultimate political sanction, impeachment. Writing in the *American Prospect*, Amy Burke adds: "Parties have long been in decline, supplanted by media, money, interest groups, and candidate-centered politics. The party platform, once the fulcrum of great national debates, scarcely matters today. It remains to be seen whether parties can recover."

Burke's list of threats to the binary Democratic-Republican system focuses on secondary problems. The real dilemma for both parties, for better and for worse, is how to address selfishness.

EXCUSES, EXCUSES

The U.S. Census Bureau surveyed some of the 40 million registered voters who didn't cast a vote in the 1998 midterm Congressional election on why they decided not to exercise their franchise. Here's what they said:

Too busy/conflicting schedules with work or school	13%
Not interested/vote wouldn't make a difference anyway	13%
Illness, disability, or family emergency	11%
Out of town	8%
Didn't like candidates/campaign issues	6%
Forgot	5%
Confused about registration status	4%
Transportation problems	2%

Source: U.S. Census Bureau, Population Profile of the United States

THE TRIUMPH OF BASER INSTINCTS

During the first half of the twentieth century, communism was universally thought to be ascendant. If Lenin had seized Petrograd's Winter Palace and toppled Russia's czar with a few thousand men, how long would it take for the Soviet Union, the world's largest nation, to conquer the whole world? The reason that their victory was inevitable, communists argued in the late teens and twenties (and many capitalists feared that they were right), was that human nature was inherently communal. Going back to the days when humans dwelled in caves, people couldn't survive as individuals; they had to cooperate in order to build shelter and a livable world. Communism, Marx had written, would bring about a "complete return of man to himself as a *social* being, not upon the egoistic self-seeking which the economists assume to be characteristic of human nature in general."

The collapse of the Soviet experiment in 1991 provoked equally sanguine assertions from commentators who claimed that capitalism had triumphed then and forever because human nature was inherently competitive. Free markets were the realization of the natural state of man, conservatives crowed over the ashes of a communist dream they declared dead forever, and anyone who said anything different was a fool and a rogue. Good or not, greed was basic.

Human nature is impossible to define so simplistically. What is certain is that the commies and the laissez faire types are right and wrong at the same time. Neither and both extremes apply simultaneously. Human beings are torn between two conflicting impulses: the individualistic and the communal.

Taking care of your family, paying your taxes, and obeying traffic signals are examples of the communal instinct at work. We human beings find it necessary to work with others in order to make things better for ourselves. We hope that others feel and do the same—if they don't, society breaks down. Unless we pass and enforce laws that say that stealing is wrong, looting breaks out and continues unchecked. Driving becomes deadly in a city where people don't universally consent to the proposition that red means stop. When you become ill in a place where communal values are not widely accepted, no one takes care of you. You don't want that to happen to you; I don't want that to happen to me. It's a matter of life and death. Because we're convinced of this, we don't stop at acting communally; we force *other people* to act communally as well. We jail people for tax evasion. We shoot looters. We berate family members who fail to fulfill what we believe to be their moral, financial, or other obligations. We shout at litterbugs. Sometimes the communal instinct goes too far, as when we criticize people simply for not behaving or dressing as we do, but there's no doubt about it: the urge to cooperate lies at the core of the human psyche.

Individualism is selfishness raised to its highest level. We demand the right to do what we want—to swing our fists, as the saying goes, to the spot where someone else's nose begins—and sometimes a little beyond. Painting your house a color that clashes with those of your neighbors, driving a gas-guzzling sports utility vehicle, and throwing food away rather than donating it to a homeless shelter are examples of negative individualism. But the same competitive instinct that allows Bill Gates to sleep soundly while a billion people starve to death creates incredible inventions like the computer software which I used to write this book as well as great art and music. You can't deny the benefits of individualism, especially in America.

For a few years after Roosevelt was dead and gone, the Democratic Party marketed itself as the home of commie lite. Because they found Stalinist repression less appealing than the utopian vision of Marx and Lenin, Democratic liberals opposed the Soviet Union in the Cold War while continuing to strive for the egalitarian economic aspect of socialism. The party became an ideological home for, along with more conservative trade union types (and for a time, southern racists), those who believed that the needs and wants of the masses were more important than those of a tiny elite. Though Democrats incorporated elements of free-market capitalist rhetoric into their platform (kowtowing to business and opposing Soviet-style communism), for the most part they supported socialist ideas like better conditions for ordinary working people, taxing the wealthy at a high rate to flatten income disparity, and providing assistance for the old, sick, and infirm.

Republicans, on the other hand, promoted a watered-down version of capitalism, favoring open markets and borders for business, low wages for workers to keep labor costs low, and reducing taxes on the wealthy people and corporations who composed most of their financial support. They incorporated bastardized elements of socialism, such as favoring government bailouts for failing businesses, into their approach. They acknowledged the popularity of liberalism; they didn't dare attack sacred "socialist" cows like Social Security, created under FDR. Overall, however, Republicans directed their appeals to the selfish half of the human instinct, which asserted that an America in which everyone had the chance to succeed without interference from the government—or being bothered to help out anyone else along the way—would ultimately rule the world.

Beginning in the fifties and sixties, the Democratic Party and its allies on the left adjusted their tactics and underlying ideology from appeals to the communal half of human nature to one that was closer in tone and approach to the GOP. Marxist-influenced class warfare—soaking the rich—was abandonned in favor of "identity politics." Democrats began taking it for granted that all black people were poorer than all white people. Women were thought to be universally—not generally—discriminated against because of their sex. These cases of historic injustice, liberals argued, could only be remedied systemically, through legislation that prohibited such discrimination in the future and reversed the effects of past wrongdoing by giving victims an advantage over the supposed heirs of their oppressors. They promulgated a national lattice of affirmative action in hiring and college admissions that granted extra points to applicants for belonging to a non-Asian ethnic minority, the female gender, or any other category deemed to have been subjected to historic discrimination. Support for affirmative action became the centerpiece of the Democrats' appeal to African-Americans and women.

Like Social Security, affirmative action has become so widely accepted that few rightists publicly call for its elimination. Newt Gingrich attacked "preferences" by calling for reform from race- to class-based quotas for those "who come out of poor neighborhoods, who come out of poor backgrounds, who go to school in poor counties." Regardless of their particular approach, proponents of *any* kind of affirmative action are engaging in attempts to buy off voters with implied promises of new advantages.

Affirmative action masquerades as an appeal to the communal instinct in politics. It asks those whom it will disadvantage to sacrifice their own career and education opportunities in order to redress historical discrimination against "disadvantaged minorities" (or, in Gingrich's case, poor people). In this political ploy, Democrats assume that the intensity of gratitude of those who benefit (their traditional African-American and female constituencies) will more than compensate for the resentment of those who lose out (white men who are likelier to vote Republican anyway). Setting aside for the moment the issue of whether affirmative action is a good idea, it is clearly an appeal to selfishness. Vote Democratic, affirmative action tells blacks and women, and you're more likely to land a better job or college admission slot. Who cares if your good fortune forces someone else, someone you'll probably never meet, to suffer?

Battles over the tax code work the same way. Republicans buy campaign contributions from wealthy individuals and corporations by promising them lower tax rates, then use the money to buy clever spots that bring in votes from everybody else. Democrats, at first glance, may seem to hold the higher moral ground by urging lower taxes on those who can least afford them: the poor and middle classes. But again, setting aside the question of who is morally right, who can deny that the Dems are buying votes too? If you're poor or middle class, and most Americans are, a Democratic victory will probably score you a bigger refund on April 15.

The truth is that both the Left and the Right appeal to the basest, most selfish instincts of human nature. Both sides have ceded the communal moral ground. Pundits have criticized George W. Bush for enacting expensive tax cuts during an expensive "war on terrorism." If we're really at war, they cry, shouldn't Americans be called to sacrifice, as our grandparents did during World War II, when they endured gas rationing and food coupons? But Bush isn't the only cynic here. Instead of calling for genuine austerity, Democrats countered the Republican giveaway to the rich with a proposal that cut taxes for their own constituents. The deficit created by their plan, which didn't even make it to a vote, would only have been a little smaller than Bush's. "Ask not what your country can do for you," John F. Kennedy urged. He'd be booed off stage if he said that now.

Conventional wisdom states that Americans can't take bad news. Don't tell the voters that taxes will have to go up. Don't ask them to make do with fewer government services. Don't admit when you're stymied by a problem. Keep on keeping on, and everything will be fine.

This ignorance-is-bliss bravado has led to what I called "The Rise of the Republocrats" in an opinion piece I wrote ten years ago for the *New York Times*. A big part of ideological blending, I argued, resulted from the parties' refusal to be straightforward. To some extent, telling the people what they want to hear worked for Clinton. But it hasn't worked for Democrats as a party, and it's failing the American people. We need a party like the Democrats used to be, one that appeals to the communal instinct while countering the Republicans' economic Darwinism. "No," the leader of a nation at war should tell us, "we can't afford a tax cut now." We need politicians who stand up and tell us that giving up and pitching in is the essence of civilization, and that that may sometimes mean—gasp!—a tax increase. We need a left that explains that citizens from states that pay more into the federal treasury than they get back aren't really being gypped, that residents of rural areas have no more right to be annoyed about paying for subways they'll never ride in cities they'll never visit than city dwellers who cough up cash for distant dams. We have to explain to African-Americans why race-based affirmative action no longer makes sense. We have to stop sneaking welfare for the poor and downtrodden into appropriations bills like thieves in the night: preventing starvation is a noble and obligatory effort in any society and particularly in one as wealthy as ours.

We have got to be as consistent as possible.

Both parties have become so narrowly focused on winning elections that they've forgotten what's important: representing their constituents' individual concerns in a way that strengthens our nation. Republicans suck up to the anti-intellectual strain in the American electorate with cheesy pledges to clutter up the Constitution with amendments on flag burning and gay marriage. Democrats are so anxious to keep female voters in their fold that they fought banning the most extreme examples of abortion, like "partial birth" procedures performed in the eighth month of pregnancy. But even as the parties scramble for votes among the idiots and single-issue extremists, they lose the vast majority of average, normal, working people who basically favor abortion but not partial-birth, who don't really care whether or not they get a tax cut, and deplore flag burners but don't think an amendment is necessary to deal with them.

We're a reasonable people, we Americans, and our moderation is mostly rooted in common sense. We want to be left alone as much as possible, free to do our thing. At the same time, we realize that government can't leave us alone if we hope to function as a society. We want to help those who are suffering, but we don't want to let lazy people live on the dole. Our national sense of self-conflicted reasonableness has fallen into a political vacuum, underrepresented and unarticulated. There is a tremendous opportunity for a Democratic Party in crisis—if they're smart enough to take advantage of it.

THE MISSING LEFT
Though it's demonstrably untrue, the Right *seems* more honest than the Left nowadays. Because we tend to respond to people who appear plain-spoken, the inarticulate, bumbling Bush looked like a natural choice over his intellectual, snotty challenger in 2000. And so, thanks to Bush's aw-shucks jus'-folks act, the United States has found its political median shoved further to the Right than any other nation in the industrialized world. True, the Right is correct about many things, at least in theory: balancing the budget and keeping government out of people's personal lives are great ideas. (It's true that the GOP only gives these ideas lip service, but that hardly invalidates them.) But just as the United States has become fat and complacent in the aftermath of the collapse of the Soviet Union, the Republicans and the rightists within the Bush administration have been corrupted by an arrogance born of an absence of competition. (How they could benefit from the slave assigned to accompany Roman emperors into their triumphal processions, whispering *mortus es*—you are mortal—into

their ears.) The free market of ideas requires ideological competition in order to thrive. Monopoly of thought, even within a democracy, is merely a friendlier form of totalitarianism.

Our country currently lives under a single-party form of government. One ideology (pro-corporate, coddling the rich, neglecting the middle class, patronizing the poor) is governing like there's no tomorrow. Should they continue, they'll be right. The triumph of the Right is driving our foreign policy, and since we are the world's sole surviving superpower, our expansionism faces no serious challenger at home or abroad. Unfettered power is dangerous to its opponents. But in the end, it's also fatal to those who wield it—for it breeds limitless resentment and hatred among people and groups who will inevitably learn to work together to bring it down, even if it means their own destruction. We saw a tiny example of this phenomenon on September 11. We must not wait until suicide attacks assume national proportions, such as a nuclear bomb launched against us by a nation like North Korea, or until we become a nation like Israel, existing in a neurotic, perpetual state of siege.

And, as my mom told me when I was nine, working people need a strong political party to stand up for them against the fat cats. The Democrats have been, and need to again become, that party.

The obvious, because it is the easiest, solution to the current crisis of American democracy is the reconstitution of a strong, viable American Left grouped within an effective Democratic Party. That revitalized party should find inspiration from the most appealing facets of conservatism and libertarianism, facets that are also going unaddressed by the GOP—both to win and because those portions of the rightist impulse are kissing cousins to classic liberalism.

A new Democratic Party should strive to become the voice of the average American, who buys into liberalism's concern for the downtrodden while shunning its penchant for overindulgence; agrees with conservatives that precious tax dollars shouldn't be wasted but doesn't go along with letting greedy corporations do whatever they want; and loves the libertarians' plea that the government should leave us alone to run our lives even if their tax policies seem a little silly. These deeply held beliefs unite our people. By definition, therefore, they are perfectly consistent.

Our current political divisions, wherein the same citizen isn't supposed to simultaneously believe in a national healthcare plan, the right to bear arms, a balanced budget, and gay marriage, are artificial. Because they don't reflect the seemingly disparate strains that form contemporary thinking, more and more Americans consider politics irrelevant. A successful synthesis of the most popular aspects of liberalism, conservatism, and libertarianism would eradicate many of the internal contradictions and hypocrisies that cause this to be so. A party that applied its approach would be unstoppable. We should build that party.

I voted for Ralph Nader in 1996 and 2000. Why not push for a bigger, better Green Party? While the formation of a viable third party, one unencumbered by stodgy personnel holding fast to out-of-date ideas, holds appeal to many progressives, the simple fact remains that the electoral system is currently configured to prevent a party like the Greens or Libertarians from achieving power. They're locked out. In some states, for example, the two major parties have conspired to ensure that only a party that obtains at least 5 or 10 percent of the vote will be listed on the next election's ballot. Granted, third-party candidates, including George Wallace and Ross Perot, made impressive showings in presidential elections, but one has to wonder how they would have governed had they been elected. (The examples of Jesse Ventura and Arnold Schwarzenegger, who won the Minnesota and California governorships via insurgent runs only to prove ineffectual, are instructive.) The rise to prominence of a viable—that is, capable of winning—third party would be welcomed by anyone who cares to see American democracy become more expansive and inclusive. But we're not there yet; we're not even close. For now, the Left's best hopes for achieving electoral success and setting the nation's political agenda rest with reforming and elevating the Democratic Party.

A great crisis of confidence has caused the Left to stop believing in itself and its ideas. Progressives can regain their faith in the justice of their cause by understanding that they represent the hopes and dreams of the overwhelming majority of the American people, while their adversaries on the Right are working to prevent those aspirations from coming to pass. These truths are addressed in chapters 2 and 4, respectively, of this book. A reinvigorated left requires a "big tent" in the form of a Democratic Party that has an exciting and relevant political agenda to sell, big ideas that will improve our lives while allowing progressives to accrue momentum for future initiatives to move things ahead still further. Chapters 3 and 5 describe the biggest problems afflicting our nation on the home front as well as abroad (and how a new and improved Democratic Party could solve them), and chapter 10 sets out a detailed platform for a party determined to represent a broad majority of the populace rather than a cumbersome alliance of ornery special-interest groups.

This book describes strategies good and bad, smart and dumb, moral and wicked, that the Left must consider in its struggle to regain the upper hand against the Republican Right. Chapters 6 and 7 analyze errors committed by recent liberal leaders and takes a look at what they might have done differently in order to achieve a more favorable outcome. In chapter 8 I argue that politics is a bar brawl, not a tea party. When one is engaged in battle against an unprincipled adversary, taking the high road is more counterproductive than noble. Chapter 9 studies strategic and tactical issues relevant to getting well-meaning Americans organized. Neither the right message nor a motivated organization can achieve anything without the right tactics.

If the United States is to continue to exist in its current form, if the ruin of autocracy is to be avoided, all American citizens, including patriotic conservatives and libertarians, should strive to make the goal of a vibrant and successful Democratic Party into a reality. The remainder of this book is dedicated to the prospect that the Left will, and must, rise again, and to the hope that the Right will come to appreciate the advantages of not winning everything all of the time.

chapter 2

AMERICANS ARE LIBERALS

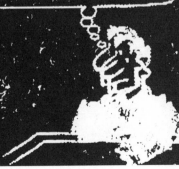

HOLY MOLEY! I GREW UP AND BECAME A PIG.

Do you want higher taxes? Do you want the government to tell you you can't do anything with your own property because you have standing water on it, making it a wetland? Do you want government imposing a one-size-fits-all solution for every problem and everyone? Do you want your elected officials continually voting against you because they're so arrogant they think they know better than you? Did you want bussing [sic] and quotas? The American people don't either, which explains the Republican landslide.

—David Tipton in the [University of Tennessee] *Daily Beacon*,
April 29, 1995

You read that chapter title right: Americans are liberals. That fat guy with the "These Colors Don't Run" bumper sticker on the back of his oversized pick-up? He doesn't know it, but he's liberal. The uptight, conservatively dressed dyed-blonde who goes on and on at the PTA meeting because "God's done been thrown out of the classroom and it just ain't right"? She votes Republican and there's an "I Support President Bush and Our Troops" sign on her immaculately manicured lawn, but deep down inside, she's a total bleeding-heart leftie. If she thought about it, if she knew enough about current events to think about it, if she could block out the TV long enough to let her brain fire off a synapse or two, she'd vote liberal every time—but she doesn't, she doesn't and she can't.

With the minute exception of a couple hundred muscle-bound freaks who shave their heads and shout out *sieg heils* to their favorite oi! songs in bucolic Montana hideouts, Americans are a nation of liberals living in a society defined by liberal values enforced by a likeminded legal system funded by a progressive tax structure with socialist roots. The truth is, American citizenship and a belief in liberal principles are so intertwined as to be virtually indistinguishable.

I know: it sure doesn't *feel* like we live in a liberal country. An increasingly right-wing Republican Party enjoys accelerating electoral successes. Conservative talk show hosts like Rush Limbaugh and Sean Hannity dominate radio airwaves; one rarely hears left-of-center opinions expressed on television or in most weekly magazines or daily newspapers. A drive across the United States takes one past countless American flags in support of a bellicose president, motels whose racist movable-type signs proudly proclaim themselves to be "American owned," and sheets draped from interstate overpasses that ask us to "support our troops"—never mind whether our troops are fighting a cause worthy of our support. Until fairly recently, I too believed that ours was a fundamentally conservative nation. But as C. Wright Mills observed, America is actually a conservative country without a conservative ideology.

Mills meant that the American style is fundamentally reserved and laconic. But just because someone buys their clothes at Wal-Mart or Old Navy doesn't mean that they favor trickle-down economics—politics are more complex than that.

THE LIBERAL LITMUS TEST
Ask any American the following questions:

- Is it morally acceptable for the head of a corporation to pay himself $40 million the same year his company lays off ten thousand people?
- Should it be legal for a drunken goon to beat someone to death merely because his victim happens to be gay?
- Should American citizens be permitted to die because they're too poor to see a doctor?

The overwhelming majority of Americans, as we'll see later, would answer "no" to all three of these questions. To the first question about CEO pay, "no" represents tacit agreement with the socialistic notion that extreme inequality of wealth is immoral; to the second one about gaybashing, "no" is the centerpiece of the demand by gays and lesbians that what they do in their own beds is of no concern to anyone but themselves; to the third about healthcare, "no" is a statement of belief that government can and should provide a safety net to people who find themselves in trouble. "No," answered to the question of whether limited government should take priority over compassion, is the quintessentially liberal answer. It is as direct a rejection of right-wing extremism as is possible to utter.

Let's turn this exercise on its head by asking Americans questions, the answers to which might initially seem to indicate fundamentally conservative beliefs:

- Should the government limit how much Americans are allowed to earn through a "maximum wage"?
- Should gay couples be permitted to get married?
- Should the government allow you keep your own money rather than squander your tax dollars on social programs rife with fraud and waste?

If you've spent any time in the United States, you probably agree that most Americans would answer "no" to all three of these questions. "Aha!" I can hear the book reviewer for the *National Review* scoff. Actually, not aha.

What these answers really indicate is that all-American character trait: common sense. We are a moderate (in the apolitical meaning of the word, descriptive solely of temperament) people. A few remote islands of cultural extravagance, places like Beverly Hills and New York City's Fifth Avenue, draw a disproportionate amount of attention from the media. But the vast ocean of American cities and towns are populated by wealthy notables who drive sensible cars and wouldn't be caught dead in fur, and working poor in debt to their ears to afford those very same mid-range automobiles. One can drive the highways and local roads of Ohio for hours without ever seeing a Jaguar or Mercedez Benz; good luck finding three-carat diamond rings on the fingers of the married women of Nebraska. Rich or poor, black or white, most people outwardly conform to a middle-class lifestyle that's so level in appearance as to seem communistic. (Their bank accounts, of course, are a different story.) Though we believe in liberal principles, we moderate those ideals with aspects of Mills's conservative style.

We Americans think of our country as the epitome of the modern capitalist state; we credit free enterprise with everything from our relatively high standard of living (though, as leftist thinkers have pointed out, other countries outrank us in such categories as literacy and infant mortality), to, less credibly, our democratic institutions as expressed through open elections (which, as demonstrated in 2000, may not be quite as democratic as we'd like to believe). Of course, the U.S. economy wouldn't function as effectively as it does without a powerful judicial and regulatory system—something the right works tirelessly to curtail or even eliminate—that limits what individuals and corporations are allowed to do with "their" money, workers, and products. Law and order provide the essential atmosphere of security that permits investors and entrepreneurs to make investments and conduct business transactions, even though it limits their ability to compete freely. Want real, pure, unfettered capitalism? Go to Russia, where the most efficient way to sell a better mousetrap is to murder its inventor and bribe a government official to have his patent transferred to you, or to Afghanistan, where banditry and drug cultivation are the primary engines of economic activity.

Americans tell themselves that the free market, minus taxes and paperwork and onerous regulations, lies at the root of their economic success. Attempts to limit CEO compensation frighten us despite our disgust at Kenneth Lay's greed: if Bill Gates's earnings can be limited, we worry, perhaps we'll be next. Americans say they believe in the miracle of laissez faire, but they're also reasonable, or moderate, about this. Most Americans are disgusted by corporate excess. Let a man preside over a company that epitomizes the computer revolution, that pays its workers decently and earns a profit for its shareholders, and few will begrudge him a salary fit for a debauched Roman emperor. On the other hand, there's Donald Carty, ex-chief executive of AMR, parent company of American Airlines. Ostentatious greedheads like Carty balance out the public's libertarian it's-my-money-and-I'm-gonna-keep-it impulse.

After a quarter in which AMR lost more than a billion dollars, Carty demanded that the Allied Pilots Association, Transport Workers Union, and Professional Flight Attendants accept a net $1.62 billion per year cut in their total pay and benefits. If they refused, Carty told union leaders, AMR would go bankrupt and their members would lose their jobs. The unions swallowed hard and convinced their memberships to go along. That was on March 31, 2003. Two weeks later on April 15, American filed a mandatory Securities and Exchange Commission report that revealed that seven executives (including Carty) would soon receive bonuses amounting to twice their annual base salaries. Carty would have gotten an additional $1.6 million. To add insult to embarassment, AMR paid another $41 million into a special trust fund to protect the pensions of forty-five executives—in case the company declared bankruptcy. We're all in it together, advocates of trickledown econimics insist, but some boats remain aloft long after the tide has run out to sea.

The unions accused Carty of "delaying the securities filing by at least two weeks to hide information that might jeopardize the votes" on the concessions. The scoundrel resigned in the end, reduced to licking his wounds on his slight million-dollar a year retirement pension.

Stephen Ross, late chairman of Time Warner (before the company's merger with America Online), was another classic example of CEOs gone wild. Ross paid himself $80 million the very same year that his mismanagement of the media giant resulted in the wholesale firing of ten thousand employees, none of whom had had a say in the decisions that led to their employer's declining fortunes. After he died of stomach cancer about a year later, Ross was reviled as a classic example of executive greed, for he had known about his terminal illness even while we was lining his pockets. He couldn't take it with him, but he didn't want anyone left behind to have any either.

Perhaps the most outrageous business story of the new century was the revelation, months after September 11 had driven the economy still further into recession, that numerous "American" companies were incorporating themselves on the Caribbean island of Bermuda in order to avoid paying federal U.S. taxes. Tyco International, previously based in New Hampshire, "moved"—actually, opened a post office box and paid a small fee—to Bermuda in order to save more than $400 million in taxes during 2001 alone. Kate Barton of the accounting firm Ernst & Young told the *New York Times*: "[Incorporating in Bermuda] is a megatrend we are seeing in the marketplace right now . . . Is it the right time to be migrating a corporation's headquarters to an offshore location? And yet, that said, we are working through a lot of companies who feel that it is, that just the improvement on earnings is powerful enough that maybe the patriotism issue needs to take a back seat to that."

Patriotism, of course, has never been much of a concern for corporate America.

There were a few muffled grumbles from Democratic politicians, but no one in Washington decided to act against these treasonous companies. (Slapping a tax on or denying government contracts to companies that transact most of their business in the U.S. yet are incorporated elsewhere might have violated free trade agreements.) Nonetheless, companies that want all of the advantages, without the costs, of doing business in the United States, remain a galling thorn in the side of regular Americans regardless of their personal political orientations.

Some might interpret this dichotomy—Americans support free markets, but only if supervised by government regulatory agencies—as a symptom of an internal conflict in our opinions concerning capitalism, but I view it as a reflection of our liberal view of fair play.

True conservatism is one of the three fundamental ideological impulses that define the American political outlook. And true conservatism, after all, stands against limits or controls on income. Americans favor *regulated* markets and mechanisms that permit the accumulation of wealth, but only within reason—i.e., only so long as the beneficiaries of the system don't behave like pigs feeding on the trough of the national community. The nineteenth-century robber barons inoculated themselves against rising communism by engaging in ostentatious philanthropy to match their spectacular lifestyles, but that approach is no longer viable: charitable contributions are plunging while the number of billionaires rockets skyward. The recognition that some wealthy people and businesses go too far, that they behave like Stephen Ross or Tyco, forces us to endorse indirect limits on wealth accumulation, typically in the form of income-redistributing taxation. The progressive tax code, which charges higher percentage rates to those in higher income brackets, isn't exactly the mob descending on Versailles—but it is a liberal approach to a core economic issue.

We see a similar ambiguity at work in my query about gay rights. A 2000 Associated Press poll, taken after the state of Vermont legalized civil unions by gay couples, indicated that Americans oppose gay marriage by a three-to-two ratio. Yet many of the same people who thought that gay marriage was too extreme nonetheless favored a broad array of new rights for gays and lesbians. Fifty-six percent, for example, believed that gay people should enjoy the same inheritance rights in the event of the death of their "life partner" (i.e., boyfriend or girlfriend) as do the widows and widowers of straight marital unions. And a Gallup poll, taken in the wake of Matthew Shepherd's 1999 Wyoming lynching, indicated that 70 percent—an overwhelming majority of Americans—wanted to see the government pass tougher "hate crime" laws that would make the murder of a gay man or lesbian a more grievous offense than killing an otherwise randomly selected victim. Almost everyone (86 percent, according to a 2003 American Enterprise Institute survey) believes that gays should not be subjected to workplace discrimination, and most folks (72 percent) would legalize the right of homosexuals to serve in the military. In all the ways that matter, Americans are as militantly in favor of gay rights as Richard Simmons.

How to explain, then, that 64 percent of the very same people think that homosexuality is "immoral"? Or that only a slim majority of the public (54 percent) believes that gay sex should even be legal?

This apparent contradiction results from an ideological disjoint at the core of the American political character. As citizens, we don't think that anyone deserves to be murdered, get their ass kicked, lose their job, or get thrown out of their homes simply because they happen to be gay. The freedom to pursue happiness your way, part of a political philosophy known as libertarianism—another of the three basic strains of American political thought—crosses party lines and has become a widely accepted part of our culture. (Libertarianism rightly has so much in common with liberalism that Democrats and left-minded activists should take up its obsessive defense of individual liberties.) But many straight people consider gay sex to be gross: the percent of Americans who tell Gallup that "homosexuality is an acceptable lifestyle" rose from 34 percent in 1977 to 51 percent in 2002. The change is significant but hardly earth-shattering. This Puritan component of conservatism sets a limit on what the average (straight) person will accept.

We're prudish but nonjudgmental.

Most straight Americans prefer not to dwell on the thought of two guys or two girls getting it on, and as long as gay people don't remind hets about the physical act that defines their sexuality, they're okay with them doing whatever they want to do—whatever the hell that is. A surprising proportion of straights believe that gayness is contagious. "I want my children to grow up and be normal people like me and my father and my grandfather was [sic]," Ziad Nimri, a foty-one-year-old salesman and Democrat from Spokane told the *New York Times*. "I don't want my children to start getting ideas. They see it's out in the open and you see men kissing men on television these days." When gay people ask to be left alone, especially when they look and act like "average" people in other respects, straight Americans are generally willing to go along. It is when homosexuals request societal approval for their lifestyle, the white dresses and announcements in the newspaper and marriage licenses issued by the state, that they get our dander up—at least for the time being.

Christian fundamentalists advocate a zero-tolerance policy on gays and lesbians. "Homosexuality is an abomination," televangelist Pat Robertson spat famously on his *700 Club* early morning television program. "The practices of those people is [sic] appalling. It is a pathology. It is a sickness." The Moral Majority's Jerry Falwell added helpfully: "God hates homosexuality."

George W. Bush, de facto leader of the national Republican Party, opposes special rights for gays, including protection from employment discrimination or hate crimes legislation. As governor of Texas, he supported a law that directed his state's child welfare agencies to revoke child custody from couples found to be gay. He even said that he would support a constitutional amendment to prohibit gay marriage.

Even in this respect, the clash in attitudes on gays results, in the final analysis, in a net positive score for the liberal column. According to polls the Right's message isn't working on the gay "issue." (My quotes arise from the fact that gay people aren't really an issue at all. They just *are*. Okay, nothing to see here, please move on.) A December 2003 *New York Times*-CBS News poll found that while 71 percent of the public was against gay marriage, only 55 percent favored Bush's idea for an amendment to the Constitution.

Despite their refusal to approve of gay sex, the American public approves of gay rights—which puts it on the opposite side of the political spectrum from anti-gay/Christian conservatives. Tolerating gays, and allowing them to live their lives free of harassment and prejudice, is all that liberalism asks of its adherents in this matter. By any standard, Americans are overwhelmingly liberal on gay rights.

(Bear in mind that attitudes about "special rights" are constantly in flux. African-Americans faced similar attitudes among whites a half century ago: they didn't object to segregated drinking fountains until the Ku Klux Klan started blowing up churches. Gays are making impressive inroads in the category of what conservatives call "special rights" on the cultural front; at this writing, the *New York Times* prints commitment ceremony announcements for same-sex couples in its snooty wedding announcements section. Can legalized homosexual marriage—something that the states of Vermont and Massachusetts, and the city of San Francisco, have begun to embrace—be far in the future?)

The healthcare debate goes to the core of one of the deepest ideological chasms between left and right. "That government governs best that governs least," wrote Thomas Jefferson, hardly a conservative himself though his words have become a credo for right-wing attacks on big government. (Big government, however, is acceptable to these folks in the form of massive defense spending and, most recently, the creation of a new 120,000-employee Department of Homeland Security.) According to Republican Party fiscal theorists like Milton Friedman, one of the salutary side effects of Reagan-style supply side economics is that big tax cuts deprive the government of the funding that it would otherwise apply to spending on "wasteful"—i.e., Democratic—social programs. "The ultimate purpose of the [Bush] Administration's [$5.6 trillion] tax cut plan has nothing to do with economics," former Nixon secretary of commerce and investment banker Peter Peterson testified to the House Financial Services Committee in 2003. "It's about politics or political philosophy. The purpose is to starve the government of revenue so that, in the long run, Congress will have no choice but to cut back spending and, with that, diminish the size of government."

Americans tend to respond favorably to the argument that the government governs best that governs on a starvation diet, at least until they think about it. Outrageous stories of government waste abound from the Left (the Pentagon paying $800 each for screwdrivers and toilet seats) and the Right (Reagan's Cadillac-driving "welfare queens") alike. Residents of rural Montana resent paying for Boston's "Big Dig" highway construction boondoggle, New Yorkers resent sending more taxes to the feds than they "get back" in spending, and everyone has their own ideas about how federal tax dollars could be better spent—ideally by and for themselves.

Healthy tax revenues, however, are essential to national security. The history of China was largely determined by the ebb and flow of tax collections. Dynasties fell whenever wealthy citizens and powerful interest groups pulled political strings to get their taxes reduced or eliminated, which starved the central government of income and ultimately led to its being defeated by internal rivals or invading armies. Any nation without a steady source of money is doomed to collapse. Conversely, the creation of the modern income tax at the start of the twentieth century provided the U.S. government with the cash to fight World War I and to replace the European imperial powers as the world's most powerful force. There would have been no American Century without the income tax.

We're all in this together; politics is the endless argument about where to go and how to get there. The last Democratic president to effectively explain to the American people how the collection of taxes allows government to do important things—pave roads, defend borders, help poor people—was Lyndon B. Johnson, who convinced us that his Great Society wasn't just fair: it was a form of revolution insurance. Republican demagogues have dominated the tax discussion since the sixties. Now we have an electorate that buys into the argument that government bureaucracy wastes every cent it gets its grubby paws on.

Yet, on a subconscious level, most people—even those who vote Republican in election after election—understand that a strong central and local government protects their standard of living, and that those agencies need a steady and significant flow of tax income in order to do their jobs. The tension between fiscal conservatism—the aspect of traditional right-wing thought that Democrats would do best to embrace—and liberalism's emphasis on compassion for people who need society's help defines a core chasm between what currently passes for Left and Right in the United States. Republicans play to taxpayers' fears that social programs are taken advantage of by the lazy and scurrilous, while Democrats imply that the price of a safety net is that a few rogues will take advantage of the system.

For the most part, Americans buy the liberal argument. Every newspaper carries its obligatory April 15 feature story about would-be tax rebels who claim that the Internal Revenue Service is unconstitutional and therefore has no legal right to demand a share of "our" money, but nearly everyone who owes taxes fills out a form and pays them on time. In a sense, the tax protesters are right: the system is voluntary. Society is voluntary. Yet, as a 2000 *Los Angeles Times* poll found, Americans prefer "smaller government with fewer services" to "larger government with many services," 59 to 26 percent. It would be easier to build political consensus around an ideology that blended the best of both lines of thinking, one that elevated liberal compassion and fiscal conservatism to the same level of priority. True, liberal social programs will always be taken advantage of, but liberals should work even harder than conservatives to root out fraud. Why should there be a conflict between the ideas that some things are worth spending money for and that wasting money is undesirable?

NEITHER WELFARE QUEENS NOR THIRD WORLD POVERTY

We're not only motivated by fear of government tyranny. Americans aren't willing—not yet, anyway—to step over the bloating bodies of the starving and sick as they walk to their offices each morning. They don't want to live the way billions of people do in the third world, constantly wondering whether they or their neighbors will have anything to eat that night. When I describe my experiences visiting Karachi during the late summer of 1999— the grim Pakistani port city where *Wall Street Journal* reporter Daniel Pearl was brutally murdered a few years later—liberal and conservative friends alike wince at the thought of children sleeping on steaming, filthy sidewalks with rusty needles sticking out between their toes because they've run out of good veins for heroin. Here in the U.S., everyone agrees: it's a damned shame that five hundred thousand of the United States' twenty-seven million vets are homeless.

Republican voters like their tax cuts, sure, but it would take one hell of a tax cut to convince them to vote to eradicate Social Security, Medicaid, or the Veterans Administration hospital system. To the contrary: the great majority of Americans, Democrats and Republicans alike, oppose schemes to privatize or cut the budget of these programs—these *liberal* programs. And, as we will see, most Americans actually favor expanding upon these liberal notions. As a nation, for example, we favor a federally subsidized solution to the health insurance crisis, though such a program would be enormously expensive and would almost certainly require an increase in taxes.

Americans want government to help citizens with their important pressing needs: unemployment benefits to pay the rent and electricity while they're "between jobs," socialized medicine that allows sick people to see a doctor even when they can't afford health insurance, food stamps that feed women whose husbands abandon them. At the same time, they deplore the scumbag doctors who rob the Medicaid system by billing the government for nonexistent patients and tests, lazy assholes who sit around the house collecting unemployment checks rather than going out to look for a job, and welfare recipients who refuse work despite being of sound body and mind. Both major parties view these beliefs as existing in opposition (or they deny the existence of the other side) but they are mistaken. To the contrary, these are entirely consistent positions.

Americans like big government, and they like big government programs. They hate waste and fraud in government. It should be, and it is, possible to believe both of these things at once.

Most people's personal lives are governed by hundreds of similar "contradictions." For example, I'll gladly lend my best friend money if he needs it to make the rent before his next paycheck, but if the son of a bitch blows the cash on drugs or stereo equipment, I'll hunt him down and cause him a world of hurt. I love my cat but can't stand the hair he leaves on my carpets. It's the same principle: we want to help the downtrodden, not coddle slackers.

liberalism (lbr-lzm, lbr-), n.: a political theory founded on belief in the natural goodness of humans and the autonomy of the individual and favoring civil and political liberties, government by law with the consent of the governed, and protection from arbitrary authority

conservatism (kn-srv-tzm), n.: a political philosophy or attitude emphasizing respect for traditional institutions, distrust of government activism, and opposition to sudden change in the established order

Which of these words looks more like America? It's certainly not *conservatism*. To hell with "traditional institutions"—we may have kicked out the Brits more than two hundred years ago but we Americans still consider ourselves revolutionaries. We admire James Dean, Elvis Presley, James Brown, and Madonna: iconoclasts who did their own thing and didn't give a whit who liked it. We look back at periods like the 1950s when "sudden change in the established order" was in short supply, and with the exception of simplistic nostalgia (the TV show *Happy Days*) think of them as boring and oppressive. The bright spots during those somnolent years were the rock 'n' rollers, the rumbling gangbangers, and the maybe-have-been-Commies who refused to name names—in short, people who went their own way.

At first glance many Americans seem to distrust government. Lefties worry that they'll be next to join Afghan jihadis at Bush's new concentration camp at Guantánamo Bay, and rightists fret about black helicopters and the creation of a U.N.–mandated New World Order. But the central complaint that underlies protests about excessive taxation is that government doesn't do enough with the money it collects—that it's wasted or goes to the wrong places. Perversely, those who pay the most taxes—upper-middle-class individuals with incomes over $100,000—believe that the government wastes less (they think the government wastes 39 cents on the tax dollar) than the working poor who earn less than $35,000 (53 cents per dollar, they think), according to a 2002 *ABC News* survey. Wealthier, better-educated taxpayers say they're happier about what they get for their money than the poorer people who pay less (and benefit more from social programs). These numbers further imply that lower-income Americans don't feel that they benefit as much from the taxes they pay.

The definition of *liberalism*, on the other hand, practically reads like a description of the word *American*. Even when presented with evidence to the contrary, most of us believe that human beings—even those with whom we disagree—are fundamentally good. Our opponents may be stupid; they're rarely evil.

We all want what's best for America, the cliché goes. We just disagree about how to accomplish that. Europeans don't share this view; in places like France and England marrying outside your political party is often more controversial than getting hitched to a member of another race. By contrast, Americans are individualistic to a fault: if I want to toss burning cigarettes out the window of my nine mile-per-gallon sport utility vehicle as I cruise through the crispy underbrush of a bone-dry national forest, that's my business. *E pluribus* my ass. MYOB is the national credo of the United States of America.

LYING TO OURSELVES, WITH GOP HELP

Liberalism is the natural state of the American republic, the dominating ideology of its first two centuries, and the approach to political and social issues that most closely suits the temperament of the American citizenry. It is what got us where we are today, what makes us who we are, and what guides where we're going. American history is the story of the continuing advance of liberal ideals, often accelerated by leftist movements like the Midwestern progressivism of Wisconsin's Robert LaFollette and the populist pseudosocialism of Louisiana Governor Huey "Kingfish" Long. True, the march of left-of-center ideals—the right to unionize, the shorter work week, women's suffrage, etc.—has on occasion been interrupted, frayed or nibbled at the edges by conservatives who wished to turn back the clock. Racists stymied, and sometimes still continue to prevent, black voters from exercising their franchise. Workers' rights have suffered as employers gained more power against labor unions. But these have been relatively minor detours from the overall advancement of progress. While it's impossible to predict the future, it's hard to imagine our country rescinding these hard-fought rights—in its present form, anyway.

Liberal dominance extends beyond domestic policy. Given the success of GOP spin, it may come as something as a surprise to hear that liberals created our current thinking on military matters. The Republican Party has seized the need for a strong defense, as manifested by high arms budgets, as its principal platform plank, and they've trumpeted this stance at every opportunity. But most Democratic presidents have also presided over periods of increasing spending, frequently in opposition to Republican isolationists. This is a well-kept secret. And the G.I. Bill, which sent millions of American veterans to college at taxpayer expense, was a program promulgated by liberal Democrats. The idea that the government should help pay for college, widely considered an optional expense, is intrinsically liberal. Many recruits are motivated to join the armed forces (which conventional wisdom claims to be a conservative force in our society) primarily because of a college tuition benefit that Democrats wrote into law.

Although it still has a long way to go before it becomes a workers' paradise, the American workplace would be a grimmer place to spend most of your waking time without such liberal reforms as the ban on child labor, the establishment of the forty-hour work week and overtime pay, the right to join a union, and regulations that force employers to consider their employees' safety during their incessant drive toward higher profitability. Liberal environmental laws have made the air safer to breathe, liberal food safety legislation has forced manufacturers to tell us what's in our food, and liberal education reformers have created a national network of public colleges and educations where the sons and daughters of the poor and middle class may obtain a college degree. Liberals brought electricity to the countryside, at public expense, when conservatives (who mostly lived in big cities) argued that it was too expensive. Liberal New Dealers created the Federal Deposit Insurance Corporation that guarantees that your money will be there to withdraw after you deposit it into your bank account. A liberal-backed agency, the Consumer Product Safety Commission, keeps dangerous toys, and flammable pajamas (not to mention asbestos ones) away from your kids. Recent liberal achievements include the Americans with Disabilities Act, which ensures that you can still get around and go to work should a mishap land you in a wheelchair, and Bill Clinton's Family and Medical Leave Act, which lets you spend some time at home (albeit unpaid) after you have a baby. Without Social Security, millions of elderly Americans would find tonight's dinner in the bottom of a Dumpster. Republican presidents, legislators, and journalists fought tooth and nail against all of these once-radical initiatives, but they wouldn't dare try to repeal them entirely.

Americans treasure these liberal achievements. Even GOP columnist David Brooks concedes: "Republicans have learned through hard experience that most Americans do not actually want their government sharply cut. Voters are skeptical of government, but they elect candidates who promise solutions for their problems, not ones who tear down departments. They do not respond to politicians whose primary message is 'No, no, no.'"

An important challenge for political activists on the left is to make people understand that their lives would suck without them—and will become far less pleasant should liberals continue, as they have these last few years, to lose political battles.

Not only are Americans unaware that they're really liberals, Democrats often seem unaware that they're Democrats. If all registered voters had voted along the lines of their stated party affiliation in the 2000 presidential election, for example, Al Gore would have defeated George W. Bush by four full percentage points in the popular vote rather than the single-point squeaker that led to the Florida fiasco. Democratic voters are more likely to stay home, or vote for the other party, than Republicans. More liberal-minded people prefer to think of themselves as conservative—even though they're really not—than the other way around. What the hell is going on?

LIBERALISM'S ORIGINAL SIN
Author and Internet pundit John Scalzi theorizes that everything boils down to original sin. "The original sin of Republicanism is greed," Scalzi told me as we sat on the back porch of his rural Ohio home during the hot summer of 2003. "Everyone understands greed. Everybody wants to get theirs. The original sin of the Democrats," Scalzi argued, "is pity. Greed is more attractive, and a better motivator, than pity."

In other words, the Left has an image problem. And a motivation issue.

So many of our nation's attitudes and politics stem from the underlying assumptions of the liberal/left/socialist/alternaculture that one would expect voters to send like-minded politicians to represent them in Washington and our state capitals. But we don't. We elect white, male, tight-assed, racist homophobes who appoint stick-up-their-ass Bible-thumpers like John Ashcroft as attorney general. We think one way—open-minded, laissez faire, low-key—and vote another. Part of the problem as Scalzi says, is that more people will pay attention to you if you promise to give them something than if you pledge to give something to their neighbor, or some stranger across town.

In a new wrinkle, politics has followed consumer culture by becoming "aspirational," in the parlance of Madison Avenue ad execs. Just as guys buy Budweiser beer because Bud's ads imply that hot chicks will dig them if they drink their swill, and just as women buy *Cosmopolitan* magazine because they think hot guys will dig them if they know how to achieve twenty-three orgasms a day, American voters vote for a look that they admire, even if it's not one they necessarily agree with. Voters have become casting directors; they vote for the candidate who most looks like he or she fits the part.

Case study: research proves that most married people cheat on their spouses, which implies that as a society we tacitly approve of infidelity but not of indiscretion. Do it; don't flaunt it. Yet Bush's pre-election pledge to restore dignity to the White House, which is , in so many words, "no more oral sex-related stains on the Oval Office carpet," hurt Gore (even though he's never been accused of womanizing). In the wake of Monicagate voters wanted someone in public life to say that cheating is wrong, even though they do it or might do it themselves. (And, according to reports circulated by the Drudge Report and *Hustler* magazine, so did Bush. In 1971 Bush allegedly paid for his underaged girlfriend to abort his unborn child—an illegal procedure at the time—in Houston.) They were looking for guid-ance, not action. Gore could have inoculated himself by taking Clinton to task for his sins, pledging not to repeat them, and noting his opponent's many indiscretions.

Most Americans know—not that deep down—that they'll never earn enough money to significantly benefit from GOP tax-cut schemes. Nevertheless, they like the idea that that might change someday. (I coined the term "wannabe Republicans" in a cartoon a while back. My phrase referred to people who worry about high tax rates that they *would* suffer in the unlikely event that they were to someday become fabulously wealthy.) Voters are deserting the Democratic Party, despite the fact that they agree with it on most issues, simply because it doesn't talk the right game.

Furthermore, Democrats don't act cool.

THE LIBERAL IMAGE PROBLEM

Republicans come across as organized, determined and aggressive—even when they're in charge of a sinking ship. "Bush's supporters," said *Time* as the occupation of Iraq turned ugly, "increasingly worry about what they see happening in Iraq, but they stand behind him because he himself has not wavered. It's as though they support his certitude more than his policies." But creating an illusion of self-confidence is hard work. Republicans stage-manage every photo opportunity, massage every constituency, ensure that their politicians get where they need to be on time, and see they remain unchallenged in the primaries.

THE ART OF REPUBLICAN STAGECRAFT

> Americans are leading busy lives, and sometimes they don't
> have the opportunity to read a story or listen to an entire
> broadcast. But if they can have an instant understanding of
> what the president is talking about by seeing 60 seconds of
> television, you accomplish your goals as communicators. So
> we take it seriously.
> —Dan Bartlett, White House communications director,
> in the *New York Times*, May 16, 2003

Every presidential administration attempts to present itself in the best possible light, but the Bushies have taken the skill of stagecraft to dazzling heights. Here's your homework assignment for tonight: as you read some of the greatest hits of spin from the last few years, consider what Bill Clinton could have done better in this regard, and how Democrats should adopt these absolutely appalling, 100 percent effective, strategies.

Piloting a fighter jet to the deck of the U.S.S. *Abraham Lincoln*, Bush's advance men ensured that a red, white, and blue banner reading "Mission Accomplished" was placed directly behind him while he was speaking. Advance men chose a late afternoon arrival time to ensure a soft, golden light, and maneuvered the aircraft carrier to obscure the skyline of San Diego in the background—they wanted it to appear as if Bush was far away at sea with U.S. sailors.

"For a speech that Mr. Bush delivered last summer at Mount Rushmore," the *Times'* Elisabeth Bumiller reports, "the White House positioned the best platform for television crews off to one side, not head on as other White Houses have done, so that the cameras caught Mr. Bush in profile, his face perfectly aligned with the four presidents carved in stone." You gotta love the subtlety.

On the second anniversary of September 11, "the White House rented three barges of giant Musco lights, the kind used to illuminate sports stadiums and rock concerts, sent them across New York Harbor, tethered them in the water around the base of the Statue of Liberty and then blasted them upward to illuminate all 305 feet of America's symbol of freedom." Lady Liberty served as the backdrop to Bush's address to the nation from Ellis Island.

At a speech in Albuquerque promoting Bush's tax cuts, GOP spinmasters "unfurled a backdrop that proclaimed its message of the day, 'Helping Small Business,' over and over. The type was too small to be read by most in the audience, but just the right size for television viewers at home."

On Thanksgiving 2003, Bush flew into Baghdad International Airport—where a plane had been shot down a week earlier—to serve Thanksgiving dinner to some of the troops fighting in Iraq. "In the most widely published image from hisThanksgiving day trip to Baghdad," the *Washington Post* reported later, "the beaming president is wearing an Army workout jacket and surrounded by soldiers as he cradles a huge platter laden with a golden-brown turkey. The bird is so perfect it looks as if it came from a food magazine, with bunches of grapes and other trimmings completing a Norman Rockwell image that evokes bounty and security in one of the most dangerous parts of the world. But as a small sign of the many ways the White House maximized the impact of the two and a half hour stop at the Baghdad airport, administration officials said yesterday that Bush picked up a decoration, not a serving plate." Handlers didn't want Bush to look like he was struggling with the weight of the real thing.

Do not scoff, grasshopper. Study and emulate.

Clinton was infamous for arriving many hours late for his appearances. I've seen him speak four times; on those occasions he showed up anywhere from forty-five minutes to two hours late. By the time he finally graced us with his presence, the buzz of anticipation had long left the crowd. People were growing resentful. "Is he still coming?" I heard a lady next to me ask no one in particular at a campaign rally in 1996. No one knew the answer. Others, late for work or whatever, packed up and left.

Senator Hillary Clinton and Bush each visited U.S. troops in Baghdad during Thanksgiving 2003. An unverified e-mail, supposedly sent from a captain serving in Gulf War II, reported that Bush got to dinner slightly late but lingered with the troops to make up for it: "It wasn't just a photo opportunity. This man was actually enjoying himself! He worked his way over the course of about 90 minutes towards my side of the room." Senator Clinton's visit, reported another soldier, went far differently: "Thanksgiving Dinner started at 3 p.m. that day, so the line was forming around 2:30 p.m. She didn't show up until around 3:30 p.m. Once she got there, Clinton and her entourage bumped everyone in line, forcing them to wait almost an extra hour." These stories are unsourced—and many such Internet missives from "soldiers" supposedly serving in Iraq later turned out to have been forged by Republican staffers—but these two ring true in my experience. Manners, class, panache: they matter.

The Left also falls short on appealing to our selfishness.

Right-wingers promise that we'll save money on taxes if we vote for them. They always say that, and it's never true. Reductions in federal income taxes inevitably lead to corresponding increases in state taxes. Tax cuts generally create deficits that have to be paid off, plus compound interest, a few years later, with even higher taxes. The few hundred bucks you save in the short run looks trivial next to the thousand-dollar repair bill for the axle that broke on the pothole that wasn't repaired by the city to finance your vote-buying rebate check.

The average American received $300 from the 2002 round of tax cuts. Because most of the money went to wealthy people, their share of the resulting deficit will be an astonishing $30,000 spread over ten years. But Republicans keep promising, and voters keep believing them, because cutting taxes is a good idea that would be really awesome if someone actually tried it someday.

Republican pledges to help the downtrodden frequently turn out to be nothing more than empty lies. Democrats, on the other hand, aren't smart enough to promise *anything* to the typical voter, who is white, lives somewhere in "flyover country," and believes himself or herself to belong to the middle class. Democratic party bosses are so stupid, so thick, and so unaware of basic human motivations that they've even stopped trying to buy votes. Not only did they refuse to promise specific benefits in exchange for votes, they wouldn't even go so far as to issue vague statements of generalized optimism to make people feel hopeful. While Ronald Reagan told Americans that a new day was dawning in 1980 and that their nation's best years were still ahead of them, Jimmy Carter spoke of "national malaise." Reagan's next challenger, Walter Mondale, pledged to raise taxes in 1984 to pay off the Gipper's deficit. Both men were honest. They were right. Both lost.

Republicans understand that the American political system is essentially indistinguishable from those of third world nations like Taiwan and Mexico, where candidates purchase votes by treating prospective supporters to banquets and free pots and pans. "Our first challenge is to let Americans keep more of their money," Bush promised repeatedly during the 2000 campaign. Democrats pledge to raise taxes in order to finance programs to help just about everyone besides the white, middle-aged, middle-class Midwesterners who decide every national election—prescription drugs for seniors, college aid for minorities. Vote for us, they promise, and we'll give your money to someone else, someone you probably don't even know. And they wonder why their sales pitch doesn't work?

Class-based affirmative action, tax cuts exclusively for the middle class, real reform for public schools: these are just some of the ways that a revitalized Democratic Party could buy votes from the long-neglected white middle class—people who actually vote.

It's also a fashion thing. Republican pundits and politicians work hard to project themselves as starchy (William Safire), dorky (Tucker Carlson's bowties), and snotty/sexy (Ann Coulter's miniskirts). They're unattractive looks, but they *are* looks. Democrats, however, are bland (Dick Gephardt), hideous (Joe Lieberman, Janet Reno), and uptight (Hillary Clinton). They're not "branded" properly. The same thing goes for leftist movements outside the Democratic Party. Leftie protesters look sloppy, disheveled, and dispirited; they don't project an image that many people want to emulate. When the Right runs wild, TV cameras record hooting jocks yelling at Florida elections officials during the 2000 recount battle. It was a frightening scene to those of us who read the minutes of the last meeting of the Reichstag in 1934, but most viewers watching at home saw the kind of hoo-ha guys who play football for their local college team before heading off to fight in Iraq when they fail to turn pro. I saw thugs on my TV screen; most Americans saw themselves.

But even for an old punk rocker like me, it's hard to identify with pierced/tattooed/branded leftists in full street regalia, whether it's rock-throwing anarcho-kids in black ninja masks chucking trash cans through the window of a Starbucks during an anti-WTO protest in Seattle or gussied-up drag queens strutting their stuff at a gay rights parade. (Don't get me wrong—the Seattle WTO and Quebec FTAA riots were unusually effective actions that saved thousands of jobs by slowing the rate of corporate-led globalization. I just don't think I would have felt comfortable hanging out with these fine young men and women.) In early 2003, protests against the U.S. invasion of Iraq drew hundreds of thousands of people to the streets of dozens of cities. This was, by any reasonable measure, an impressive display of dissent for a movement that was attempting to stop a war that hadn't yet begun. But the antiwar rallies failed to resonate, either with reporters assigned to describe them or the folks back home watching the images from San Francisco on their televisions. The message was diffuse and the image was unattractive. The protesters didn't look like America.

"One morning soon, before too many surfers or joggers are out, dozens of women in their fifties and sixties will gather on a beach somewhere in San Diego County, take off their clothes, lie on the sand, and arrange their bodies to spell 'peace,'" wrote Copley News Service's Dana Wilkie in February 2003.

The paragraph above was the lead of a story headlined, incredibly, "U.S. Antiwar Movement Based in the Mainstream." Only in an article about the American Left could old ladies stripping for peace be considered "mainstream." There isn't anything wrong with such outré stories per se. The trouble is, what ought to be presented as the kooky extremes of progressivism all too often appears to be its norm. Liberal actress-comedienne Janeane Garofalo put it like this: "[Network news] tends to marginalize [antiwar protests] by only interviewing the guy dressed as a carrot on stilts or [hippie and self-described "Clown Prince of the Counterculture"] Wavy Gravy. You know what I mean? Like some guy with no teeth and a tie-dyed Grateful Dead shirt, because they want to marginalize it. It doesn't seem fair that the heartfelt opinions of millions of people were ignored by a media circus whose center ring was a few dozen freaks and usual suspects."

I attended a few of the antiwar demonstrations in New York. I was struck by how many "normal" people were marching for peace, but their presence was aesthetically overwhelmed by the tattooed butch lesbians, giant skeleton puppets, and performance artists. It was unfortunate to have to note that, as usual, marchers refused to remain focused on the issue at hand: the imminent war. There were signs urging the state of Pennsylvania to free Mumia, asking states to ratify the Equal Rights Amendment, and decrying the disadvantaged status of bisexuals within the gay community, causes so worthy that they ought to have been the beneficiaries of their own rallies rather than diluting the power of the opposition to the war in Iraq.

Would Republicans tolerate the presence of similar distractions (pro–free traders, Christians marching for school vouchers, anti-abortion groups) at their rallies *for* the war? Certainly not.

Like it or not—and I don't—mainstream American voters are significantly less likely to identify with stilt-walking, flag-burning, purple-haired retro-hippies than a bunch of stuffy bald white dudes in suits. They may not like the suits—the suits are usually the guys who turn them down for a raise and fire them at the earliest sign of lagging stock prices—but they're used to them. The shock troops of the left come off as freaks, fringe lunatics, or worse.

Americans are liberals at heart, but the challenge for the Left isn't to convince voters that their ideas are the nation's. They are, but there's no way to explain that to an ahistorical electorate whose attention span peeters out halfway across the last bumper sticker they've read. One way liberals can send the message that they're regular people is to look like regular people, talk like regular people, and act like regular people.

When blacks marched for civil rights during the early sixties, they wore suits and ties. When redneck sheriffs sicced German shepherds on these clean-cut young people and blew them down the street with fire hose blasts, TV viewers in faraway northern suburbs were appalled. They finally understood why blacks had been complaining all of those years. A bunch of redneck lowlifes were beating the crap out of nice, well-groomed people who wanted nothing more than to eat a burger at Woolworth's. It pissed them off. Of course African-Americans really wanted much more than a burger, and they got it. But because of their actions the national mood changed. Segregation was doomed. And it would have taken a lot longer had civil rights protesters insisted on dressing and acting like slobs.

STOP PLAYING DEFENSE

Progressive-minded citizens need to stop manning their rhetorical Maginot Line.

Conservatives look like activists flogging new ideas because they are; they're for-ever presenting new ways to attack the prevailing social and political structure. (Yes, there's a difference between new ideas and trying to tear down old ones. But the distinction is a subtle one, and subtlety doesn't go far in politics.) The existing legal and social structure is predominantly liberal, because *liberals won the culture wars*. Liberals have spent the post-Vietnam era holding the line against Republican assaults, doing everything they could in order to protect their previous gains. But working the defensive line makes Dems look weak and insecure. It also costs them some of their own supporters, since humans prefer insurgents, crusading of activists, over stodgy same-old, same-olds.

The Left has fallen for the trap of the former revolutionary who turns reactionary in his old age. Ironically, liberals have become small-c conservatives—those trying to maintain the status quo—as conservatives present their rehashed, retrograde antipopulism as something novel and revolutionary. Liberals would do better were they to recognize that victory in American politics goes to those who express a forward-looking vision over those who cling to the past, no matter how glorious, fair-minded, or recent that history may be. As difficult as it is to do, some previously acquired ideological territory must be given up in pursuit of new victories. The current string of defeats must be brought to an end. Liberalism has arrived at a crisis decision. Winning is its own reward, whining a road to ruin.

WHAT TO DO
The American Left can take back America from the right-wing Republican minority, but only if it embarks on the following courses of action:

- Lefties must convince a sizable majority of the public that they share similar opinions on the most pressing issues.
- They must stop refighting the old culture wars of the sixties, seventies, and eighties.
- Democrats must create and publicize a slate of exciting new ideas and candidates that would improve the daily lives of ordinary citizens.
- They must abandon identity and special interest political agendas.
- They must establish that while Republicans are a party of selfishness and greed, Democrats stand up for the common good of most Americans.
- They must act cool.

In our mass media–saturated culture this last point may ultimately prove the most potent. One of the few things I knew for certain when I was a kid, before I even realized that I liked girls better than boys, was that I would never join the Shriners. Based on my observation of those old farts driving around in their miniature cars at my town's annual "Holiday at Home" parade every Labor Day, there was no way on earth that I could ever have seen myself wearing one of those ridiculous hats or making a fool of myself—at least not making a fool out of myself in that particular manner. From what I hear, the Shriners are responsible for many good works. They fund hospitals for desperately sick children, and that's just swell. But no matter how valuable its mission or how collegial its membership, I would never consider joining any organization whose members wear stupid fezes or drive those dumbass little cars.

Few like to admit it, but self-image is a critical component of human personal development. Like many teenagers, I enjoyed drawing cartoons. But what made me decide that I wanted to take things beyond the hobby stage was meeting an actual cartoonist and coming under the impression that both he and his life looked cool. Mike Peters, who later won a Pulitzer Prize, had invited me to his office at the *Dayton Daily News* to watch him draw and teach me a few basics about issues of taste (you can make fun of dead dictators but not dead presidents) and which types of paper work best with what kinds of ink. What struck me most at the time, however, was that Mike dressed great—hip-hugger jeans, retro-cowboy shirt with big pointy collar, boots—and that he worked in a funky, ink-stained corner room adjacent to the sports department. "Now that's cool," I remember thinking.

Most adult men I knew wore hideous suits to work. Whether or not their constrictive clothing was to blame, they looked depressed and uncomfortable. Peters, on the other hand, looked like he was having the time of his life. That made a big impression on me; the thought that I could have that life—his life—motivated me to keep going during the many years it took me to become established as an editorial cartoonist. Novices ask me how to deal with rejection, and my short answer is: keep your eyes on the prize. For me the prize was a way of life. Everything I did was directed towards getting that lifestyle for myself.

Personal ethics are impacted by similarly subjective stimuli. As much as I'd like to believe that my current political outlook reflects the culmination of decades of logical analysis of current events, trends, and historical precedent filtered through an objective lens of logic and moral rectitude, the truth is that image played a big role in my political development. When I was first becoming aware of the world around me, around the ages of eight to ten, the Republican Party was epitomized by President Richard Nixon, an unappealing man who looked smug, mean, vicious, and scary. Furthermore, when my fourth grade class held a mock presidential election in 1972, all of the kids who spoke up for Nixon were the bullies and morons. He was ugly, and his fans were scum. Unlike a future conundrum presented by the Ramones—whose music I loved despite the violent idiots who attended their concerts—my choice was easy.

And, of course, my mom was a Democrat.

Like most Americans, she counted Democrats and Republicans among her friends. With few exceptions, her liberal pals were noticeably cooler. They wore form-fitting turtlenecks, like Mary Tyler Moore (whose character on TV was obviously a liberal Democrat). They cracked funnier jokes, cooked better food, and laughed louder when laughter was called for. Her Republican friends often made more money at their jobs and had bigger homes in nicer neighborhoods, but they were a stiff and stuffy lot; if we accidentally broke something at their houses, they'd make such a big deal about it that we would be afraid to return. And sometimes we wouldn't get invited back.

Democrats didn't go crazy because you had deep-sixed a glass. They cleaned up the mess and went on talking as if nothing had happened.

My childhood impression—that Democrats were more fun, intellectually curious, and more charitable than Republicans—was mainly reinforced, albeit with subtle adjustments, during college. At Columbia the conservatives were a tiny, freakish minority on campus, loudly represented by the bow-tie-wearing Young Americans for Freedom and their anal-retentive weekly newspaper, the *Hamilton Report*. In the manner of young Republicans everywhere, Columbia's young conservatives wore suits to class and worked to affect a faux upper-class accent reminiscent of the films of the 1940s. Their newspaper was a sea of text presented in a miniscule eighteenth century–style font containing lengthy rants liberally sprinkled with yawn-inducing quotes from, appropriately and dully, the *Federalist Papers*. Campus rightists had devolved all the way through dorkdom and emerged from the tunnel of self-congratulation as fully realized freaks. (One of the right-wing girls, a tall platinum blonde who frequently claimed that her Welsh ancestors had suffered every bit as much in their mines as blacks had in the antebellum South, would have been downright hot had she not walked around with a furrow permanently glued to her forehead.) I didn't want to know these people, much less hear out their vision for the country.

The Right, then, was out. However, choosing the specific variety of leftism with which I wanted to affiliate myself proved difficult. One of my friends, who had impressed me with his encyclopedic knowledge of rock and punk music, was a strident Trotskyist who decorated his dorm room with posters of Lenin and a Soviet map of the world (in Russian, no less) tacked to the ceiling. At first I thought the red bunting look was cool, but after spending hours in there listening to a scratchy original pressing of Phil Ochs's second LP, I got sick of Kremlin chic. I couldn't imagine living like that every day. Also, the more Trotsky I read, the more I thought the little counterrevolutionary had had that ice pick coming: he couldn't write for shit.

Some of my college buddies called themselves Democratic Socialists, after the influential book by Michael Harrington. They aligned themselves with the French Socialists then led by President François Mitterand and strutted around College Walk wearing DSA T-shirts sporting the party's red rose logo. I wasn't too excited about their sportswear—in all seriousness, I remember hating the cheesy Cooper Black font they used—but what finally did in my interest was the interminable meetings. Kids would pull chairs around in a circle and spew theory quoted from books I hadn't read and had no interest in reading, more to impress one another or hear themselves talk than to enlighten.

More damning, they never had any plans to do anything. Protests, they replied to my inquiries about marches against Reagan, were an ineffective tool of political action. And there were no chicks! Had I wanted to hang out with a bunch of skinny white guys, I could have tossed back beers in the TV lounge.

That ended my dalliance with the radical Left.

I worked for Ted Kennedy's presidential bid in 1984, and after he lost at the convention, for Walter Mondale. At least the Democrats had a real organization. Unlike the D-Socs, they were *doing* stuff. They were pretty open-minded, too. As New York coordinator, I organized guerilla campaigns plastering anti-Reagan posters designed by a radical leftist ("the bombing begins in five minutes," they read in mock homage to an open-microphone gaffe) throughout the city. Nevertheless, I never felt quite at home with the Democrats either. Too many of my fellow campaign staffers were square, a little lackadaisical, and not a little witless. Here we were, fighting the evil Ronald Reagan for the future of the world (or so I thought), and these people showed up at campaign HQ with the same enthusiasm I mustered up for my latest hateful day job.

I ultimately developed much of my current political outlook, particularly concerning economics, after college and outside of the political process, during the six years I worked at Bear Stearns & Co. and the Industrial Bank of Japan Trust Company. (I wrote about this experience in an essay for *Might* magazine called "Confessions of an Investment Banker," which was reprinted in my book *Revenge of the Latchkey Kids*.) Observing the gross inefficiency of a free-market system shattered my assumptions that free markets were well-tuned (if amoral). I marveled how even the most well-intentioned cog was driven to become an evil part of the machine. I used to think that capitalism was more evil than inefficient; now I believe the opposite. Free from the influence of organized political groups, I formulated many of my current opinions about economic justice and efficiency. These years in the political wilderness allowed me to see how and why unfettered capitalism was a force that does more harm than good. I spent most of my long days toiling with businesspeople whose politics often surprised me, ranging from hard left to hard right but all wearing the same uncomfortable suits. They weren't the problem. The system was.

To this day my take on the capitalist system remains more of a reaction to the nepotism and egoism that drives the engine of free markets than adherence to any neatly formulated philosophy. Still, I'd be lying if I dismissed the influence of those early impressions from my childhood. For most of my life, Dems have tended to enjoy better style—if not always substance—than the Rs. That has had a lot to do with who I am today.

THE BLIGHT OF IDENTITY POLITICS

Lefties began to lose their mojo during the 1970s, when the identity politics craze began dominating the college activist groups whose alumni entered the worlds of journalism and politics.

The Vietnam-era New Left coalition of antiestablishment causes splintered into narrowly focused organizations obsessed with single issues. For instance, feminists who had previously found common ground with environmentalists found more strength in their identities as womyn striving to replace Hemingway with Toni Morrison in their local college campus English curriculum. If alliances require compromise, compromise necessitates moderation. The opposite is also true. The National Organization for Women, a mainstream, if somewhat milquetoast, feminist outfit founded by Betty Friedan in 1966, became increasingly radical under the presidency of Patricia Ireland. The vanguard of the contemporary environmental movement is no longer the Sierra Club—too moderate—but rather the tree-spiking, SUV-torching radicals of Earth First! and the freeform ecoterrorists of the Earth Liberation Front.

It says a lot about the state of the feminist movement that Americans are likelier to legalize gay marriage than pass an Equal Rights Amendment that would guarantee women equal status under the Constitution. But let me be clear: radicalization isn't NOW's problem. Perception is. The last thing any feminist organization needed was a president that feeds into the worst conceivable stereotypes equating gender rights with lesbianism; even worse, Ms. Ireland is hardly the "lipstick lesbian" Anne Heche type.

After NOW Ireland went on to become chief executive of the Young Women's Christian Association, which unceremoniously let her go after six months. The *New York Times* reported that conservative groups had pressured the YWCA to fire her because of her "tenure as president of the National Organization for Women, which supports gay and lesbian rights, as well as a woman's right to seek an abortion, and Ms. Ireland's living with a woman in the early 1990s while remaining married." Ireland's sexuality had been so effectively used to smear NOW that right-wingers were able to use NOW—which had been thought of as stodgy and mainstream before she came along—against her after she'd left.

Patricia Ireland is an intelligent, hard-working woman fervently devoted to the cause of equal rights for American women. She was amply qualified for the position she held, and I personally admire her. But for the same reasons that an upscale restaurant might do better than to hire an overweight, poorly groomed maitre d' to greet its patrons, a political group selecting a president whose job requires her to make frequent appearances on television should consider issues beyond mere qualifications. (For instance, few would argue that the Sierra Club found its most able candidate for president in Adam Werbach, who was twenty-three when picked for the top job at the venerable environmental group. But the club's board of directors wanted to send a message that it valued the involvement of young activists.) Most people who heard about Ireland's ascent to the presidency of the National Organization for Women mistakenly believed that it signaled a shift from moderate feminism to the kind of radical man-hating lesbianism espoused by figures like Andrea Dworkin. It turned them off, and away from NOW.

The point is simple yet important. When politics intersects with an infotainment culture, style frequently matters more than substance. It's unfortunate, but it's reality. In debates with the right, progressives often win on the facts and lose on image—where's the glory in that? Once left sts show independents/soccer moms/NASCAR dads/Reagan Democrats/ swing voters that they understand their cultural references as well as their abstract political desires, they'll be much more likely to be attracted to them, and thus to their message.

Presenting a pretty face isn't necessarily a sellout, by the way. Like a great CD with a great cover, if you offer a positive message, spin is an honest use of aesthetic propaganda. Presenting a great product in an ugly package is the ultimate betrayal of the all-important principle of truth in advertising.

COURTING THE NEGLECTED MIDDLE CLASS

Let's assume that the big issues—attitude, organization, public relations, all the rest—are under control. The question remains: how do Democrats and their fellow travelers explain to us Americans that we're—gasp!—liberal?

The first step on the road to recovery is to make Americans understand that they're not conservatives. The vast self-identified "middle class" (as opposed to the smaller, actual, middle class, this group includes many poor and wealthy citizens who prefer, for whatever reason, to think of themselves as earning an average income) receives far more attention from Republicans

---

IF YOU'RE POOR BUT YOU DON'T KNOW IT . . .

The National Center for Opinion Research finds that:

> 36 percent of Americans who earn $15,000 a year define themselves as "middle class"

> 49 percent of people who earn between $35,000 and $49,999 say they're "middle class"

> 71 percent of those who earn more than $ 75,000 think of themselves as "middle class"

According to Worth-Roper Starch:

> The median annual income of the top one percent of American workers is $330,000. Most of these people do not consider themselves "rich," but rather "middle class."

The U.S. Census Bureau says:

> Median income in the U.S. is $22,000.

than Democrats, who direct most of their campaign rhetoric toward the extremely poor down-and-out sorts who don't bother to vote.

I grew up fairly poor—my mother's mid-1970s starting salary as a teacher was less than $8,000 a year—and some of my friends were doing still worse than us. Yet I never heard of, much less met anyone who participated in, Head Start. No doubt, it's a great program. But most people don't take advantage of it or know anyone who does, so they don't relate to it.

Head Start, Head Start, Head Start—when is Hillary Clinton going to stop talking about goddamn Head Start?

Democrats spend far too much time talking up worthy programs that most people don't give a shit about. Gays in the military, midnight basketball, standing up for the rights of prospective flag burners: these are the stupid, narrowly-focused faux issues that the right uses to distract gullible leftists from infinitely more pressing matters. Of course, Republicans don't actually *do* anything more for the middle class than the Democrats; the truth is, neither party cares about middle-class concerns enough to devote a government spending program to them. The GOP, however, is smart enough to *talk* to what Marx called the petty bourgeois and to address their concerns, albeit with empty election-year rhetoric. Trickle-down/supply-side economics has been repeatedly proven to be a crock; the theory that cutting taxes to the rich in the hope that their spending will stimulate the economy for everyone else has been thoroughly debunked. Yet many members of the middle class vote Republican because they buy into the trickle-down scam. Republicans promise that they'll stimulate the economy and that a rising tide will raise all boats, and middle class Americans believe it. And why not? No one else even bothers to *lie* to them.

That has got to change.

CREATING AN ASPIRATIONAL IMAGE

I worked several years as a staff writer for one of the first glossy "lad" magazines during the late nineties. (*Maxim* and *FHM* remain the successful relics of that era.) Marketing and advertising experts kept harping on magazine publishing rule number one: glossies are an aspirational product. While titles like *Men's Health* are read by males who hope to pick up information niblets they can use to improve themselves and thus attract women, most male-oriented magazines create a the illusion of a lifestyle, an image that they hope readers will want to emulate. Their implicit promise, that reading a magazine will teach you how to get laid or pick the perfect car, is an inherent tease.

First and foremost, it isn't possible to orgasm for an hour straight and you probably can't afford $120,000 for a car. For most readers, however, reading about sex and money and what a Ferrari feels like rounding a curve doing 140 is enough. Readers experience what they crave vicariously, then head back to their boring jobs. Mission accomplished.

It's easy to forget now, but the most successful politicians didn't just talk voters into supporting them. They made them want to be them.

The perfect political image blends an impression of thoughtfulness and élan. Protestants took a chance on electing America's first Catholic president because John F. Kennedy promised, overtly with a speech pledging to ignore the Vatican on political issues and subliminally with a calm speaking style, not to do anything rash. JFK balanced his message of prudence with an easy wit and graceful charm at press conferences, and made-for-proto-TV moments like a "spontaneous" stop at Baskin Robbins on a hot day. Deliberation and pizzazz—you see it in the leaders that Americans consider their favorites. FDR, Ike, and Reagan all had it. So did Martin Luther King Jr.

The other trait these men projected was cool. Their clothes, hand gestures, and oratorical ticks were carefully calibrated to appeal to our national lust for Steve McQueen's calmness and occasional willingness to go over the top when it's appropriate. In recent years, Senator John McCain and General Colin Powell both came close to the American masculine ideal of quiet, determined dignity, but blew it. "Straight talk express" veteran McCain lost his grip on the popular imagination—many of my liberal friends said they would have voted for him despite his consistently conservative voting record—when he decided to endorse Bush after a bitter primary battle. McCain yielded to GOP pressure but lost the people in the process; what kind of man would endorse a man who had falsely accused him, during a crucial Bible Belt primary, of fathering a black child out of wedlock with a hooker? Calmness, yes; wimpiness, no.

Powell, on the other hand, lost his rep for even-tempered dispassion by signing on as secretary of state to the most radically right-wing White House in memory. His association with Bush, his integrity-sacrificing lie-filled performance before the United Nations on Iraq's fictional weapons of mass destruction, plus reports that he lost his temper in meetings with fellow cabinet members and journalists, have probably ruined his chances of becoming our first president of color, as my PC pals would say. We appreciate Powell's role as a moderating influence to hotheads like Rumsfeld and Cheney, but he's no longer the relaxed know-it-all we once thought he was.

It's hard to recruit charismatic candidates to high office. Even more difficult is remaking the image of a party itself.

Democrats last achieved this in 1932, thanks to FDR's visionary understanding that the Great Depression had created an opening for a new kind of majority political party. Republicans did it in 1980 by channeling Barry Goldwater's purist conservatism into the easy smile of former actor Ronald Reagan and packaging the same-old same-old as something brand new. Clinton revitalized the classic tax-and-spend Democratic image in 1992 by pledging to temper traditional liberalism with traditionally Republican platform planks like free trade, welfare reform, and balancing the budget. (He also played the Baby Boomer card, relying on early footage of himself as a young man meeting Kennedy at the White House—it's destiny, see?—and referring to himself as "the man from Hope.") Television coverage of national political conventions, thirty-second attack ads, planted opinion pieces, and a host of other strategies to project a unified image are necessary to communicate to the public that one's message or approach has changed. What should that image be? That comes later. Right now, the important thing to remember is that a new Democratic Party must adopt a new image, that image has got to be cool, and the marketing of that image must be relentless.

STOP TAKING ABUSE

Few Americans have ancestors who were pioneers of the Old West, but the mythical spirit of rugged individualism helps define what it means to be American. The film *Death Wish* framed the masculine zeitgeist of our times. The character of the quiet, well-armed architect played by squinty-eyed actor Charles Bronson, who goes berserk after criminal loons go too far once too often, is us. We don't start fights, but we finish them. Bush played the vengeance card after September 11: they attacked us, now they're gonna pay. Who cares whether we bomb the right country or kill the guilty people? Close enough is good enough when you're going gangbusters and walking tall. All too often, as when Clinton failed to intervene in Rwanda or to push for his 1992 campaign platform, Democrats hesitate when shooting first is what's called for.

The silly tank photo is what we remember most from Michael Dukakis' 1988 presidential campaign, but what really did him in was his answer to the question of what he'd do if his wife Kitty were raped. (He hemmed and hawed before settling on a perfectly reasonable, cold-blooded response about letting the courts take their course.) But we didn't want to hear a rational response to an irrational question. We wanted to hear him say what we'd say: "I'd hunt the bastard down and kill him with my bare hands if I had to. If I spent the rest of my life in prison, I'd sleep just fine knowing that I had ripped that scum's head clean off." In reality, of course, few Americans resort to vigilantism when their loved ones are murdered or raped. Ninety-nine point nine percent of us do, as Dukakis said he would, let the system do its thing. But vengeance is a powerful fantasy, so powerful that we asked ourselves: if a guy doesn't get angry at someone who rapes his spouse, what will he do if someone attacks the country? Call the cops?

Looking out for you and yours is selfish, but it's expected. On the national political scene, Republicans understand this principle far better than Democrats. In 2002, for instance, GOP congressmen and senators demanded that the president of Germany fire a cabinet official who had compared Bush's aggressive foreign policy to that of Adolf Hitler's. They also demanded the dismissal of an aide to the Canadian prime minister for calling Bush a "moron." Recently they extrapolated the sacred-cow protocol to the point of protecting the legacy of a former Republican president.

When CBS announced plans to broadcast a "biopic" miniseries called *The Reagans* about the former first couple, Republican politicians and their media allies immediately screamed bloody murder. Word had it that *The Reagans* would discuss Nancy Reagan's reliance upon an astrologer when she was First Lady. Though Ronald would be given credit for ending the Cold War (undeserved credit for a dubious achievement at best, given the chaos and rising Islamism that filled the power vacuum created by the fall of the USSR), conservatives were furious that the movie would make no mention of the eighties economic boom (probably because most economists believe the "boom" to have been nothing more than a chimera, having benefited pitifully few Americans). "They were mocking a president while he was ill!" shouted conservative TV talk show host Bill O'Reilly on Fox News. "Show me one instance of a Republican doing that to a Democrat! One!"

Ultimately, CBS yielded to political pressure and canceled the miniseries. ("CBS officials acknowledged a sense of awe, if not shock," reported the *New York Times* in a coy reference to Defense Department bombing strategies employed against Iraq, "at the fury of the conservative response through cable news shows, radio talk shows and, most notably, the Internet. The network, they said, received about eighty thousand angry e-mail notes, protesting the miniseries.") It may seem like a relatively minor victory, but as Bruce Springsteen sang, from small things big things one day come: after CBS canceled *The Reagans*, Congressman Matt Salmon's long-stalled crusade to carve Reagan's face into Mount Rushmore began gathering renewed attention.

Senate Minority Leader Tom Daschle and other Democrats tried to rouse public anger at the network for engaging in censorship, but no one much cared. Truth was, Americans understood what the Republicans were doing. Reagan was their man; they were protecting their party's image by looking out for him. If CBS gave into their pressure, that was their problem. They could have, after all, said no.

The CBS-*Reagans* story is a lesson for liberals to emulate. (Imagine such a program, featuring lurid details of the Monica Lewinsky scandal, being aired while Clinton lay on his deathbed. Could Democrats generate enough heat to force a major television network to cave in? Would they bother to try?) Whether you're a liberal politician or just an ordinary citizen, stand up for what's yours, even when you're not absolutely certain that you're morally entitled to do so. After all, your values are majority values. Moreover, you want what's right. Fight tooth and nail to protect the battles you've won, the people who've been there for you and those you want in the future. Don't let a day pass without working on a liberal-minded initiative, even if it's just writing a letter to the editor. Don't concede a thing to the Republicans. If you lie down and take abuse, after all, how can people trust you to protect them against enemies foreign and domestic?

chapter 3

THE TROUBLE WITH AMERICA

With its population comprising only five percent of the world total, America produces 27 percent of the world's total economic output . . . In the past 20 years, the wealth of America grew from $7 trillion to $32 trillion, a rate that exceeded federal expenditures by 400 percent.
— Former Secretary of Labor Robert Reich, 2000

God, don't let me die! I have so much to do!
— Last words of Louisiana Governor Huey Long,
September 10, 1935

Aside from rainy days, riptides, and occasional shark attacks, we shouldn't have any problems.

The United States of America is wealthier than any nation-state has been in the history of the world. Millions of illegal immigrants cross our borders every year, but that's only because the INS allows them to pass at the behest of American businessmen who want to hire illegals as cheap foreign labor. The truth is, our frontiers are secure. We enjoy excellent diplomatic and economic relations with our two immediate neighbors, Mexico and Canada, and there is no imminent threat of a devastating military attack by any rival nation.

No one can touch us when it comes to military prowess. "The United States spends more than all of its allies—including the next most potent military powers in the world—combined," Ivan Eland, director of policy studies at the Cato Institute, noted before the start of the Iraq war. "At most, the Russians and Chinese each spend $70 billion to $80 billion per year, and the actual total may be much less. The most unfriendly nations— Iran, Iraq, Syria, Libya, Cuba and North Korea— spend a paltry $15 billion per year combined." No one can keep up with us. Moreover, everyone is dependent upon us to defend themselves. U.S. military equipment is the world's gold standard, making us the world's number one arms dealer. (In 2002 we raked in $13.3 billion, amounting to 45.5 percent of the world's conventional weapons sales, of which $8.6 billion went to third world countries.) We can enact regime change simply by turning off the flow of arms to our client states.

September 11 made us feel vulnerable, but it could have been avoided. Had our government deployed its resources more intelligently, paid attention to the warnings of our allies, and scrambled fighter jets as soon as it became obvious that they had been hijacked, it wouldn't have happened. It was a tribute to incompetence rather than intrinsic weakness. Terrorism, crime, drugs—we have our problems, but they're all of our own making.

We are, in short, da bomb.

Given our enormous wealth and outsized military strength, it stands to reason that the fortunate citizens of the American empire should enjoy the world's highest standard of living. And our average per capita income—though skewed internally due to increasing disparity of wealth—is in fact ranked first among nations (we're tied with Norway). Yet a growing gap between rich and poor has, by some measures, reduced us to second and third world status. Moreover, many poorer countries do better than us, especially when it comes to providing such basic needs as medical care and affordable housing for their people. It's not right and it doesn't make sense. Why should Germans enjoy six weeks of paid vacation every year while we make do with two? Why should Americans skimp on medical care because of cost? Who won World War II, anyway?

According to opinion surveys, these same thoughts annoy Americans year after year. They concern problems and complaints, all of them solvable if we care enough to try, that drive tens of millions of Americans nuts. Yet nobody does anything. It's all virgin territory for the leader, or political party, that chooses to stake it out, and it presents an amazing opportunity.

Theoretically either major party could exploit these longstanding concerns and complaints, but Republicans suffer from the smugness of victory; like the Great Society–era Democrats, they're unlikely to change course as long as they believe that everything is going well. Also, taking on these issues would force them to address a fundamental ideological conflict. Tackling most of these issues in a meaningful way would require asking business, a traditional Republican ally, to remit higher taxes and make other concessions.

Democrats, on the other hand, are desperate for new, winning issues. They've already taken baby steps in most of these areas. Most importantly, taking on long-neglected concerns offers the chance for Democrats to prove to typical voters that they care about them. These are, after all, the problems that Americans citizens would most like to see fixed. Who doubts that voters would show their gratitude on election day?

Of course, identifying the biggest irritants is only a beginning. Progressives need to get organized and channel popular support for their proposed solutions. But they can't exploit big issues until they understand them. This means:

- *Selecting issues of importance to a wide social and political spectrum of the population.* Narrowcasting (for example, appealing to senior citizens with a prescription drug benefit specifically targeted towards them) catches fewer fish and risks alienating members of other constituencies who inadvertently become the collateral damage to your solutions (for example, young people who don't get a prescription drug benefit from the government but pay higher taxes nonetheless). Affirmative action is perhaps the ultimate example of narrowcasting.
- *Addressing chronic problems instead of trendy ones.* While addressing temporal issues may have a topical appeal and garners headlines, voters will remember a leader who reduces crime over the long run more fondly than one who takes credit for a single year's drop in burglaries. More importantly, his or her party will coast on the credit for a long time.
- *Keeping the list short.* An imaginative analyst can come up with thousands of matters of concern to the American electorate, but the Rule of Three that governs the human attention span—if you ask people who don't follow basketball to name basketball stars, most can recall no more than three—governs politics. Former Clinton chief of staff John Podesta says, "The question I'm asked most often is, 'When are we getting our eight words?' [Conservatives] have their eight words on a bumper-sticker: 'Less government. Lower taxes. Less welfare.'" Eight words or three slogans, whichever comes first, is a good limit for a politician trying to present an easily recalled agenda.

- *Mixing it up.* The key to rebuilding the Democratic Party is recognizing that Americans won't support a party that addresses a single constituency. (The perception that Republicans don't care about anyone but the rich is their Achilles' heel.) Those big bumper-sticker issues have to appeal to as broad a group of Americans as possible—ideally 100 percent of them.

Following is a look at the most consistently highest-ranking responses to the classic pollster's question: "What problems are you personally most concerned about?" You may be surprised to discover what these issues are. Only a liberal electorate, you may murmur, would care about this stuff. If you say that, you're exactly right. Americans, after all, are liberals—they just don't think of themselves that way. If the Left presented popular solutions to neglected problems, if they took a gun to the elephant standing there in the room wearing a big insolent grin, they'd tap into the electorate's inner liberal. If Democrats use these issues to get elected, and then use their power to make good on their promises, they'll kick GOP ass for years to come—whether or not Americans care to use the *L* word.

THE SHAME OF AMERICAN HEALTHCARE

If you need an organ transplant, the United States is the best place to live in the world. Should you contract some obscure yet-to-be-identified virus, your chances of being correctly diagnosed are probably better here than anywhere else.

Odds are, however, that you will never journey to these extreme limits of your local hospital ward. The overwhelming majority of Americans visit doctors, dentists, and specialists in order to treat their sore throats, fix their prostates, and fill their cavities. They need new glasses and contact lenses. They want moles whacked and frozen off, broken bones mended, infections controlled by antibiotics.

For a variety of reasons ranging from the rising costs of medical school and malpractice insurance to plain old greed on the part of HMOs and insurance companies, healthcare costs keep rising faster than just about anything else. The average monthly premium for employer-sponsored health care plans is currently increasing between 10 and 15 percent per year—in addition to the inflation rate.

I'm forty years old and in excellent health. I've never smoked, I drink alcohol in moderation, and I run about fifteen miles a week. Not to brag, but what the hell—most people say I look more like thirty-three than forty. I look good, I feel great, and I typically see my doctor twice a year, once for a physical before traveling overseas and again to treat an ear infection or similar minor annoyance. My wife, who is a year younger than me, is also a picture of perfect health and enviable personal habits. Yet the cheapest quote we've been able to find for our crappy HMO plan—one that only partially covers a visit to see our long-time family physician, doesn't cover dental or glasses, and requires us to pay an additional $250 per category deductible per annum—is $600.88 per month.

That sucks. In New York City, where we live, you have to earn at least $1,000 in order to keep $600 after taxes. Therefore, we dedicate $12,000 per year in pre-tax earnings just for health insurance. That doesn't include all the stuff our crappy plan doesn't cover, like the deductible, a $20 co-pay per visit, etc. Of course, I probably shouldn't complain. Given that millions of people *earn* less than that for a year of backbreaking full-time work (the minimum wage now works out to $10,300 a year), it's no big shocker that 44 million Americans don't have any health insurance whatsoever (in 2002 alone, the last year for which statistics were available at press time, more than two million people lost their coverage) and that another 40 million are considered "underinsured," i.e., only "partly covered" for certain maladies and injuries or unable to maintain insurance for twelve months out of the year. More than a third of Americans aren't fully insured!

Health insurance is an incredibly crappy deal. Since I became self-employed in 1995, I've spent roughly $60,000 on insurance premiums. But with the exception of 1999, when I underwent a $2,500 hernia operation (watch that bench-pressing, guys!), I've never spent more than $500 a year on doctors—that makes a total of about $7,000, for a net insurance company profit of $53,000. Incredibly, "managed care" is even a bigger nightmare for hospitals than for individuals.

You might decide, as many Americans have, to forego health insurance and hit the ER in the event that you break something. But government budget cuts, closing hospitals, an aging population, and uninsured patients who wait longer than previously to seek care are creating an unprecedented explosion in the number of sick people being crammed into the nation's emergency rooms. Trusting your health to the ER isn't wise.

HEALTH INSURANCE:
A NATION OF HAVES AND HAVE-NOTS

	Insured Privately	Medicaid or Government Insurance	Uninsured
All	69.6%	11.6%	15.2%
Children	67.5	23.9	11.6
Adults	72.2	6.9	19.5

Source: U.S. Census Bureau, 2002

"We see just over 50,000 patients a year," attests Dr. Tom Scaletta, emergency department chairman at Chicago's West Suburban Hospital. "We're starting to get to the point where we're underproviding. Hospitals reach capacity and have to turn away ambulances."

Because federal law prohibits hospitals from refusing to provide patients with care, indigent people have traditionally relied on ERs for their basic medical needs. Because of the healthcare insurance crisis, the typical ER patient has become markedly more upscale. "The profile of an uninsured patient is that of somebody who is working, sometimes two jobs—usually they're low-wage jobs, however—in a situation where the employer may offer the option for the employee to purchase insurance and they simply can't afford it," says Scaletta.

Even if you make $36,000, a fairly decent salary in most parts of the country, who can spare a third of their salary just for health insurance? And it costs more—sometimes twice as much—if you're older, suffer from a preexisting condition, or have kids.

Together, the third of our population who make do without insurance are driving up costs, clogging hospital emergency rooms, and dying prematurely due to lack of adequate care. But that doesn't mean the rest of us, those with insurance, are much more fortunate.

Some political analysts, bedazzled by the Republican defeat of Bill Clinton's healthcare plan, have been fooled into thinking that healthcare isn't the issue it once was. Nonetheless, during the 2000 election some 44 percent of voters identified healthcare as their single biggest worry (the state of the education system was the only issue that came ahead). By July 2002, after the September 11 terrorist attacks, a Harris poll saw that number drop to nine percent, compared to 37 percent for terrorism, 37 percent for the economy and jobs, and 13 percent for war and defense.

Of course, people's minds turned to foreign affairs as fighting continued in Afghanistan and the Bush Administration began to make its case for war against Iraq. But healthcare as a concern never disappeared, and poll numbers expressing that worry began rising as soon as the shock of September 11 began fading. After all, even people covered by insurance despised their HMOs. Sixty percent of respondents to a post–September 11 survey said that healthcare was too expensive and difficult to obtain. "Physicians should recognize that their patients are still concerned about rising healthcare costs and access, even though this survey shows that there are other things on people's minds besides healthcare right now," said Mollyann Brodie of the Kaiser Family Foundation.

I got sick a lot as a kid. My mom never had any trouble getting an appointment to see our pediatrician, the genial Dr. Palmer. More often than not, we got an appointment a few hours after my mom called his receptionist.

Dr. Palmer always had more than enough time for us. I remember that he always gave me a lollipop from a drawer under the examining table and that I always took one even though I didn't like them. Insurance was a breeze. My mom flashed her Blue Cross/Blue Shield card and Dr. Palmer earned enough money to pay his mortgage on his very big house. He filled out the forms, not my mom. Sometimes he'd recommend tests, or a visit to a specialist. Blue Cross paid the bill. Again: no forms, no wait for reimbursement, no frustrating phone calls to some clerk in Hartford, Connecticut.

Now—well, you know all about now. Now is a nightmare. First you have to beg for an appointment because doctors impoverished by low insurance reimbursements cram in dozens more patients a day in order to meet their expenses. Choosing a doctor means picking a name at random out of a book. Big-city HMO clinics are dingy and grim. Furthermore, more and more, you have to pay your bills out of your own pocket because an increasing number of doctors refuse to deal with the HMOs. With luck, a check for perhaps 80 percent of the bill will appear several months later; more typically your HMO will refuse payment altogether, for no reason whatsoever, simply because it can. The idea is transparently cynical: the longer your HMO avoids paying out reimbursements, the more interest it earns on the "float." They say you'll get paid if you insist, but why should you have to insist?

God help anyone who should require drugs or an appointment to consult with a specialist. Now some bureaucrat, not your doctor, decides whether a prescribed test was absolutely necessary. Because they're paid to keep expenses low, rather than to keep you healthy, HMO bureaucrats routinely deny legitimate requests for payment. And this all assumes that you're happy picking your "care providers" from a list of names arbitrarily selected by a corporation, rather than, say, because a friend or relative recommended them.

An NPR-Kaiser-Harvard poll taken in 2002 shows that 80 percent of the electorate favors a radical overhaul of the nation's health care system. Twenty percent thinks that minor changes are necessary. That adds up to 100 percent. *Nobody* believes that the state of medical care in the United States is just peachy. Despite such distractions as the war on terrorism and the recession (the latter actually contributes to concerns about health care costs), the dismal state of health care in the United States remains a massively potent political issue that remains oddly underexploited.

This may be due to the bitter defeat suffered by the Clintons in their 1993 attempt to overhaul the nation's health care reimbursement system. But the Clinton plan didn't fail because people were satisfied with the state of healthcare. The problem with the 1993 plan was that it tried to accommodate the insurance companies at the expense of patients and doctors alike. It was too complicated for individuals and too expensive for business. Typical of such compromises, the plan's unwillingness to pick sides meant that it didn't have a constituency. Nobody stood to gain, so nobody fought for it. Polls have consistently demonstrated that Americans want something done about the sorry state of healthcare in the world's richest nation. They just didn't believe, with good reason, that the Clinton plan would have solved the problem.

THE MINIMUM WAGE FARCE

"All but the hopeless reactionary will agree that to conserve our primary resources of manpower, government must have some control over maximum hours, minimum wages, the evil of child labor, and the exploitation of unorganized labor," President Franklin D. Roosevelt said in 1937. Sadly the hopeless reactionaries have been getting their way ever since.

Created in 1938 in order to stop businesses from undercutting their competitors by slashing workers' pay, the minimum wage has the potential to become a rare bulwark of civility and economic decency in a workplace where labor-management relations most closely resemble the slave ship scene in *Ben Hur*. Instead businesses have used their cozy relationships with federal lawmakers to keep the federal minimum wage so low that eleven states and the District of Columbia have passed legislation mandating higher rates in order to prevent their regional economies from slipping into third world status.

American workers are among the most productive in the world. They produce more "value added"—the dollar value assigned by economists to a worker's efforts with raw material—than those of any other nation. Yet it is still possible to wallow in poverty while doing an honest day's work five days a week, fifty weeks a year, for the rest of your miserable life.

Every now and then some forward-thinking Congressional Democrat proposes a modest increase in the national minimum wage. (In December 2003, Democratic presidential candidate Howard Dean proposed an increase to—party at my place tonight!—seven bucks an hour. And he was the "leftie.") Because two-thirds of minimum wage workers are adults, the vast majority of minimum wage increases goes to support families that are struggling to remain afloat, not to fund CD or Gameboy purchases for spoiled teenagers as some pundits assert. Raising low-end wages helps the states reduce welfare rolls by making work pay more than sitting at home. Perhaps most importantly, raising the minimum wage benefits higher-wage workers by pushing up the entire pay scale, as well as by increasing the overall consumer spending that propels two-thirds of the U.S. economy. Unlike wealthy citizens who dump their surplus cash into numbered accounts in the Cayman Islands, poor people put all the money they earn directly back into circulation in the form of rent and groceries.

There's a basic moral principle here. Working forty hours a week ought to enable an individual to provide for basic expenses like food, shelter, and medical care. The food doesn't have to be fancy and the shelter can be a run-down apartment in a marginal neighborhood, but it's nothing short of obscene that a citizen who works every bit as hard as a CEO doesn't receive enough on payday to take care of his bills.

Unsurprisingly as well as unfortunately, too many employers don't believe that they have any moral obligation to pay their workers a living wage. If infinite cash and zero work is the ideal situation from the standpoint of workers, management's perfect world of work would reinstate legalized slavery and hundred-hour weeks. Counting on the good will of bosses to do the right thing voluntarily is a mug's game; left to their own devices, employers would allow wages to spiral forever downward, dragging the economy along into something that looks more like the Philippines than Philadelphia. Naturally employers wouldn't be able to sell their products if no one earned enough money making other products to afford theirs, but few executives are smart enough to understand that simple truth. The minimum wage is a perfect example of a liberal program that saves capitalism from its own wretched excesses.

The Right invariably trots out the same tired arguments whenever it fights liberal-backed proposals for increasing the minimum wage. People will lose their jobs. Companies teetering at the razor's edge of solvency will be pushed into the abyss of bankruptcy. These bogus claims should have been laid to rest during the late seventies, when the claim that minimum wage increases caused layoffs was thoroughly debunked by the Congressional Minimum Wage Study Commission, a detailed review of the economic impact of the minimum wage conducted by a blue-ribbon panel of national economists. Naturally, there is a limit to the benefits of raising the minimum wage: a hike to a million bucks an hour would obviously precipitate economic ruin. But the Carter-era commission ultimately found that each incremental increase in the minimum wage had caused only minor (between one and three percent) cuts, and even then only among workers age seventeen and under. Even teen employment—and the idea that kids should work is hardly universally accepted—quickly rebounded in every historical example. There was *no effect whatsoever* on adult employment—employers, it turns out, need the number of workers that they need, and they pay more for them if forced to do so. There is no evidence that a single business has ever failed in the history of the United States due to a rise in the minimum wage.

As is the case concerning so many economic issues, conservatives have been repeatedly proven dead wrong about the minimum wage. Yet, as is also often true, Republicans' fallacious reasoning, when coupled with relentless campaigning and red-baiting attacks on progressives, resonates with a public too busy working multiple jobs to take the time to figure things out for themselves. The end result is a minimum wage that goes up but fails to keep up with inflation—much less one that allows working families to get ahead.

When the current minimum wage of $5.15 an hour was enacted in 1996, the rate already paid below the federal poverty line for a family of three. Two presidential terms later, inflation has eaten away 21 percent of that paltry sum. Depending on how you prefer to look at it, today's minimum wage is either worth $4.07 in 1996 dollars or, if it had increased along with inflation, should now be $6.23. And that's merely a short-term example of how inflation—during the low-inflation turn of the century—eroded the minimum wage.

Oregon State University (OSU) compares the minimum wage to the rate of inflation by adjusting historical minimum wages to the value of the dollar in the year 2000. According to OSU, the minimum wage peaked out in 1968, when it was worth $7.84 in 2000 dollars. With the exception of small increases during the late seventies and late eighties, the inflation-adjusted minimum wage has plummeted ever since. (Still buy the GOP's rhetoric about a high minimum wage stifling economic growth? Consider the state of the American economy during the fifties and sixties, when the wage was going up, versus the next three decades, when it was dropping.)

A wage hike is long overdue. Considering that American workers are more than twice as productive as they were in 1968, a relatively minor lift, to ten dollars per hour, is the very least companies can do to show that they appreciate the people who cook their fast food and clean their offices.

Not only is a substantial minimum wage hike the right thing to do, it's also damned smart economics. It would stimulate consumer spending, creating a ripple effect up the income ladder as higher-income businesspeople sell more goods and services to working-class Americans and in turn earn profits to be reinvested and used to hire more workers.

Another way to consider the minimum wage is to ask where the world's biggest economy stands next to other industrialized nations.

Luxembourg pays Europe's highest minimum wage, $9.48 per hour. The Netherlands pays $7.13, Belgium $6.71, and France brings up the rear at $6.55—low by European Union standards but still 27 percent above the lowest-paid workers in the United States. European unemployment is higher than ours—8.5 percent next to our 6.0 percent—but economists

VALUE OF THE FEDERAL MINIMUM WAGE
ADJUSTED FOR INFLATION

Year	Nominal Dollars	1996 Dollars
1955	0.75	4.39
1956	1.00	5.77
1957	1.00	5.58
1958	1.00	5.43
1959	1.00	5.39
1960	1.00	5.30
1961	1.15	6.03
1962	1.15	5.97
1963	1.25	6.41
1964	1.25	6.33
1965	1.25	6.23
1966	1.25	6.05
1967	1.40	6.58
1968	1.60	7.21
1969	1.60	6.84
1970	1.60	6.47
1971	1.60	6.20
1972	1.60	6.01
1973	1.60	5.65
1974	2.00	6.37
1975	2.10	6.12
1976	2.30	6.34
1977	2.30	5.95
1978	2.65	6.38
1979	2.90	6.27
1980	3.10	5.90
1981	3.35	5.78
1982	3.35	5.45
1983	3.35	5.28
1984	3.35	5.06
1985	3.35	4.88
1986	3.35	4.80
1987	3.35	4.63
1988	3.35	4.44
1989	3.35	4.24
1990	3.80	4.56
1991	4.25	4.90
1992	4.25	4.75
1993	4.25	4.61
1994	4.25	4.50

FEDERAL MINIMUM WAGE (CONT.)

Year	Nominal Dollars	1996 Dollars
1995	4.25	4.38
1996	4.75	4.75
1997	5.15	5.03
1998	5.15	4.96
1999	5.15	4.85
2000	5.15	4.72
2001	5.15	4.56
2002	5.15	4.49
2003	5.15	4.40

Source: U.S. Department of Labor

figure that the higher tax revenues that result from higher salaries more than finance a social safety net for those who can't find jobs. Furthermore, EU unemployment is calculated differently than U.S. figures, which stop counting jobless workers who become discouraged and stop looking for work. There's no evidence that European employers would hire more workers if wages were to fall.

Here in the United States, every dollar hike in the minimum wage directly impacts the living standards of at least 10 million potential voters. According to numerous polls, even people who aren't subject to the minimum wage would prefer to see it increased. "It's noteworthy that support for the wage increase runs high even among those who don't stand to benefit directly," says Daniel Merkle of ABC News, who marvels at the idea's consistent popularity over time. "Eighty-eight percent of lower-income Americans like the idea, but so do 79 percent of those in the higher-income range of $50,000 and up. It may be altruism based on a recognition that $5.15 won't go far; or, perhaps, hopes for a ripple-up effect."

The issue of higher wages for the people who do the hardest work used to belong to the Democratic Party, but thanks to decades of neglect by the former "party of the people," it's now wide-open. Doing well by doing good is basic economics as well as smart politics, but Democrats must ratchet up their rhetoric if they hope to make an impression on a jaded electorate. To hell with pushing for *an* increase in the minimum wage—regular increases ought to be permanently indexed to the real rate of inflation. (The current inflation rate, by the way, is a fiction. Under the Reagan administration, the Bureau of Labor Statistics was ordered to virtually eliminate the proportion of the consumer price index attributed to housing costs. Since rent or mortgage bills account for 25 to 40 percent of the typical consumer's monthly expenses, and they've been soaring since the seventies, the actual inflation rate is significantly higher than the official figure.)

COLLEGE TUITION MADNESS

Average tuition at a private four-year college or university in the United States is $19,710. Oh, and don't forget the cost of housing, textbooks and student activity fees. All are skyrocketing. While the Consumer Price Index rose just 1 percent during 2003, public university tuition jumped 14 percent.

Meanwhile what students call "real" financial aid—grants and scholarships that never have to be paid back—are fewer and far between. In 1980, the average Pell grant covered 77 percent of the cost of an average four-year college. Now it covers just 40 percent. This is partly because, when adjusted for inflation, tuition has doubled.

Replacing loans with grants would have a two-fold positive effect. The Rand Corporation estimates that, unless officials do something to solve the education problem, six million young Americans will be "priced out of the system" during the next two decades. As for those who bite the bullet and take out loans anyway, more kids than ever (from 46 percent in 1990 to 70 percent in 2000) end up saddled with staggering loads of debt.

With tuition and housing totaling $40,000 per year at the most prestigious colleges, student loan balances of more than $100,000 are becoming increasingly commonplace among newly minted undergraduates. The *average* twenty-one-year-old graduates after having borrowed a staggering total of $27,600, payable at an average rate of $350 to $420 per month, every month, for ten years. That's as much as a cheap house or an expensive car, with only a scrap of parchment to show for it. There's no way to get out of it, either—under federal law, student loan debt cannot be relieved by filing for personal bankruptcy. Even if you drop out of school before graduation, it doesn't matter: you still have to pay off your loans.

If a student loan debtor loses his job during his repayment period, he can apply for a deferment. I wouldn't recommend it, though. I filed for an eighteen-month deferment during the early-nineties recession. The interest charges accumulated exponentially; as a result I paid off my last student loan last year, at age thirty-nine.

The rising cost of college tuition takes a terrible hidden toll on American society as its best and brightest young people are forced to defer their hopes and dreams so they can pay off their loans. Kids major in economics instead of art history. They pass up chances to backpack through Asia or volunteer in a soup kitchen. They defer buying their first homes and cars. Worst of all, many don't attend the best schools for which they qualify academically.

I met one such young man, a senior preparing to graduate from Lima High School in Ohio. He had just returned from a visit with his mother to an art college in Pittsburgh. "I had no idea it would be so expensive," he marveled sadly. "I'll have to go somewhere else, maybe do something else." No one's dreams should be crushed like that at seventeen.

Whether or not you feel sympathy for students' plight, a country that churns out generation after generation of pre-bankrupted youth suffers from an increasingly sluggish economy—who's going to buy houses from "empty nesters" whose adult children have moved away?—and a real but immeasurable increase in social alienation and cynicism.

Fortunately, the attitudes of typical American voters have evolved in a positive direction since the dismal days of Ronald Reagan's 1981 federal financial aid cuts—a move that he made partly to *improve* his popularity rating. Nowadays even the most anti-education politicians have to at least pay lip service to Americans' new advocacy of post-secondary education.

When Clinton took office in 1993, most people actually thought that too many young people went to college. However, a Public Agenda poll taken at the end of his second term showed that three-quarters of Americans believed that there "cannot be too many people with education and training beyond high school." Eight-seven percent agreed with the statement that "a college degree is now as important as a high school diploma used to be." And more than 60 percent said that their own children would fail in the workplace without one.

Interestingly, pollsters John Immerwahr and Tony Foleno found, "African American and Hispanic parents give college an even higher priority than do white parents." Historically disadvantaged minorities see a college education as the best way to overcome systemic discrimination in the workplace. But 69 percent of all parents—the number is even higher among the minorities who place such a high emphasis on the importance of higher education—were worried that they wouldn't be able to afford tuition at any college, much less the school of their choice.

And the choices for students on a tight budget are becoming less appealing. Per-student administrative spending at state colleges fell from 70 percent of that of private schools in 1977 to 58 percent in 1996, reflecting an increasing quality gap between private and public higher educational institutions. You'll save money but your schooling will suffer.

Concern over high college tuition is a potent political issue for the party that chooses to seize it. Ironically, Republicans—who have worked tirelessly to unravel federal financial aid programs—planned to exploit education sticker shock during the 2004 campaign. "President Bush would accuse colleges of closing the doors of higher education to students from low- and middle-income families, by making it unaffordable," reported the *Chronicle of Higher Education* about a new campaign strategy being considered by GOP tacticians. "The president would also reprimand colleges for allowing too many students—especially low-income and minority students—to drop out and remain without the skills and knowledge they need. In addition, he would question the quality of education that most students receive." Congressman Howard McKeon, an influential education committee chairman, fired the first salvo in this Republican broadside in October 2003 by introducing a bill that would deny federal funding to the most expensive colleges and universities beginning in 2011.

Bush's bash-the-colleges strategy relied on an interesting statistic: fewer than half of incoming freshmen at four-year institutions obtain degrees within the next five years. The number falls to 20 percent for minority students.

Regrettably the Republicans' spare-the-cash approach wouldn't address two simple truths: Americans overwhelmingly consider a college education essential, and most people don't think they can afford this essential product. Eighty-two percent of respondents told a 2003 *Chronicle* survey that a college education was becoming "very difficult" for a middle-class family to afford. McKeon counters: "There's always demands for more money, but money itself doesn't guarantee a solution to every problem."

Perhaps not. But, as David Ward of the American Council on Education says, "percentage increases [in tuition] don't tell the whole story." Indeed, the College Board confirms, "tuition at public colleges rose so fast [in 2003] to compensate for the declining government support of state campuses." Professors, classrooms, and computer equipment aren't free. If government won't pay for higher education, schools are forced to pass on the bill to students and their parents. Only money will solve a problem centered around unaffordability.

The federal government currently doles out more than $105 billion in student loans and grants—mostly loans—to qualifying low- and middle-income college students each year. Considering that the Bush administration is spending more than $100 billion per year to occupy Iraq—an optional and unnecessary war, as the failure of U.S. forces to find weapons of mass destruction has proven—the decision to let young men and women shoulder this immense financial burden is just that: a choice. Replacing all student loans with grants that would never need to be repaid would add roughly 10 percent to the currently projected $6 trillion, ten-year federal budget deficit—a small price to pay to address such a pressing political and fiscal problem.

Democrats could also frame free college tuition as a form of reverse trickle-down economics. The for-profit student loan system currently generates hundreds of millions of dollars in annual profits for the Student Loan Marketing Association, also known as Sallie Mae. Few Americans are aware that Sallie Mae is owned by Citibank—and that the typical student loan has to be paid back at a usurious rate of 13.5 percent, more than the rate of interest on home mortgages or the cheaper credit cards. Citibank and other student loan lenders make a fortune on the backs of students and their parents: $50 billion in loans generate some $100 billion in interest charges over ten years—money that could otherwise have been pumped back into the economy by recent college grads.

Government should also lean on colleges and universities to start spending their tuition revenues more frugally. For example, the salaries of university presidents are approaching CEO levels of greed. During the 2001–02 academic year, for example, Vanderbilt University president Gordon Gee received an appalling $852,023 in total compensation, more than the president of the United States. The University of Michigan, a public institution, paid $677,500 to Mary Sue Coleman in 2002-03. "[High college president salaries are] certainly not helpful at a time when public higher education is facing fiscal stringency, raising tuition by double-digit numbers," says Patrick Callan, president of the National Center for Public Policy and Higher Education. "It's particularly hard for these high-paid presidents to go to the legislature and make the case for higher funding." Legislators are reacting to such sybaritic behavior. A new Florida law slapped a cap on presidential pay at public universities; at this writing Ohio was considering a bill that would prevent it from rising higher than what the governor receives. One thing's for sure: it's unreasonable to ask students to assume massive debt burdens while universities are so profligate with their tuition money.

An even more aggressive step could involve slapping federal price controls on college tuition. From 1980 to 1999, universities raised tuition by an average total of 334 percent. During that same period, inflation increased just 98 percent. A system that replaced loans with grants would serve as a direct taxpayer subsidy to these institutions, forcing them to become dependent on government largess for their financial health. This relationship would give the feds leverage they could use to impose inflation-adjusted limits upon the "free market" of college tuition.

THE VACATION TIME CRISIS

Joe Robinson, founder of the Work to Live campaign and author of the book *Work to Live: The Guide to Getting a Life,* says: "We have the shortest vacations in the world—and they're getting even shorter." Between short vacations, long work weeks and a low number of federal holidays, the International Labor Organization calculates that Americans work eight to twelve more *weeks* a year in total hours than Europeans or Aussies, who are guaranteed at least four weeks paid vacation by law. (Most people take six.) "The U.S. is the only industrialized country in the world without paid vacation laws on the books," points out Robinson. "There are real benefits to vacations. They allow you to rejuvenate, recover your health and diminish stress. You come back refreshed and with higher productivity."

God knows we need the rest. We're stressed out and burnt out. Christian churches are reporting drop-offs in attendance as more and more people put in seven-day workweeks or sleep off a hard six during the Sabbath. This is no way for members of the world's most productive workforce to live.

Longer, guaranteed, paid vacations would also allow us to improve our reputation as citizens of the world's most untraveled and ignorant modern nation. You can't climb the Himalayas without bumping into a German, but I've spent hours at international borders waiting for the guards to stop passing around my U.S. passport because they'd never seen one before. Part of why "they hate us" is because we don't know them, and "they" don't know us.

Even the hard-working Japanese are slowing down. Worried about high rates of heart disease and suicide among the nation's famed salarymen, the Japanese government has created a cabinet-level Ministry of Leisure. Tokyo

Nation	Legally Mandated Vacation Days per Year	Average Days Actually Taken Off per Year
Australia	20	25
Austria	25	30
Belgium	20	24
China	15	15
Denmark	25	30
Finland	24	25
France	25	25–30
Germany	24	30
Greece	20	23
Ireland	20	28
Italy	20	30
Japan	10	17.5
Netherlands	20	25
Norway	21	30
Portugal	22	25
Spain	25	30
Sweden	25	25–35
Switzerland	20	25–30
United Kingdom	20	25
U.S.	0	10

Source: Work to Live

office buildings are locked promptly at 5 P.M. on Friday. If you need to get something from your desk during the weekend, you have to ask a local cop to accompany you to your desk—to ensure that you don't do any work!

Consider this irony: while employers laid off more than 3 million workers from 2001 to 2003, the average work week kept rising and vacation time shrunk for those who survived downsizing. Companies are making do with less—by making you do more for less.

According to the Bureau of Labor Statistics, the average worker with one year's seniority at the same company receives 8.1 days of vacation per year; one with three years under his belt gets a whopping 10.2. Incredibly, we're allowed to take fewer vacation days than citizens of any other country, but we don't even take those. "Nothing illustrates the stranglehold of overwork on American lives today than the fact that 175 million vacation days each year are not taken by employees who are entitled to them," Robinson says. And all of those "hard workers" aren't doing anyone any favors. To the contrary, their "hard work" is helping keep millions of other people under- and unemployed.

Yeah, but won't we lose our competitive edge if we start taking time off? You know, in the "global marketplace"? Longer vacation time doesn't seem to have hurt the economies of France, Germany, or the Netherlands, all of which have seen their hourly productivity skyrocket as the number of total hours worked per employee falls.

Clinton administration Treasury Secretary Robert Reich recently pro- posed "a federal law requiring that every company in America give every employee at least four weeks paid vacation per year" in an article for the *American Prospect*. "Think about all the new jobs that will be created when more Americans have more vacation time—hotels, restaurants, recreation, and travel," wrote Reich. "I'm not running for office, but I offer my pro- posal to anybody who is. Make it part of your platform: a minimum four weeks paid vacation for every working man and woman in America. You'll be elected in a flash."

Conservatives cite polls that show that workers, when offered a choice, tend to pick more money instead of more time off. But that's not an honest choice—most workers can produce the same total quantity of value-added product using less "face time" than they do at present. Most Americans say that they don't receive enough time off, and 20 percent fess up to calling in sick on Fridays or Mondays in order to create ad hoc three- or four-day weekends. More important, younger voters are far more devoted to the lat- ter half of the money versus time equation: 37 percent of those under thirty- five would trade higher pay in favor of more time off, as opposed to 15 per- cent of people over fifty-five. Time over money is the wave of the future. Reich is on to something.

PRICE FIXING

If you've ever shopped for an airline ticket, you know about price fixing: the practice of (supposedly) competing businesses colluding to offer identical prices. The main point, experts say, is for the biggest players in a business to lock out potential new competitors that could hurt all of them.

Try to book, say, a round-trip direct coach flight between my home- town of Dayton, Ohio, and New York City's LaGuardia airport. At this writing, these flights are offered by, among other carriers, U.S. Airways and Delta. It's a fairly safe bet that the quoted fare for this trip is exactly the same on both airlines, down to the penny, for any given departure and

HOW I LOST MY LAST REAL JOB

I don't blame them for firing me. My bosses were so paranoid about sharing information—they were convinced that everyone was out to stab them in the back—that they didn't assign me any work. I was so idle that I spent an hour a day working the knobs at a pinball alley a few blocks away from the office. The rest of the time I worked to develop my skills as a writer. (This was before the Internet, the friend of slackers everywhere, became a staple of every office.) I would say that I stayed at the job because I needed the work, but since there wasn't any work it would more accurate to say that I stayed because I needed the paycheck. As Patti Smith would say, forty-two hours a week, thirty-two thousand dollars a year doing nothing as a financial analyst in San Francisco beat working in a piss factory.

My bosses could have come to me and said that things weren't working out, that they didn't need me anymore what with me not doing any work and all, how about two months severance and let's call the whole thing off. That would have been peachy. Why they didn't do that, I'll probably never know.

But first, a flashback. When my father was a young officer working for the United States Air Force, he came back from a vacation to find his desk gone. Just . . . gone. "We've done some rearranging while you were gone, Fred," his commanding officer explained. "Just find someplace to do your work." The thing was, there wasn't any place to sit. Everyone else in the room had a desk. Just not my dad.

The message wasn't subtle. Get out. Still, my dad refused to get lost. He scrounged a cardboard box from the trash, sat down on the floor, and got to work. Or pretended to; I don't remember whether they had given him any assignments to do or not.

At any rate, this humiliating state of affairs went on for a few weeks until some general happened to visit the office on business. "What in God's name is that man doing on the floor?" he demanded to know. "Reorganization . . . waiting for a new desk . . ." the C.O. stuttered lamely. "I don't want to hear any excuses, goddammit!" the general shouted. "Get that man a desk now!"

My father rose through the ranks, eventually becoming a very important asset to the defense of our great nation. Yet he never forgot that incident. "Going on vacation," he'd say, "is asking for trouble." Unless he couldn't possibly avoid it, he never took a day off again. And then he'd schedule leaves to coincide with his boss's absences.

My father's words of wisdom would come back to haunt me.

One afternoon I came back from "lunch" at the pinball joint to find a pink while-you-were-out message on my desk. Ethel Kennedy, widow of the late Robert F. Kennedy and all-round martyr, had called to notify me that I had won the 1995 Robert F. Kennedy Journalism Award for Outstanding Coverage of the Problems of the Disadvantaged. Besides this being a big deal—it was the first major award of my nascent cartooning career—winning the RFK meant a free trip to Washington to hobnob with the Kennedys. I sent an internal e-mail to my boss asking for a couple of days off, got a message back saying it was okay—what, was I going to be missed?—and headed off to D.C.

Upon my return, pleased as punch that I'd gotten to talk history with Arthur Schlesinger, there was a message on my answering machine at home from my boss. "Why aren't you at work?" she asked, pretending to be all confused. Uh-huh. She knew damn well that I wasn't due back until the next day. After all, we'd exchanged written electronic memos on the subject, with copies sent to the company president. It was obvious that she was trying to set me up. She followed up with a second message, a few hours into mid-morning, with a faux stern tone: "We'll talk about this tomorrow." Yeah, right.

The next morning, the shrew calls me into her office and fires me for taking an unauthorized day off. I didn't bother to argue. When someone's screwing you and both of you know it, what's the point of keeping up appearances? As Mao Tse-Tung said, whether or not you try to make nice, a hungry tiger will bite. I quietly gathered my stuff, went to the state "job development" office and filed for unemployment benefits.

In California you can't collect unemployment if you were fired "for cause"—that is, doing something wrong like taking an unauthorized day off. You only get the money if you're laid off or fired without due cause. Since your former employer pays part of your benefits, they prefer to have the state rule each firing as legitimate. So my application became something of a he-said, she-said kind of thing. Fortunately a buddy of mine who still worked at my former company intercepted some e-mails between the top honchos at the company congratulating each other on their successful firing, conceding in so many words that they'd lied about my taking "unauthorized" time off. I faxed the damning e-mails to the state and my checks started coming a few weeks later.

By the time the money ran out, I was making enough from cartooning and writing columns to not have to find another day job. But, heeding my father's advice and my personal experience, in more than a decade of syndication I've never missed a deadline.

return day. Ask both companies and they'll say that they don't talk to each other about prices. They may even be telling the truth. But dropping or raising your prices to match your "competitor" cent for cent doesn't happen in other industries—and it's still a form of collusion.

Competition is the essence of free-market capitalism but lately it has been in short supply to American consumers. Whether it's a row of gas stations offering the same exact price for regular and premium unleaded, cereal companies gouging supermarket customers to the tune of five bucks a box or the fact that most cable TV viewers have the choice of exactly one service provider, the biggest corporations are engaging in an unprecedented amount of price-gouging collusion. Economists call it an "imperfectly competitive market."

Thanks to antitrust legislation passed a century ago, it's also illegal.

After a judge found that the Microsoft computer corporation had violated antitrust laws, 62 percent of Americans told ABC that the company shouldn't be broken up as the Clinton Justice Department had requested. Yet 91 percent said that antitrust laws were a good idea. Most people wanted action taken against Microsoft, to see it put on double secret probation and carefully monitored by government watchdogs to make sure that it didn't get the chance to misbehave again. Whether it's disgust at the recent wave of accounting and corporate scandals epitomized by Enron or something deeper in their character, the American people believe that big business has far too much power and they want their government to rein it in. Nowhere does the impact of corporate power affect the ordinary lives of Americans more than it does in their capacity as consumers.

This is politically potent stuff, and Republicans are exceptionally vulnerable. Even at the height of Bush's post–September 11 popularity, 75 percent of Americans told CBS that big business had "too much influence" on the GOP-controlled Congress. Four times more people blamed Republicans than Democrats for the Enron and other corporate accounting scandals. And 57 percent said that out-of-control corporations were an important problem that needed to be dealt with. The party that successfully channels Americans' sense of impotence and outrage into a realistic platform for corporate reform stands to pick up millions of votes in a national election. Such a legislative package should include, among other things, harsh sanctions against companies that engage in price fixing and other anticompetitive practices that hurt consumers—up to and including being nationalized or shut down.

FREE TRADE RUN AMOK

Americans don't mind free trade in the abstract. Depending who does the asking, anywhere between 55 and 69 percent of Americans favor reduced tariffs and improved communications, including the exchange of products through commerce, between nations. Nonetheless, most favor getting rid of the agreements that have already been signed by President Bill Clinton and

George W. Bush, including the North American Free Trade Agreement (NAFTA) between the U.S., Canada, and Mexico. Americans want us out of the World Trade Organization, according to a 2000 Harris/*Business Week* poll, because free trade isn't just about business. An overwhelming 80 percent of people think protecting the environment should be a top priority of such agreements, 77 percent say we shouldn't sign any deal that costs U.S. jobs and 74 percent are against "unfair competition by countries that violate workers' rights."

Such has been the case with all of the recent major free trade deals.

NAFTA has allowed polluters to set up shop along the Mexican side of the Rio Grande in filthy *maquiladoras* and forced the U.S. to accept the importation of dangerous products. During the nineties, for example, Canada sued in trade court to enjoin us to lift our ban on asbestos importation as "an unfair restriction of free trade." They won, forcing us to compensate them for our refusal to import a proven carcinogen. The Department of Labor estimates that NAFTA alone has cost the United States a net job loss of about 500,000 since 1994. (The Economic Policy Institute puts the figure at closer to 766,000.) And everyone's aware that most of the people hired overseas by American corporations are abused and poorly paid, even by local standards.

When the American economy is relatively healthy, it generates some four hundred thousand jobs per month. Compared to that, the loss of less than a million jobs probably doesn't seem like a big deal. But workers feel more besieged by their employers than ever. They're working longer hours for less money, being asked to pay for the cost of their medical insurance (which for the most part sucks at any price), doing without pensions and matching-fund 401(k)s, and watching their bosses lay off thousands of coworkers only to hand them the extra work. With union representation hitting new lows, it doesn't matter that Ross Perot's "giant sucking sound" may or may not have materialized precisely as predicted by early-nineties doomsayers. American workers feel downward pressure on their wages and upward stress on their workload. And while employers may not be exporting the entire American workforce overseas, they're adept at using the threat of cheaper overseas labor to keep U.S. salaries low.

The sound you hear, of wages steadily declining as high-wage manufacturing and technology jobs leave forever, is more of a slow, steady hiss.

A cleverly worded party appeal to radically revise or pull out entirely of lopsided trade agreements like NAFTA and the World Trade

Organization could appeal to Seattle-style anarchists on the left as well as nativists on the right. Moreover, it would be the right thing to do. After finally conceding that unregulated free trade causes loss of jobs and reduced prosperity, Russell Roberts, a professor of economics at George Mason University who favors such agreements claimed: "The bottom line is this: NAFTA has caused hardship for some Americans in certain sectors, but it's made for a more stable and integrated Mexican political system—and that's a real good thing for the world." If that's the best case that can be made for taking part in free trade—and that's Roberts' number-one argument—why are we playing the game?

CRISIS IN THE SCHOOLS

Everyone agrees that American public schools are in a state of crisis, though people differ on what the crisis consists of and what can and should be done about it. As the son of a teacher and a possible future parent living in New York City, however, I've given more thought to this problem than the average bird.

For the most part, residents of middle- and upper-middle-class suburbs, where nearly half of the U.S. population lives, enjoy access to excellent, well-funded public schools. To be sure, there are persistent problems: bullying, aging equipment, and a concern among religious-minded parents that spirituality has been banned from the public forum. Kids drop out at sixteen—why is that legal? But these are relatively minor problems. Suburban schools are in fairly decent shape.

The real crisis affects poor and big-city urban middle and high schools, where teachers and administrators find it nearly impossible to cope with a constant threat of violence, underfunding, overcrowded classrooms, and a lack of adequate equipment. Ironically, a Teachers College study of New York's schools by Francisco L. Rivera-Batiz found, "Overcrowding is not associated with lower academic achievement in all schools . . . Among schools with low proportions of students who live in poverty, the study actually finds a positive correlation between overcrowding and achievement. What happens is that schools which have high academic achievement attract more students and therefore are overcrowded," she explains.

Few parents would agree with Rivera-Batiz's assessment—overcrowded classrooms are obviously less than ideal learning environments—but her observation is nonetheless worth noting. The worst schools are so bad that they drive good students away to the good ones—thus overcrowding (and eventually ruining) them as well.

Another dangerous trend, largely the result of budget cuts, is "differentiated instruction," in which students of widely varying skill levels are placed in the same classes. Advocates agree that this hare-brained scheme benefits special needs children by removing them from the ghetto of tracking. But gifted kids, who are forced to waste time helping other children rather than learning themselves, are getting the shaft. A forty-year study by James Kulik at the University of Michigan came to the inescapable conclusion that "gifted students benefited more when put in a separate class and given advanced material than when in a mixed group in which all the students got the same material." Well, duh.

Taxpayers are understandably frustrated. When New York City's schools chan-cellor announced a $6.9 billion rebuilding plan for the system's overburdened infrastructure, it seemed that relief for overcrowded students was finally at hand. But the proposed plan—which was ultimately pared back—would only have meant thirty-four new schools, or 32,953 new classroom seats. That would have been enough for a city one-third the size of New York, and it didn't account for immigration that adds to the city's million-student population.

Conservatives like to point to these statistics as evidence that money alone won't ease the troubles of urban school districts. But they're mistaken. While these sums seem staggering *in toto*, what really matters is spending per student. Any teacher will tell you that more funding would make an enormous difference to her school: it would allow it to buy new books and computers, and let administrators place fewer kids per classroom. Money is destiny, but no matter where you look, struggling urban schools aren't getting their fair share per pupil.

In 2001, for example, New York's city and state governments each spent about $4,500 per student on public schools, for a total of $9,000. In Westchester County, home to the upscale northern suburbs of Rye and Scarsdale, local property owners paid $11,000, added to state spending of $2,000, for a total of $13,000—44 percent more per pupil. Moreover, the average cost of living is lower in Westchester than in the boroughs of New York City.

A New York Supreme Court judge has ruled that the state's funding system violates the Civil Rights Act of 1964 by disproportionately affecting minority students. Seventy percent of the state's minority students live in the city.

Similar statistics plague the rest of the country. In 1998–99, Milwaukee spent $506 less than the state average per student while suburbs spent $748 more. If you attended school in the Portland, Oregon, metropolitan area in 1995–96, they spent $10,447 on you in the Bonneville School District but only $4,505 if you went to class in Beaverton.

These disparities in spending per pupil have a dual, equally destructive effect: run-down and overcrowded schools send a message to children of disadvantaged minorities that society doesn't care about them. Kids thus neglected by society are more likely to become alienated, drop out, and engage in criminal behavior and drug use than their luckier suburban counterparts. They also drive upper-income whites out of the cities or to enroll their children in expensive private schools.

Where I live in New York I must choose between sending my child to an expensive private school and a substandard public one. If I go the private route, it will cost me an annual kindergarten-to-grade-12 expense of $20,000 in present 2004 dollars, which adds up to a total bill of a quarter of a million dollars—which certainly adds to the challenge of saving for college. Alternatively, I can send him to a public school where he'll be beaten up at worst and undereducated and unchallenged at best. With luck my kid might qualify for one of the system's well-funded "charter" schools, but those usually require parents to decide what field of concentration their children will want to work in after graduation. I didn't know what I wanted to do for a living at age eighteen, much less six; I don't foresee forcing my child to make such a decision.

Millions of families on both sides of the income divide face similar dilemmas. Even if you're not personally affected by inner-city poverty, you live with the results whenever someone breaks your car window to steal your radio or winds up in jail, gobbling down "three hots and a cot" at your tax-funded expense. Providing an affordable high-quality education to every American child is a top national priority for all of us. Whether or not you have a kid is immaterial.

The root of the public education crisis is unequal funding. Wealthy suburbanites fund their local schools with high property taxes whereas inner cities, where most real estate is rented, rely on an ever-shrinking pool of state aid. As Denis Kennedy wrote in a 2001 article entitled "The Case for Reforming Public Education," "Lower income school districts, whose residents typically pay a larger percentage of their meager incomes to support education, are still incapable of providing the level of education found in their more affluent neighboring districts. Their children are being penalized, not for the districts' lack of trying, but for the economic inability to support a comparable education system. Students in these disadvantaged school districts must endure crumbling school buildings, overcrowding, underpaid and underqualified teachers, and, in general, less funding for education. And, despite these iniquities, disadvantaged students must still pass nationwide standards and compete nationwide for spots at universities."

Kennedy continues:

"Teacher quality varies considerably, and directly corresponds with teacher salary. In [poor districts], only 37 percent of the teachers possess master's degrees, compared with 57 percent of teachers in [affluent districts]. The Northeast, which boasts a remarkable 60 percent of its public school teachers with master's degrees, pays extremely well. In fact, Connecticut, New Jersey, New York, and Pennsylvania average the top four highest teacher salaries in the nation, paying an average of $50,000. Conversely, the South and the West maintain only 39 percent and 38 percent of their teachers with master's degrees, due to the low salaries in states such as Mississippi, which pays teachers an average of only $29,530 per year. Due to overcrowding and small budgets, these cash-poor school districts have neither teacher quality nor quantity. Lower income students also enroll in college in vastly differential rates. Students in families earning less than $25,000 are accepted to colleges at a rate of only 46.4 percent, compared to the rate of 77.3 percent enjoyed by the progeny of families earning in excess of $75,000."

Most common alternatives to our flawed public school financing system are intrinsically flawed. Few parents have the patience, demeanor, or intellectual background to educate their children as effectively as trained public school teachers, yet the U.S. Department of Education estimates that 850,000 children are being "homeschooled" by parents disgusted with the public schools—up from 360,000 ten years ago. Those who try rarely have the time or energy to do so properly. Parochial and religious schools are often less pricey than other private institutions but remain out of reach (economically or geographically) to the urban poor. And school vouchers are plainly unconstitutional because they transfer public funds to private religious institutions. It's only a matter of time before the Supreme Court overturns these programs entirely.

The long-term solution, as Kennedy suggests, is obvious: federalizing our national system of public education. Oversight by the U.S. Department of Education would replace local control and funding of public schools. Money would be distributed evenly so that a junior high school in Oakland, California, would receive the same exact per capita spending, adjusted for local cost of living, as a student in Beverly Hills. This would, he says, "resolve many of the inequalities in funding, teacher quality, overcrowding, class-room size, and course offerings, raising the bar for education as a whole." In addition, a unified national school curriculum would allow students in our increasingly mobile society to change schools with a minimum of disruption to their education; the seventh week of Algebra II ought to be about the same whether you're studying it in Montana or in Maine. Federalized control would also help to temper the influence of regional curiosities like the bizarre Kansas state school board, which voted to teach creationism as science.

France, Germany, and other western European nations all outrank us in student achievement in mathematics, the sciences, and foreign lan-guages. These countries all apply a federalized, uniform structure to fund and run their public schools. While inequities continue to exist—injustice will, obviously, always be with us—students have access to the same quality of books, school buildings, and teachers whether they live in the tony First Arrondissement of Paris or the grimy immigrant-filled slums of Nanterre. Theirs is an egalitarian vision: no matter where you come from, you can make something of yourself if you're willing to work hard. Ideology aside, federalized education is the only solution to America's messed-up schools. It is the future. The leader who points the way to a better system will be recognized as a visionary who eased the misery of millions, even by those who clung to the phantom of local control.

Of course, conservatives may have blocked education financing for good reason. In 2003, 53 percent of college graduates were Democrats, as opposed to 44 percent for Republicans. Those with a high school diploma or less education favored Republicans 49 to 45 percent. The more you learn, it seems, the more liberal you are.

LEGISLATING LIFE'S PETTY ANNOYANCES

In past elections, rightists made plenty of political hay out of issues so minor that they were very nearly nonexistent: going after burners of the American flag with a Constitutional amendment, for instance. (When's the last time *you* saw someone burn an American flag here in the U.S., where such an

amendment would be enforceable?) These little micro mini-issues—
Republicans recently began promoting an amendment to ban gay marriage—remain great electoral fodder. But why not push for votes by
improving the lives of ordinary people in small yet meaningful ways?

In 2003, for example, the federal government finally ended the menace
of the dinnertime telemarketing call with a "Do Not Call" registry. This is
merely anecdotal, but what used to be a constant annoyance—I got anywhere from twenty to thirty calls a day, many from the same exact companies I'd said no to a few minutes earlier—has slowed to a minor trickle.
Knowing that I can answer the phone without having to fend off a sales
pitch has improved my quality of life, and if the registry hadn't been a
bipartisan effort, I would have eternal gratitude to the party that made it
happen.

Similarly, New York City Mayor Michael Bloomberg's anti-smoking
legislation has made going to bars and nightclubs a pleasure for the majority
of the city's population. Although I suffer from mild asthma, I now spend
many happy hours drinking in establishments I formerly avoided because
acrid cigarette smoke used to sear my eyes and lungs and stink up my clothes
and hair. To be sure, secondhand smoking doesn't rank with such scourges
as global warming or the bubonic plague, but smoking in bars bothered the
hell out of me. Now it's gone; for that reason alone, I'm considering voting
for Bloomberg if he runs for reelection in 2005. This would—for this very
small, virtually insignificant, reason—be the first Republican ballot I've
ever cast.

Here are but a few of the little quality-of-life platform planks a revitalized Democratic Party could use to recapture the House and Senate:

- A real "Do Not Email" registry for spam (one with teeth,
  not like the fake one passed in 2003) that addresses the 70
  percent of Internet users who say e-mail advertisements
  have made surfing the Web less pleasant and the 25 percent who actually stopped going online entirely;
- Order corporations to offer free toll-free tech support for
  a set number of years after purchase of their products (if
  you've ever had to cough up twenty bucks for useless
  technical assistance about computer software, you know
  of what I speak);

- Ban online "Trojan horse" programs, cookies, and other subtle violations of personal privacy on the Internet;
- Force airlines to give away empty first-class and business-class seats to coach customers using a random-selection lottery; make them refund your tickets for non-weather-related delays;
- Fine businesses that fail to hire enough service clerks to handle their customers;
- Eliminate ATM fees;
- Revive the Better Business Bureau's old consumer-complaint bureau, but under the auspices of the federal government with the results to be posted online for all to see;
- Require all elected officials to issue personal, timely responses to correspondence from their constituents.

We Americans are the kings of the world. Not so deep down, we expect to be treated accordingly: "Every man a king" was the slogan Huey Long used to propel his Louisiana political machine. "If you want to live like a Republican," the Democratic line goes, "vote Democratic." Better yet: "If you want to live like an American deserves to live, vote Democratic." There are big openings, unexploited gaps, in the marketplace of ideas. People feel that their concerns are being ignored by the major parties, and they're pissed off. But anger can be channeled into electoral success. Whoever gives the people what they want, in the immortal words of the Kinks, will own the future.

chapter 4

~~CONSERVATISM~~
~~is~~
~~UNAMERICAN~~

IT'S BAD OUT THERE.

THE CONSERVATIVE

I wanna tell you, ladies and gentlemen, that there's not enough troops in the army to force the southern people to break down segregation and admit the nigger race into our theaters, into our swimming pools, into our homes, and into our churches.

—Senator Strom Thrumond,
Republican of South Carolina, 1948

He carried out a life clearly unmatched in public service.

—Senate Majority Leader Bill Frist,
Republican of Tennessee, upon Thurmond's death in 2003

Strom Thurmond was my father. I have known this since 1941, when I was 16 years old.

—Essie Mae Washington Williams,
Thurmond's illegitimate African-American daughter,
December 17, 2003

If conservatives always got their way, we'd still be living in caves. "Stay inside! What the hell are you doing? There are *animals* out there! The cave god will become *angry*! We'll all DIE!"

Think about it. Conservatism is, by definition, an ideology dedicated to preserving the status quo. Of leaving well enough, and not so well enough, alone. Of leaving things one way because that's the way they always have been. There's a lot to be said for refusing to fix what ain't broke, but that philosophy is the exact opposite of what America is, and always has been, about.

Contrary to popular belief, it's impossible to call yourself a red-blooded American as well as a rock-rib conservative. Liberals have to get out this message, for it doesn't matter how hard they work to develop an attractive political platform, reorganize themselves, or adopt ass-kicking tactics if their opponents succeed in selling themselves as the living embodiment of Americanness. Liberals must have a positive message to promote; at the same time, they have to tear down their opponents. Yes, there's a case to be made for tit-for-tat smearing of Republicans as unpatriotic and reckless—

if they say that about us, we can say the same about them—but that approach, if successful, only cancels the effect of their attacks at best.

The Achilles' heel of the GOP is its underlying conservative myth. (I call it a myth because Republicans, who since Reagan have proudly declared themselves the bearers of the conservative standard, no longer even pay lip service to the bedrock principles of true conservatism: limited government, fiscal austerity, isolationism, and respect for individual rights. Nevertheless, the Republican-conservative link remains a powerful fiction.) Here are the basic arguments that Democrats should make in order to destroy the foundation of the Right's propaganda: its claim to being more patriotic, more mainstream, and more American than the rest of us.

Every substantial improvement in the lives of the American people has been initiated by liberals, and opposed by conservatives.

Democrats are far more conservative in the ways that most self-declared conservatives care about—fiscal responsibility and keeping the government out of your life—than Republicans.

The "conservatism" that Republicans espouse—fighting new programs like national health insurance and cutting taxes on the wealthy to please their corporate donors—goes against everything America (Left and Right, liberal and conservative, moderate and extremist) stands for. The values espoused by true conservatives are closer to Democratic liberalism than Bushist neo-conservatism, which is something entirely different.

Republicans refuse to help you pull yourself up by your bootstraps, and they defend the people who are trying to keep you down. Democrats give people the tools they need to help themselves.

Since its inception, the United States has been a nation whose people have devoted themselves to progress for its own sake. The assumption shared by most Americans, one that unifies us whatever our religion or ethnic background, is that life should improve over time, that children should always do better than their parents. Whose parents, here in the U.S., ever told their kids to settle for good enough? Shoot for the stars, we tell our kids, and if things don't work out, you can settle for the moon.

Europeans, burdened by the weight of history—it's hard to make your mark when you're born in a town built around Roman ruins with a medieval cathedral down the block—and a residual aristocracy that inhibits class mobility, accept early in life that they'll probably live just like their parents, possibly even in the same house. Sons take a job performing the same tasks at the same plant as their fathers and consider themselves fortunate. Poor workers in Europe exhibit "class pride" because they have no other choice—their class, their parents' and grandparents' class—is all they'll ever have.

You probably shuddered at that last thought. Our national obsession with moving forward, ever forward, is the big difference between Americans and Brits—whose language, culture, and system of laws we otherwise most resemble for obvious historical reasons. Most citizens of the United Kingdom came to accept their nation's declining fortunes after winning World War II left them shattered and poor; they've never been quite the same after the Blitz or losing India. Every lost square mile of empire added another drunken soul to the dole queue, and no one expects that trend to change any time soon.

The disintegration of the British Empire left us and the Soviets, whom we killed to make ourselves God.

If our grandparents made the last one an American Century, many of us hope and expect to continue that upward trajectory—*faster cars! bustier women!*—well into the twenty-first. Our leaders, under popular pressure to make things better, better, always better, repeatedly ask anxious Americans to be patient, as President Bill Clinton did in his final State of the Union address. "Let us remember," he cautioned in 2000, "that the first American revolution was not won with a single shot. The continent was not settled in a single year. The lesson of our history—and the lesson of the last seven years—is that great goals are reached step by step; always building on our progress, always gaining ground." But, as the last line of Clinton's speech acknowledged both political reality and basic physics, "you can't gain ground if you're standing still."

At the time when Clinton delivered that address, he had presided over seven years of an economy so robust that employers suffering from widespread labor shortages had to bus in workers from distant towns. Eighty-four percent of Americans were able to tell pollsters that they were either better off or in the same financial condition as they had been in 1992. (Ronald Reagan's 1980 question, "Are you better off now than you were four years ago?" has since become a boilerplate bellwether of the public's mindset.) With the exception of minor military interventions in Somalia, Kosovo, and Haiti (two out of three of which ended in virtually bloodless victory), the nation had enjoyed peace and prosperity from 1993 to 2000. But Al Gore—Clinton's political proxy—still lost. How could that be?

Voters did believe that there had been progress under the Democrats. Their wages had risen. Many people achieved the American dream by purchasing their first homes. Undeniably, Gore's campaign was hobbled by lingering resentment over Clinton's behavior during the Monica Lewinsky scandal as well as his own schoolmarmish oratory. (Republican pundit David Brooks conducted a survey of voter attitudes in 2000. "They didn't trust Al Gore because they thought he looked down on them," he reported. "They felt Bush could come to their barbershop and fit right in.") And there is a historical tendency of voters to throw out one party simply to give the other guys a chance. But weighed against his impressive advantages, those were relatively trivial problems.

The truth is, most Americans saw the Clinton years as a series of lost opportunities, as a period when billions of dollars were earned and lost with little to show for them in the end. The information economy had proved ephemeral. Sure, there'd been progress. They just didn't think that, given the rewards society could have reaped from the dot-com boom, there had been enough progress. Life had not improved dramatically. In the final analysis, just under 50 percent of the electorate voted for change—risking a deviation from the Clinton-Gore record of peace and prosperity— because change for its own sake is a corollary of the drive towards progress.

To be sure, Americans hold wildly divergent views on how progress should mani-fest itself. Right-wingers hope to build military bases through-out the world, intimidate potential international rivals, and occupy some nations outright. Building empire and increasing corporate profits are their primary objectives. Their opponents on the left prefer to fight poverty, want to do something about the shameful lack of a national healthcare system and protect hard-won civil rights here at home. Goals, and ways to achieve them, differ, but every shade of the American ideological spectrum claims to be devoted to what it calls progress.

PROGRESS IS PERSONAL

When Democratic strategist James Carville famously scrawled "It's the econ-omy, stupid" on a wall in Clinton's campaign war room in 1992, he distilled to four words the five-word adage: Americans usually vote their pocket-books. True, a myriad of factors that are impossible to define, such as how "likeable" a candidate is perceived to be, or the sense that one candidate would "stand up" for the United States against its enemies more effectively than his rival (the impact of the 1980 Iranian hostage crisis on Jimmy Carter's reelection bid is a case study of the tough guy syndrome in American politics), affects how we vote. In the final analysis, however, the state of the economy—or, more accurately, the state of your personal economy—determines whether you eat and sleep inside. And that's usually what typically determines our political allegiance.

To sum up: we Americans are obsessed with progress. We judge the state of our nation, and the competence of our political leaders, based on whether or not we perceive things to have improved.

Furthermore, we care more about the economy, specifically how we are doing personally, than anything else. You can see where I'm going with this. People who make more than they earned the year before feel that all is right with the world; people who earn less tend to feel insecure. Naturally, it's all relative. About a year ago, I met for dinner with a friend of a friend to try to convince him to invest a tiny fraction of his fortune in an idea for a business. He was a straightforward guy. When he said he liked my idea in principle, I believed him. But he didn't plan to invest in anything until the economy—his personal economy—improved. "I know this is going to sound a little strange," this venture capitalist told me over dinner, "but I was worth $80 million a few years ago. Now that the stock market has tanked, I'm worth $45 million and I feel broke." He didn't fund my business plan.

Around the same time one of my best friends was strutting like he owned the town. He bought a new computer although his previous one, only a few years old, still worked perfectly. Like one of those scurrilous loafers conservatives love to hate, he rented a villa on the French Riviera for a month "because I can." He had lost a full-time job a month earlier and, thanks to the vagaries of the unemployment compensation system and his ability to pick up part-time work off the books, the sum of his income and his jobless benefits exceeded his previous salary. His annual pay had effectively risen from $25,000 to $34,000—just a temporary increase, since unemployment benefits expire after six months. By any objective standard he was barely a member of America's struggling lower middle class. Some might have said he was in trouble. But he felt wealthier than the multimillionaire venture capitalist.

The VC, a lifelong Democrat, admitted that he had cast Republican votes in the 2002 midterm elections. "I feel weird about it," he allowed, "but I really need those irresponsible tax cuts." My friend, the jobless denizen of the French Mediterranean, voted the straight Democratic Party line as usual.

Americans obsess on progress.

Coasting isn't good enough. Merely keeping your head above water, staying on top of the bills, is equivalent to failure. If you have two cars, you want a third. If you have a Sony Trinitron, you want a plasma screen TV. More, better, repeat as necessary. In the most recent presidential election, polls showed, voters supported the candidate they thought would be most likely to protect their personal economic interests. Voters who earned more than $50,000 tended to support Bush, largely because they anticipated receiving tax cuts. "But [Bush] was not successful among African-American and lower-income women who know government policies will affect their pocketbooks," noted Martha Burk of the Center for the Advancement of Public Policy. Self-interest was the determinant factor.

In some respects our progress fetish can seem absurd. Presupposing continuous technological advancements that allow improved efficiency, economists note that Americans vote to remove an incumbent president during election years when the U.S. gross domestic product *fails to increase* by at least three percent. At some point in the future, of course, logic dictates that efficiency will go as high as it can, that it will approach perfection and level off. Inevitably, no matter what happens, increases will someday fall below three percent—and that will be as good as it gets. It's simple logic, as certain as the fact that the sun will someday go supernova and blast this planet and everything on it into cinders. But no one wants to think about that.

John Pitney, a political scientist at Claremont College, argues that September 11 changed everything, that personal economics will henceforth take a back seat to the fear of terrorism in voters' minds. "In the past couple of years," he says, "I think we've seen a shift from rough parity [between the two parties] to a slight Republican advantage, which I think reflects a shift in public interest to national security, which Republicans own. If you think about bombs and rockets most of the time, you're probably going to vote Republican."

But, few people spend their nights lying awake worrying about al Qaeda. Self-interest didn't vanish along with the World Trade Center. Admittedly, the September 11 attacks on New York and Washington had an immense political impact. They created an opening for rightist ideologues within the Bush Administration to radically reshape American foreign policy, to transform the world's last remaining superpower into a nation hell-bent on vengeance and expansionism. A semipermanent war footing, however, doesn't change the fact that American citizens have bills to pay. While U.S. foreign policy and its effect here at home motivates the electorate to some extent, the majority of Americans continue to prioritize the health of their bank accounts ahead of dangers from abroad. The threat to the stability of Central Asian oil reserves posed by the insurgent Islamic Movement of Uzbekistan's attacks against the government of President Islam Karimov, a U.S. ally in the "war on terrorism," may have grievous future consequences for Joe and Jane Sixpack, but such esoteric developments aren't likely to cross their minds as they consider their choices inside the voting booth. "Am I better off now than I was four years ago?" will.

No political party should hope to remain in power primarily by pointing to foreign policy successes real or imagined. Winning wars, capturing dictators, and spreading American influence gives a president a temporary boost in the polls, as George Bush #41 discovered in 1991 after the Gulf War. Then he learned a year and a half later that the way to an American voter's heart is to convince him that the quality of life of himself and his family, followed distantly by those of his friends and neighbors, is improving—and will get even better.

LIBERAL VALUES HAVE WON

Politics is a retail game. While appealing to the narrow interests of tiny constituencies can make a critical difference in a tight race, long-term victory goes to the party whose candidates appeal to the broad mainstream of citizens who regularly turn up to vote.

Eight polls of "leaned party identification" showed that, through 2002, self-identified Democrats outnumbered Republicans 46 to 37 percent. (Independents, who make up the remainder, tend to split their votes evenly between the two parties.) Interestingly, Columbia University professor Todd Gitlin writes, the general public is "less affluent, less educated, less white, less Republican than the private club of regular voters." The conclusion is inescapable: until a couple of years ago, American voters overwhelmingly identified themselves as Democratic. Americans, including those who don't vote, are more liberal still. (The fact that Americans are more liberal overall than the subset of Americans who vote explains why high voter turnout benefits Democrats.)

The war in Iraq, however, marked what *ABC News* calls "a rare point of political parity" in its twenty-three years of tracking the opinions of the American electorate. For the first time, in November 2003, the network found that Americans had become evenly divided by party affiliation: 31 percent Democratic, 31 percent Republican, 31 percent independent. Leaned party identification, however, continued to favor Democrats, albeit by a smaller 46 to 43 percent margin. Democrats remained steady. Republicans, meanwhile, convinced six percent of independents to declare themselves in their camp.

The American liberal paradigm goes much deeper than mere party affiliation. When asked where they stand on important "values" issues like abortion, college financial aid, Social Security, and healthcare, Americans overwhelmingly concur with the liberal-left-Democratic segment of the political spectrum. On the other hand, one might expect voters to side with conservatives on economic matters. We are, after all, a culturally libertarian and aspirational people to whom cries for "class warfare" are supposedly anathema. Nonetheless, we continue to favor a progressive tax code that redistributes wealth from rich to poor, as well as caps on CEO compensation.

If Americans voted by party affiliation, Republicans would *never* win a national election. If voters' choices were determined by their systems of individual values, Republicans might not even win local elections.

Yet few can deny that the American Left, which encompasses a diverse range of political opinion represented by the Democratic Party along with progressives, pacifists, leftist libertarians, and other allies, is getting its collective ass kicked. As of the beginning of 2004, Republicans and their allies (which include every strain from the Christian Right and racist militia groups to Reagan Democrats) controlled the White House as well as both houses of Congress. Writing in the *Weekly Standard*, Fred Barnes notes that Republicans held 229 seats in the U.S. House of Representatives, up from 176 in 1992. The number of Republican governors had risen from eighteen to twenty-seven. And the gains aren't just on the federal level. The GOP controlled just eight state legislatures in 1992; now it has twenty-one. "For the first time in 50 years," the *New York Times* reported in 2003, "a majority of state legislators are Republican."

Electoral gains aside—and George W. Bush's success at getting virtually every piece of legislation he proposes enacted into law demonstrates how sweeping those gains have been—the Right has successfully shifted the mainstream of public discourse to match its agenda. Remember the statistic I cited at the beginning of this section? Democrats represent 46 percent of the nation's voters. When FDR was president, the number was 63 percent.

THE TRIUMPH OF THE RIGHT

Nothing illustrates the rightward shift of the Republican Party more succinctly than the career of the late Arizona Senator Barry Goldwater, who lost his 1964 presidential bid after being, as he later recalled, "branded as a fascist, a racist, a trigger-happy warmonger, a nuclear madman." GOP pundits lauded him during the eighties as the father of modern conservatism and crediting him for popularizing many of the ideas espoused by Reagan. By 1994, however, the Republican Right had turned against him. They became so extreme that they passed Goldwater on the right and kept right on going.

"A lot of so-called conservatives today don't know what the word means," Goldwater told the *Los Angeles Times*. "They think I've turned liberal because I believe a woman has a right to an abortion. That's a decision that's up to the pregnant woman, not up to the pope or some do-gooders or the religious right. It's not a conservative issue at all." If Goldwater ran for president today, his pro-abortion and gay rights stances—which were entirely consistent with old-school conservative dislike of government intrusion in people's private lives—would be derided as those of a wild-eyed leftist. It is highly unlikely that a candidate espousing his positions on the issues would be permitted to rise to prominence by Republican Party leaders, much less survive the earliest primaries to become the presidential nominee.

The rightward shift of American political discourse has been reflected in the so-called Left. Bill Clinton ran for office in 1992 as a "New Democrat" who, in the words of Lorraine Woellert, "moved the party toward the political center through an artful fusion of conservative economics and liberal social policy." The programs established by LBJ's War on Poverty were unwound by a "welfare reform" bill—signed by a *Democratic president*—that threw millions into the streets. Clinton's greatest legislative achievement was NAFTA, a tariffs-reduction treaty whose passage had long eluded his Republican predecessors. If it took a hawk like Nixon to go to China, it took a Democrat like Clinton to drive the last nails into the coffin of organized labor, a traditionally Democratic constituency.

A few decades earlier, in 1972, George McGovern promised Americans that he would establish a system of socialized medicine. (The point isn't that he lost. The point is that the notion became part of mainstream political discourse.) In 1994, even Clinton's watered-down national HMO scheme, considered "too radical" by the new centrist Democratic leadership, went down in flames. Now that more people than ever can't afford a doctor's visit or prescription medications, you'd expect possible solutions to the crisis to be proposed by politicians and discussed in the media. But they're not. Healthcare is still troublesome to millions of Americans, but it's no longer an "issue." Pundits don't talk about it, legislators don't propose bills to do anything about it, and the media hardly covers it.

Inside the two parties, conservative factions are winning. They're also winning in the struggle between the two parties. How can we tell? Because everything is going backward—in opposition to the American way.

CONSERVATIVES HAVE ALWAYS FOUGHT PROGRESS

Whenever progressives have suggested that there might be a better way of doing things, whenever they demanded that we stop discriminating against some class of citizens, whenever they've argued that something could be done to improve the lives of ordinary, average Americans, some right-winger has told them to shut up. Conservatives fought tooth and nail to keep blacks in slavery, to prevent women from voting, and to stop gays from serving in the military. If pro-slavery conservatives had succeeded in making their vision of America our own, Colin Powell would be plowing fields and picking cotton while they were raping his wife.

Of course, conservatives can also be found in the Democratic Party, especially in its racist southern wing. Southern "Dixiecrats" so ferociously opposed the Civil Rights Act of 1964 that the debate led to a political realignment: so many angry white racists flocked to the GOP that, as Johnson famously predicted, he had lost the South for the Democratic Party "for a generation," or possibly forever.

Watergate set the stage for the right-wing hijacking of the party of Lincoln. After the disastrous 1974 Congressional elections cost them forty-three seats in the House of Representatives, six governorships, and 21 percent of state legislators, and incumbent President Gerald Ford lost to a virtually unknown Georgia peanut farmer in 1976, GOP officials decided that they needed to revamp their ailing party. After studying the problem, party leaders determined that the best way to rebuild was to attract right-wing extremists—true believers who had never been able to get excited about milquetoast moderates like President Ford. "For us to prevail, the party was going to have to be hospitable to people far out to our right," recalls Nancy Dwight of the party's Congressional campaign committee.

The Democrats' current situation may not seem quite as grim as the Republican rout of '74, but you shouldn't wait until the whole ship goes down before realizing that hitting that gigantic iceberg may have caused a problem. And the state of the Democrats is pretty grim. The Left has already lost momentum. Now it's sinking slowly, which makes it more difficult for guys like Al From (the Clintonista head of the centrist Democratic Leadership Council that has dominated the party's leadership since the early nineties) to understand the gravity of the problem. Slow illness, being more easily ignored, is more dangerous than spurting blood gushing from an artery. Can you imagine Mr. From echoing Nancy Dwight by encouraging his party to move back to the left, to recapture the liberals who've been taken for granted, allowed to sit out elections, and set twisting in the ideological wind?

Nowadays, after a twenty-year revitalization program, the "mainstream" Republican Party espouses positions that would have once been held only by the organization's extreme right wing or wacky fringe groups like the John Birch Society. Mainstream GOP politicians oppose both *legal* immigration and the separation of church and state, forcing teacher-led prayer upon children in public schools and replacing the teaching of evolution with the creationism myth promoted by fringe Christian fundamentalists. They favor running up the budget deficit by more than a trillion dollars, merely to pay for tax cuts!

Conservatives are right when they say that they have more ideas than liberals. They certainly have a lot of ideas, but few of their proposals help the average schlub, the man and woman struggling to get by from month to month, hoping to save up enough to buy a new house or car or maybe send their kid to college. Quite the contrary: with the exception of empty gestures like Bush's $300 per person tax rebate checks a few years back or his "ownership society" initiatives to privatize and jeopardize Social Security trust funds, Republicans *never, ever* come up with an idea that can be credibly said to help ordinary Americans.

We've heard the rhetoric. When rich people spend their big tax cuts, jobs are created. But that's nothing more than spin. That trickle-down economics was debunked twenty years ago doesn't change the fact that only fools believed in it in the first place. The truth is, conservatives don't want life to improve for the average American. Keeping the rest of us down, working to widen the divide between rich and poor, is a strategy transparently designed to increase their wealth at our expense. Bush's tax cut is an excellent example.

Princeton economist Paul Krugman calculates that "most families . . . will see their taxes fall by less than $800 [from Bush's tax cuts]—in many cases, much less so. Meanwhile, a handful of people will benefit hugely: the top one percent of families, with incomes averaging more than $1 million, will get tax breaks to the tune of $80,000 each." Tax cuts, like freedom, aren't free, not when you have to issue bonds to foreign investors to pay for them. The federal government must pay compound interest on those tax cuts. Each American's share of the resulting deficit will be roughly $30,000 paid over the course of ten years—higher if rates go up. The big tax cuts, therefore, went disproportionately to the superrich (who will net an average of at least $50,000 even after interest is paid on the resulting debt) but the burden of the big debts will fall disproportionately on the rest of us (who will pay a net average of at least $29,200).

There are countless hidden costs to trickle-down tax cuts. When government slashes spending on road maintenance and police protection, after all, we pay in the form of broken axles on bigger potholes and having our homes rifled through by rampaging burglars. Things go to hell, but not for everyone. The rich drive sturdier, more expensive cars. They take helicopters. Private security guards protect their estates.

Americans who vote conservative come in two varieties: privileged people dedicated to protecting their prerogatives, and wannabes who, though currently disenfranchised, hope someday to ascend to fiscal Mount Olympus themselves. Both the rich and the poor strivers wish to retain a state of affairs that benefits a class to which they either belong or to which they aspire. Economic and social entropy, the widening gap between rich and poor, relies on the existence of a class of people content to live with less and less.

When I give a public talk I sometimes issue a challenge to my audience. "Please identify," I'll ask them, "one conservative or right-wing idea that has moved American society forward." (In true capitalist form, I offer the winner a free book or T-shirt.) Believe me, people try to win. College campuses, more conservative than ever, are full of enthusiastic laissez faire libertarians. Nonetheless, usually nobody collects. Emancipation, women's suffrage, anti-discrimination laws, improved working conditions for workers, the minimum wage, Social Security, and every social program you can think of are concepts dreamed up by liberals.

A rare exception to the conservative losing streak at Ted Rall events occurred when a student at Carnegie-Mellon University offered "balancing the budget" as an example of a positive conservative contribution to American political thinking; I gave him a copy of *Revenge of the Latchkey Kids* because I'm a firm proponent of fiscal responsibility in government. Actually, I shouldn't have paid up. It's one thing to pass laws that get enacted and funded, as FDR did with a host of New Deal programs, and quite another to merely talk about them. No one has driven the federal budget further into the red than Republicans Ronald Reagan and George W. Bush; in recent history only Bill Clinton managed to accrue a surplus. "Conservatives" don't balance budgets. On the other hand, fiscal responsibility is a good idea—one that, until Clinton, only conservatives talked about.

Republican ideas fall into two categories: bad, and good but insincere.

Not only are they the enemies of that all-American principle of progress, conservatives spend every working hour scheming to reverse previous improvements in the lives of ordinary working people while blocking ideas that might do them some good in the future. To think that these are the people who wrap themselves in the trappings of patriotism and accuse those who disagree with them of anti-Americanism! They love America, but they hate Americans.

Conservatives are a perfect manifestation of Rall's Theorem, my observation that anyone who, unprompted, claims to be (insert adjective here) *is actually exactly the opposite*. The man who prattles incessantly about what a great husband he is inevitably turns out to be an abusive philanderer; the woman who brags about how good she is under the sheets is a pillow queen. Similarly, conservatives fly flags and wear them in miniature but despise everything the United States stands for. They disdain the Constitution and the Bill of Rights, they hate our national sense of egalitarianism, and they can't stand We, the People. They're not devoted to the fundamental American value that everyone, no matter who their parents were, deserves to see their children live better lives than they have. They pursue their self-interest at the expense of the national community. They don't see the point of helping fellow Americans simply because they *are* fellow Americans. They're un-American, nay, anti-American, in every sense of that inglorious word.

AMERICANS ARE LIBERAL II

If Americans are liberal, if conservatives are opposed to core American values, why is the conservative political agenda doing so well?

"Liberals have no ideas and no remedies," Ann Coulter, the fiery neoconservative columnist, repeats as a mantra. She's right. They don't. Of course, that's just how things seem now. It's not that liberals never had ideas—quite the opposite. Not only did lefties have a vision for how America could reach its full potential, most of their ideas were wildly popular. They caught on. They became law. They made America what it is today.

Early-twentieth-century American progressives realized that the exploitation of workers at the height of the Industrial Revolution was the worst unresolved problem of their time. As Upton Sinclair depicted in his muckraking novel *The Jungle*, tens of millions of Americans worked in the foulest of conditions six days a week, twelve hours a day. Exhausted, dirty, and sick, they lived in primitive shacks without running water, paid rent to the same employers who abused them, and bought their food from said employers at extortionist prices in company stores. Kids as young as eleven and twelve dropped out of school and went to work in coal mines and factories. There were no safety regulations.

When workers agitated for the right to join a union and to strike, work reasonable hours, and keep children out of factories, police in the pay of local businessmen shot at strikers and provided protection for scabs who crossed their picket lines. Conservative Congressmen passed laws that made it illegal to strike, essentially forcing people unsatisfied with their salaries to work for less or risk losing their livelihoods. If there's a better term than wage slavery for that, I don't know what it is.

Later in the American Century, when the Great Depression prompted down-and-out Americans to look to Soviet-style communism as a possible alternative to the joint scourges of capitalism—its boom-and-bust cycle and rapacious employers—FDR came along to calm things down. Herbert Hoover, a classic do-nothing conservative Republican, had watched idly as the Washington Mall and New York's Central Park filled with the tin-roofed sheds and shabby tents of the destitute. The nation plunged into ruin; conservatives did nothing. Nothing is what conservatives do.

Roosevelt's sweeping New Deal reforms enshrined liberal ideas in American law and government institutions and reduced the impetus for a radical uprising. "The New Deal was a revolution, peaceably accomplished," the great liberal New York governor Herbert Lehman remembered in 1958. "Part of this revolution consisted of the establishment of the responsibility of government for the basic economic welfare of Americans not only as farmers, laborers, and businessmen, but as individuals. The Social Security system which provided a program of old age and unemployment insurance, and for the support of the blind, the needy, and of mothers with dependent children—was a revolution all in itself. I am convinced that liberalism saved America in the 1930s, first from violent and subversive revolution, and then from defeat by the gathered forces of fascism."

McCarthyism, the spearpoint of a quintessentially conservative attempt to marginalize liberals by smearing them as socialists and socialists as subversives (this tactic continues unabated on right-wing sites on the twenty-first-century Internet), proved to be but a short detour in the mostly successful crusade led by political progressives to improve the lot of the downtrodden and the oppressed. African-Americans fought their own battles and lost countless martyrs in the struggle for equality, but northern white liberals contributed the critical impetus for successes of the civil rights movement. Liberals were crucial allies in the fight for fair treatment for blacks, women, and gays, inevitably over the pained howls of right-wing conservatives anguished that the America they loved—an America of lynchings, rampant discrimination, and hopelessness for millions—was being "destroyed."

Conservative southern Democrats and northern Republicans fought the constitutionally guaranteed right of black people to vote, arguing that "states' rights" precluded the right of the federal government to stop racists from committing lynchings and acts of voter intimidation. Liberals in the Kennedy and Johnson administrations said that that was absurd—and acted, states rights or no.

After winning the civil rights battles of the sixties, liberals went on to win victory after victory in the culture wars of the seventies and eighties. Adherence to feminism and opposition to the Vietnam War became widely accepted. The overwhelming majority of Americans now favor the rights of women to work and earn wages equal to those of men (though this goal has yet to be fully achieved). Most citizens back abortion rights. Many men privately confide that they still look down on women, but the expression of such retrograde opinions is considered socially unacceptable.

Even after Americans have repeatedly made clear that they don't share their values, conservatives keep trying to turn back the clock. The war in Vietnam has been retroactively rehabilitated (thanks in part to the Rambo-Reaganite "they didn't let us win" myth of the eighties, which echoes Hitler's interwar "stab in the back" leitmotif), and Bush's wars against Afghanistan and Iraq were initially well received. But the aspect of the Vietnam conflict most despised by the Left, the military draft, remains so unpopular that even the generals oppose conscription. Gays still get beaten up in dark alleys now and then, but it's happening less—and the leftie concept that people's sexual choices are their own business will forever be the norm in polite company.

Reagan's election in 1980 pushed liberals to their current defensive posture. As the Gipper beggared old New Deal and War on Poverty programs through tax-cut-driven deficit spending, Democrats fought sometimes and, more often, went along with what they inaccurately perceived as the popular will expressed by the Reagan Revolution. They quickly became exhausted from fighting off a blizzard of new Republican initiatives and, for the most part, Reagan got his way: runaway military spending, a ratcheted up Cold War, nasty secret conflicts in El Salvador and Nicaragua, assassinating Libyan leader Moammar Khaddafi's young daughter. On the domestic front, Republicans eviscerated spending on public education, decimated labor unions and the rights of workers, gutted the progressive tax code, and deregulated business to the extent that corporations, not government, was put in charge of our destiny. People began asking the question from this book's first chapter: Where are the Democrats?

In a cogent analyses of the status of the two parties for the *New York Times*, Adam Clymer ventured an answer: once they went on the defensive, the Dems doomed their chances for political success. "The Democrats have generally spent their energy defending past accomplishments, from Social Security to Medicare, rather than seeking to refocus that basic commitment to the middle class and the poor into ideas that reflect how the nation has changed," he wrote. In a phenomenon that would have been familiar to defenders of a castle under siege, Democratic thinking became short-term. "We think tactically and not strategically—one election at a time," Democratic pollster Peter Hart told Clymer. "We take the issue we can exploit, but we don't take the party and say this is what we are about." Lack of long-term vision inhibited change. Ossification set in.

Initially, liberals viewed Clinton's election as an opportunity to reverse some of the losses they had suffered during twelve years of Reagan-Bush. But Clinton, never much of a liberal in the first place, quickly gave up on big programs as politically unfeasible. Opting instead for the path of least resistance espoused by his adviser Dick Morris, he resorted to pushing micro-mini ideas like school uniforms and a V chip to protect kids from seeing icky images on television. Then his first term was hobbled by Newt Gingrich's Republican Revolution of 1994, which led to a long year of humiliating cohabitation with the GOP firebrand. Clinton spent his second term fooling around with intern Monica Lewinsky, and then managing the fallout from that idiotic dalliance. When he wasn't in full-on defensive mode, Clinton was trying to co-opt swing voters, the former "Reagan Democrats," by pushing for traditionally Republican ideas. Liberals watched "their" Democratic president unravel welfare and pass free-trade legislation they fiercely opposed. Union leaders threatened to take their votes elsewhere, but where else could they go? Now the liberal Left, the soul of the Democratic Party, found itself defending past achievements (the New Deal, Fair Deal, and Great Society) from Democrats as well as Republicans. New ideas? Who had time think of those?

Liberals may not have been inspired by many new ideas during the nineties, but it wouldn't have made any difference if they had. There hadn't been a liberal president to pitch them to since 1968.

Despite recent setbacks, progressive-minded Americans should take pride and comfort in the fact they've won the war of ideas that defined the last half of the twentieth century. That's right: *won*. Whenever an African-American walks into a restaurant or a bus and sits wherever he wants, he's living the realization of a liberal idea. Whenever a woman casts a vote, she spits in the eye of President William Howard Taft, a conservative Republican. (Taft opposed women's suffrage because he believed that the fairer sex was too emotional: "It is fair to say that the immediate enfranchisement of women will increase the proportion of the hysterical element of the electorate.") Liberals shouldn't forget, and shouldn't stop reminding America, where conservatives stood on rights they now take for granted.

Conservatives have always been like that—playing on people's fears to keep the downtrodden underfoot, dividing and conquering to make sure that they keep the biggest piece of pie for themselves. And the rest of us have often been fooled by their clever rhetorical devices. But we Americans always strive to improve, to grow. Progress, you know.

More than two centuries after Thomas Jefferson posited that we are all created equal, we're beginning to act like we believe it. We still have a long way to go before our society achieves anything approaching perfection. But this much is certain: we wouldn't have gotten this far if we'd paid attention to conservatives.

The Republican Party, it's worth noting, is the political heir to the Tory party of Great Britain. Had the early American colonists followed the advice of such great Tories as Benedict Arnold, we'd be singing "God Save the Queen," eating shepherd's pie, and drinking warm beer in brightly lit bars. If that's not un-American, what is?

chapter 5
STABBING
THE NEO FASCISTS

Historians in the future will reflect on an extraordinary, undeniable fact: over time, free nations grow stronger and dictatorships grow weaker. Liberty is both the plan of Heaven for humanity, and the best hope for progress here on earth.

—George W. Bush, 2003

The Left, using the Democratic Party as its mainstream political vessel, hopes to recapture its rightful place as America's dominant force and engine of political progress. Domestic issues (specifically the economy and more particularly our individual standard of living) usually determine the outcome of elections. Liberals tend to demonstrate more concern than conservatives for the prosperity of the common man and woman; when elections become referenda about compassion, they usually get credit for it. This book concentrates on domestic policy because it's so often a key determinant of electoral and political success. Moreover, a focus on domestic issues offers the path of least resistance for an ideology that finds difficulty in making its case as being strongest on international affairs. Liberals don't have to do as much to convince Americans that they have their best interests in mind on the domestic front as they do concerning matters related to foreign policy.

I fervently believe that the main thrust of a liberal drive to recapture the forward momentum it lost during the eighties and nineties, coupled with a Democratic attempt to retake the White House and Congress, as well as state and local seats across the nation, should be centered around a domestic economic agenda. "We care about you and your children," the liberal/Democratic message should say. "They only want to use you."

Voters don't trust Democrats to fend off foreign threats. "The public strongly prefers Republicans on national defense," affirms Adam Clymer, "and even though most Democrats in Congress backed the war on Iraq, at least a third of the rank and file was unhappy with it, which makes it difficult for party leaders to get too far out in front." Adding to the Democrats' otherwise pressing woes, the historical perception that they're weak on defense—an assertion belied by rapidly increasing defense budgets and the frequent use of military force under Presidents Carter and Clinton, but whatever—has been magnified in recent years by the same Bush-era polarization that has afflicted the electorate on taxes and other domestic issues. According to a November 2003 poll conducted by the Pew Research Center for the People and the Press, "Republicans have become more hawkish on national security, in support of Bush's policies, while Democrats have become more dovish, reflecting their growing disapproval of the war in Iraq. In the middle of President Bill Clinton's two terms, the difference between Republican partisans and Democrats was nine percentage points in agreeing with the statement that 'the best way to ensure peace is through military strength.' Now the gap is 25 percentage points."

Nonetheless, the Pew study does find reason for optimism for Democrats. Swing voters prefer the liberal approach to foreign policy: "The views of self-described independents fall much closer to those of Democrats."

The immediate aftermath of September 11 seemed to tighten the Republican's lock on their main strength: being perceived as strong on defense. As Americans reeled from the first major terrorist act on U.S. soil since Pearl Harbor, Bush's job approval rating shot to a staggering 89 percent, handing him nearly limitless political clout that he exploited to get everything from new free trade agreements to tax cuts through Congress. His administration launched a number of foreign and domestic policy initiatives during the year following September 11, its main projects being Operation Enduring Freedom, the invasion of Afghanistan that toppled the Taliban in favor of the Northern Alliance, and an attack against and subsequent occupation of Saddam Hussein's Iraq.

The invasion of Iraq began with giddy optimism. Journalists who had abandoned all pretense of objectivity, some even stooping to wearing the Bush administration's trademark American flag lapel pins on the air, predicted that grateful Iraqis would greet their American "liberators" with flowers and that order would be quickly restored. A nascent Iraqi democracy, neocons claimed, would serve as an example to repressive Middle Eastern neighbors, encouraging them to liberalize or be toppled by their own people. Michael Ledeen, who published a book titled *The War Against the Terror Masters,* summarized their point of view: "We are at war with a group of tyrants who sponsor a network of terrorists. Our most potent weapon against them is their own people, who hate them and wish to be free. We don't need to invade Iran or Syria or Saudi Arabia, but we certainly need to support the calls for freedom coming from within those tyrannical countries."

Big promises inevitably lead to shattering disappointment. The invasion of Iraq proved no exception. Only a few months after the U.S.-led coalition captured Baghdad, more American soldiers had died during the "occupation" than during the invasion, which had been declared ended May 1, 2003. There were no roses or cheering crowds. Even the high point of the war, the toppling of a statue of the Iraqi dictator, turned out to have been staged. Museums and libraries were looted and burned. A guerilla insurgency reminiscent of Vietnam launched, by the end of 2003, an average of thirty-five attacks on coalition forces per day—killing an average of one to two troops and wounding many more. Soon even Iraqis who had been jailed under Saddam were calling for the Americans to go home, saying ruefully that life had been better under dictatorship than anarchy.

There were no indications that the Iraq war had inspired Middle Eastern dictatorships to democratize. The medium-intensity war between Israel and the Palestinian Authority escalated. Administration officials pointed to Libya's decision to unilaterally destroy its weapons of mass destruction as evidence of a deterrent effect, only to later concede that Colonel Khaddafi had approached the U.S. long before the build-up to war. And the main impetus for the invasion, to disarm Iraq's biological, chemical, and nuclear weapons, proved pointless.

In interviews six months after the start of combat, Bush accentuated the positive: "If I could step back and maybe think out loud here about some of the stories or some of the speculation that was going on before we went into Iraq—one, the oil revenues would be blown up, the oil fields would be destroyed. They weren't. As a matter of fact, oil production is up to 2.1 million or 2.2 million barrels a day, to the benefit of the Iraqi people." (That wasn't true. Production peaked at 1.3 million barrels.) "That's a very important point. Remember, there was speculation about sectarian violence—that the long-suppressed Kurds or Shia may [sic] take out their anxieties and their frustrations on the Sunnis. That didn't happen." (Actually it did.) "There was talk about mass starvation—it didn't happen—refugee flows that would be unmanageable—that never happened. And so a lot of the contingency [sic] that we had planned for didn't happen."

Not all Americans bought Bush's claim that all was well on the Middle Eastern front. A *Los Angeles Times* poll taken on the six-month "anniversary" of the fall of Baghdad found support for the Iraq war at 48 percent, down from 77 percent at the beginning of the invasion. Only 35 percent thought that "the cost to the U.S. in military lives . . . was worth it." "My biggest fear is: is this thing going to end up being like Vietnam?" asked fifty-year-old Alan Geleske of Michigan City, Indiana, one of those polled. "It doesn't seem like there are any clear-cut objectives . . . and the casualty list is growing. It's a concern. I have a son and a son-in-law in the army."

As Nixon faltered by prolonging Vietnam, Bush and the Republicans may find that the Tigris has become their foreign policy Rubicon. It would be too much to claim that the Right's traditional advantage on defense issues is trickling away along with the blood of young men and women in the sands of what U.S. occupation troops refer to as Vichy Mesopotamia, but the Iraq debacle—coupled with the administration's abandonment of Afghanistan to the warlords—has created a potential opening for liberals hoping to score points on foreign affairs. If it's smart, the Left will concentrate the bulk of its efforts to seduce the hearts and minds of American voters with exciting pro-posals designed to solve economic and other problems here at home, while opening a secondary front on matters of war, peace, and the role of the United States in the international community to keep Republicans off bal-ance on their home ideological turf.

Forming a coherent foreign policy argument for liberalism could make the difference between success and failure in countless contests. Infinitely more important, it could save America from the greatest threat it currently faces: homegrown Republican extremism.

The gap between prewar expectations and postwar disappointment in Afghanistan and Iraq has forced the Right to concede that it doesn't have all the answers when it comes to national security. It has further exposed the Republicans' willingness to lie when it suits them, even to the extent of endangering our safety. If Democrats are a party in search of Big Ideas, however, gotcha politics—what happened to the WMDs? huh? well?—fall far short of what's needed to eradicate the historical conservative advantage on defense. Primary contender Howard Dean, for instance, stumbled with his assertion that the capture of Saddam Hussein hadn't made Americans any safer. He was correct but failed to explain why: Saddam hadn't ever been in charge of the Iraqi resistance, publicly humiliating a former Arab head of state with a televised louse inspection angered Muslims, and Iraq had never been affiliated with the Islamist radicals who carried out September 11 or the U.S.S. *Cole* and 1998 embassy bombings in East Africa.

Off-the-cuff gibes won't draw Republican blood. Liberals must explain, to score political points and to save the republic, that the Bush administration and the new Republican leadership it epitomizes are not conservatives at all, but radical extremists determined to change the United States in fundamental ways that are dangerous and unpalatable to most Americans. As Chalmers Johnson cogently argues in his 2004 book, *The Sorrows of Empire,* the Bushies represent the final triumph of a new aggressive U.S. militarism over our traditional homegrown values. Preemptive warfare doesn't fit our cultural predisposition for refusing to start unnecessary wars. We prefer to build infrastructure at home than empire abroad. And we prefer spreading democracy by example to creating phony pseudodemocratic puppet states at the point of a rifle.

American citizens continue to believe that their language, political influence, and popular culture has spread across the globe due to their inherent appeal to billions of clueless foreigners, but the dominance of our consumer-based culture has piggybacked on an aggressive, expansionist military posture about which most of us remain blissfully unaware. McDonald's may have the best fries, but more than half a million permanently stationed servicemen at U.S. military bases around the world have a greater impact on spreading American influence abroad than the Hamburglar. Chalmers Johnson believes that America is so far along the trajectory that ancient Rome followed from city-state to republic to empire that it may be impossible to stuff the genie back into its bottle, but the essence of optimism—the core of being American—is to understand that we're not doomed until the Visigoths start streaming up the Appian Way. Liberals can still save America from the Right, but in order to do it we must explain to people that their current leadership is dangerously out of control and must be replaced. Liberals must also educate voters, the majority of whom will never travel outside the United States, about how and why we are perceived as arrogant and vicious.

Using the Second Gulf War as a case study, this argument that today's "Republicans" are nothing like Dwight Eisenhower, Barry Goldwater, or even Ronald Reagan flows in logical reverse:

- Bush and the Republicans lied about Iraq's weapons of mass destruction and underestimated the cost in cash and corpses of occupation. They screwed up the war.
- If the GOP doesn't know how to fight the war on terrorism abroad, an endeavor that ought to be relatively

trightforward, it stands to reason that it probably isn't doing such a fabulous job here at home.

- Didn't we give the Bushies everything they wanted after September 11: the USA-Patriot Act, a Department of Homeland Security, the suspension of privacy rights and individual liberties for the sake of increased security? Sure we did—but we still don't feel any safer—and we aren't.
- Could it be that the government knew that its policies would do nothing to reduce the likelihood of future terrorist attacks—that, in fact, making us safe wasn't even the point of those policies?
- What kind of people would demand such a radical reordering of our societal priorities without good reason?

The answer to this last question is simple. These Bushist neocons are people who do not care about America, or at least America as we know it. They are further outside the ideological mainstream than any administration in our nation's history.

WHO DARES SPEAK THE F WORD?

Bush said he'd be an isolationist. During the 2000 campaign, he promised that, as president, his foreign policy would avoid the kind of "nation-building" Clinton had undertaken in Haiti and Kosovo. Analysts anticipated that he would continue to expand international business while shying away from U.N.-led peacekeeping operations, much less launching full-scale military confrontations halfway around the world. True, his cabinet read like a who's who of hard-right hawks. With the benefit of hindsight, Bush's intentions were plainly obvious to anyone who cared to pay attention.

In 1997 a group of right-wing bigwigs met to form the Project for a New American Century, a Washington-based advocacy group that advocated a more aggressive foreign policy stance. Of the twenty-five original PNAC founders, four would later land top jobs in the White House occupied by George W. Bush: Vice President Dick Cheney, Defense Secretary Donald Rumsfeld, Deputy Secretary of Defense Paul Wolfowitz, and U.S. Ambassador to Afghanistan and Iraq Zalmay Khalilzad. The following year, the PNAC wrote open letters to Congress and President Clinton demanding "the removal of Saddam Hussein's regime from power" and the use of military force, if necessary, to achieve this goal. Eighteen people signed the letter, including Rumsfeld, Wolfowitz, Khalilzad, Deputy Secretary of State Richard Armitage, *Weekly Standard* editor William Kristol, and Richard Perle, the GOP-connected chairman of the semi-governmental Defense Policy Board.

These men would soon lead America to the brink of fascism.

The PNAC clique advocated ramping up America's military posture from one of deterrence to the brand of preemption Israel used to justify its 1981 bombing of an Iraqi nuclear reactor. In the past U.S. presidents had waged war in self-defense, or at least the pretense of it. Potential enemies, the PNAC argued, should be taken out before they had a chance to strike first. War, necessary to defend the "homeland" and potentially beneficial to business as an American empire expanded, could be justified on the flimsiest of evidence. The United States, the hawks said, must pursue its self-interest without concern for international opinion, with or without the imprimatur of organizations such as the U.N. This vision was so radical that, despite stacking his cabinet with PNAC adherents, Bush didn't try to sell it to the American people before the fall of 2001.

"Before 9/11, this group . . . could not win over the president to this extravagant image of what foreign policy required," says Ian Lustick, Middle East expert at the University of Pennsylvania. "After 9/11, it was able to benefit from the gigantic eruption of political capital, combined with the supply of military preponderance in the hands of the president. And this small group, therefore, was able to gain direct contact and even control, now, of the White House."

"What started as a theory in 1997," reported ABC News' *Nightline*, "was now on its way to becoming official U.S. foreign policy."

The PNAC crowd began to echo the theory promoted by British historian Niall Ferguson in *Empire: The Rise and Demise of the British World Order and the Lessons for Global Power* that the U.S. was "an empire in denial" that needed to overcome its wariness of the "formal rule over subject peoples" that characterized British imperial rule until the Second World War. "Like it or not," Ferguson wrote, "and deny it who will, empire as much a reality today as it was throughout the 300 years when Britain ruled, and made, the modern world." If the U.S. was an empire, in other words, it had might as well behave like one. The September 11 events added a Machiavellian twist to the preemption argument: failure to assert power given an opportunity to do so,neocons claimed, is a statement of weakness that terrorist groups and rival states will inevitably view as an invitation to attack. Neoconservatism incorporated this nakedly imperialistic philosophy—for the first time in a generation or two, the word *imperialist* was bandied about with implicit approbation—and demon seed of this marriage became "The National Security Strategy of the United States of America," published by the State Department in 2002. The repackaged Bush Doctrine manifested itself after September 11 via invasions of Afghanistan and Iraq, a War on Terrorism at home and abroad, the creation of military bases in new spheres of influence historically controlled by Russia, closer alliances with various nations overseas, and the stifling of domestic political dissent, both by mainstream Democratic politicians and leftist opposition groups.

The wars against Afghanistan and Iraq were the first major tests of the new Bush Doctrine. Though marketed at first as an attempt to capture Osama bin Laden (blamed without evidence for the September 11 attacks) and later as a war to liberate the Afghans from the oppressive Taliban regime, the campaign in Afghanistan was, as I documented in my book *Gas War: The Truth Behind the Occupation of Afghanistan*, actually dedicated to establishing a foothold in Central Asia with an eye towards future exploitation of Caspian Sea energy reserves. (In 1999 Kazakhstan struck a pocket of oil estimated to contain as much as 260 billion barrels—more than six times current Saudi reserves—at a drilling platform on the eastern shore of the Caspian Sea. Officials in the Clinton and Bush #43 administrations hoped to build an oil and gas pipeline across U.S.-controlled Afghanistan to secure strategic control over these new resources.) The PR campaign promoting the invasion of Iraq morphed from fear-mongering about weapons of mass destruction to fictional ties between Saddam and bin Laden's al Qaeda organization to liberating the Iraqi people from Baathist oppression to, hilariously, establishing a model of Western-style capitalism and democracy in the Middle East. However, the fact that Iraq possesses the world's second largest oil reserves after Saudi Arabia played a greater role than these constantly shifting rationales for war.

The Bush administration cut unsavory deals with repressive nations including China and Pakistan, whose leader Pervez Musharraf deposed his democratically elected predecessor in a military coup, to convince them to endorse a War on Terrorism that was nothing but a thin cover for American expansion. In return for signing on to the U.S. agenda, nations extracted tacit consent to escalate oppression within their own borders. China requested and received Bush's approval to expand its suppression of Muslims in its western

Xinjiang province. Xinjiang's long-suffering Uyghurs, who had long hoped that America would help them work towards their goal of an autonomous Republic of East Turkestan, saw their worst fears realized with this arrangement. Bush agreed to turn a blind eye to human rights violations in the autocratic (and oil-rich) Central Asian republics of Uzbekistan, Kyrgyzstan, Kazakhstan, and Tajikistan in exchange for temporary or permanent American military bases. General Musharraf welched on a promise to hold elections.

The USA-Patriot Act, signed into law without substantial public debate on October 26, 2001, permits law enforcement agencies to obtain wiretaps and other forms of domestic surveillance on U.S. residents and citizens without being required to obtain a warrant from a judge. All cops need to do, according to former Clinton chief of staff John Podesta (now teaching law at Georgetown University), is to supply "a mere certification that the information likely to be obtained is relevant to an ongoing criminal investigation." Section 216 of the act authorizes "the installation of devices to record all computer routing, addressing, and signaling information" and Section 206 "allows a single wiretap to legally 'roam' from device to device, to tap the person rather than the phone." Civil libertarians who recall Nixon's abuse of the FBI to spy on Democrats and antiwar activists fear that these sweeping powers could easily be used the same way again. Based on the way the new law is written, it's less likely now than in the 1970s that we would find out if such abuses were taking place. And given the unscrupulous nature of the current regime in control of Washington, it's more likely that they are.

Fearing that their radical policies couldn't withstand public scrutiny, top GOP officials smeared those who questioned Bush as the moral equivalent of Osama bin Laden, on par with the terrorists who killed three thousand Americans in New York, Washington, and Pennsylvania. Senator Don Nickles, reacting to the news that two Democratic Congressmen had traveled to Baghdad before the war on a fact-finding mission, said that "both sound somewhat like spokespersons for the Iraqi government [of Saddam Hussein]." A Republican National Committee ad prepared for the 2004 Iowa caucuses accused liberals of "attacking the president for attacking the terrorists." (Actually they had accused Bush of wasting resources on attacking Iraq *instead* of attacking the terrorists.) Emboldened by their out-of-control leaders, rightist Republicans have abandoned any pretense of civility. It's open season on anyone who has a problem with Bush, whether

the issue is tax policy, civil liberties, or his wars in Afghanistan and Iraq—
especially the latter.

"There is a virulent strain of anti-Americanism in this country," prominent right-wing blogger Andrew Sullivan—now a *Time* magazine opinion
columnist—wrote. "Some, like [Ted] Rall, are now urging the murder of
American troops in defense of Islamist terrorists and the acolytes of one of
the most brutal dictators in history."

As if.

As Sullivan well knows, I have never said or thought or implied anything of the sort. The essay that he was referring to was my attempt to
explain that the Iraqi resistance was motivated more by Iraqi nationalism
than blind hatred of the United States, and to argue that any country
occupied by a foreign power would likely fight a guerilla war against its
occupying troops. I have repeatedly written that Saddam Hussein was a
reprehensible dictator, albeit one who would never gotten the chance to
inflict as much misery had he not been propped up by the United States for
so long. The mere fact that a liar like Sullivan could publish such extremist
tripe in formerly respectable venues proves that the monkeys are in charge
of the ethical zoo.

The analogy isn't perfect, but the closest historical precedent for the current foreign policy of the Republican Party—the party of Lincoln, hijacked
by lunatics who think that the world becomes safer when one country
reserves the right to declare war without justification, even to launch
nuclear weapons preemptively as General Tommy Franks requested the
right to do—is fascism. (Franks gleefully predicted the "militarization" of
the U.S. government here at home.)

Fascism is an ideology that favors dictatorial government, the obsessive
creation of an economic climate favorable to big business, repression of
political opposition, scapegoating of political enemies and ethnic minorities,
and extreme nationalism channeled into a policy of military expansionism.
Bushism isn't exactly identical to fascism, but it comes uncomfortably close
to its dictionary definition.

(Mussolini, who famously observed that "fascism should more properly
be called corporatism because it is the merger of state and corporate power,"
elevated the privileges of businesses to enjoy direct representation in the
Italian legislature's *Camera dei Fasci e delle Corporazioni*. Many see parallels
between this marriage of government and business interests in the Bush

administration's invitation to pro-business lobbyists to write the exact language of bills to be voted upon in Congress.)

In his classic 1998 essay "The Five Stages of Fascism," Columbia University professor and fascism expert Robert O. Paxton (who supervised my honors thesis on Vichy France, another illegitimate regime with interesting similarities to the Bush phenomenon), wrote: "Fascists despise thought and reason, abandon intellectual positions casually, and cast aside many intellectual fellow travelers." The Republicans' shifting rationales for invading Iraq, before and after the start of combat, provide a clear example of this phenomenon.

Paxton identifies seven "mobilizing passions" characteristic of traditional fascism:

1. A sense that one's group or country is superior to others. (I was struck by this aspect of American culture, which dates back at least to Woodrow Wilson's assertion that America should make the world safe for democracy, during a debate about the occupation of Iraq at the Yale Political Union. Liberal and conservative speakers alike accepted as a given that the U.S. had a God-given right and duty to guide other nations in their internal affairs, which might sometimes "require" military intervention. When I asserted the importance of national sovereignty by arguing that the U.S. has no more right to order other countries around than Liechtenstein, the audience reacted with the empty sheep-eyed stare that I call "the Simpsons blink." They didn't get it.)

2. A victim mentality that "justifies any action against the group's enemies, internal as well as external." (Septermber 11 has become the Right's Reichstag fire, an all-purpose trope to justify dubious attacks on two sovereign nations, oil drilling in Alaska, tax cuts, the lagging economy, deficits, and opposition to campaign finance reform. We were attacked on September 11, liberals are reminded in order to justify a reaction—any reaction—to real and perceived threats, have you forgotten that?)

3. "Dread of . . . decadence under the corrosive effect of individualistic and cosmopolitan liberalism." (Free

Republic pundit John Huang, who bashes "traitorous DemoRATS" still pushes the conservative standard line that "Bush restored dignity and respect to his office, after the battering it took during the Clinton years." The conservative myth that liberalism goes hand in hand with all manner of sexual debauchery and assorted thought-crime, while the Right epitomizes noble virtue, explains why Bush supporters continue to attack former President Clinton years after he went into retirement.)

4. The creation of a national community self-defined by purity and unity and, if necessary, violence against those who disagree. (Fortunately, despite the Bush Right's penchant for death threats and outrageous slander, we haven't seen much actual violence against liberals.)

5. "An enhanced sense of identity and belonging, in which the grandeur of the group reinforces individual self-esteem." (Post–September 11 patriotic bunting and symbolism, from "United We Stand" posters and billboards to car antenna flags, to the administration's American flag lapel pins, function toward this end.)

6. The "authority of natural leaders (always male) throughout society, culminating in a national chieftain who alone is capable of incarnating the group's destiny." (Running the sentence "Bush is the best president ever" through the Google Internet search engine yielded forty-two hits. Lest you believe that this toadying is old behavior, "Clinton is the best president ever" gave zero results.)

7. "The beauty of violence and of will, when they are devoted to . . . success in a Darwinian struggle." (Beginning with Johnny "Mike" Spann, a CIA interrogator killed during the November 2001 prison uprising at Mazar-e-Sharif, Afghanistan, the U.S. has elevated the status of those killed in the War on Terrorism to sainted martyrs, far exceeding the praise for the valor and sacrifice of those who fell in such previous conflicts as Somalia and Panama. Both bin Laden and neoconservative thinkers assert that we are engaged in a clash of civilizations

between militant Islam and the West. To these people,
the fate of the planet hangs in the balance.)

No, the United States is not a fascist state. Not yet.

Nevertheless, many of the most influential figures in the Bush administration espouse policies and strategies for promulgating those policies that
rely on fascist impulses. As David Neiwert writes: "This is not to argue that
the Bush Doctrine is fascist *per se*—but rather, that it has enough elements
in it to appeal strongly to the right-wing extremists who are increasingly
becoming part of the mainstream GOP fold. It plays out in such manifesta-
tions as its utter disregard—indeed, clear contempt—for the United
Nations and multilateralism generally, a stance that resonates deeply with
the John Birch crowd . . . These kinds of appeal clearly resonate with the
proto-fascist Patriot element that have been increasingly finding common
cause with the Bush regime." Men like Rumsfeld, Cheney, and Perle have
blended elements of old-school fascism with mainline conservative rhetoric
to create an ideology that can fairly be described as *neofascism*. Bush &
Company don't goosestep or wear jackboots, but as Paxton notes, "one can
not identify a fascist regime [solely] by its plumage." Actions define this
quintessentially activist ideology.

To lift a page from the Bush Doctrine of preemptive defense, right-
thinking, Right-hating Americans needn't wait until swastika banners are
hanging from their local city hall before acting to save their country.
Traveling part of the way down the road to fascism, as the Bush neofascists
have already done, is already going too far. Sure, if Democrats and progressives stand by and do nothing to stop them, there's a chance that the hard-
right PNAC faction running Washington may turn back on its own. On the
other hand, they may not. We can't trust in the good intentions of officials
whose resumes are nothing short of terrifying. The United States sacrificed
too many soldiers to defeat Fascist Italy, Nazi Germany, and imperial Japan
during World War II to allow their successor ideologies to triumph here in
the "homeland."

No one disputes that September 11 called for a response or that military
force may have been the most appropriate expression of such a reaction. I
argued in my book *To Afghanistan and Back* that Bush should have reacted to
the attacks with both carrot and stick, the former in the form of statements
acknowledging that American foreign policy often has deleterious effects
upon the peoples of other nations, especially in the Muslim world. Bush

ought to have understood that September 11 was an urgent warning that Islamists would continue to attack American civilians unless the United States stopped propping up corrupt tyrants in places like Saudi Arabia and Uzbekistan. He should have begun trying to act as an honest broker in the Israel-Palestinian conflict—changes that, terrorism notwithstanding, we should have undertaken long ago. Convincing the Muslim world that we understand their rage would have deprived Islamist radicals of their millions of moderate supporters, reducing their base of political and financial support. Of course, there would still be some hardcore anti-American types out there. This is why we should also have pressured the Saudis and Egyptians, the home nations of the nineteen hijackers and likely sponsors of the group Islamic Jihad, to which all nineteen belonged, to extradite suspects related to September 11 for interrogation and possible prosecution for conspiracy to commit mass murder. "We get it," we should have told the Muslim world. "We will stop supporting the evil regimes that oppress you. But don't mistake kindness for weakness. We will track down anyone who has anything to do with harming Americans and bring them to justice."

Had Bush been certain of bin Laden's involvement in September 11— which he was not—he should not have threatened the Taliban with an invasion of Afghanistan. First he ought to have quietly worked with the governments of neighboring Pakistan, Iran, Turkmenistan, Uzbekistan, and Tajikistan to seal their borders with Afghanistan so that U.S. Special Forces paratroopers could enclose and capture the al Qaeda leader. After capturing bin Laden, he should have ordered our soldiers out. The Taliban were a reprehensible regime, possibly the worst on the planet, but respecting the territorial integrity of other countries ought to be a top priority of every leader who cares about the sanctity of his own national borders.

Bush certainly should not have attacked Iraq, which had no ties whatsoever to September 11 and presented, by all account, no credible threat to the United States.

The wars against Afghanistan and Iraq were inappropriate, illegal follow-ups (one can hardly call them reactions) to September 11. However, they do not present prima facie proof of the Bush Administration's extremist tendencies. With the exception of the preemptive strike doctrine vis-à-vis Iraq—an application of naked aggression morally indistinguishable from the 1939 invasion of Poland—the mere fact that we invaded Afghanistan and Iraq does not *per se* establish Bush's wars as the beginning of America's neofascist era. After all, President Clinton invaded Haiti and Kosovo; one of his greatest regrets was failing to intervene in the Rwandan genocide. Bush the First was first to go after Saddam, as well as the architect of a bizarre assault on Panama. Reagan bombed Libya, invaded Grenada, and mined Nicaraguan shipping lanes. One could reasonably argue that Dubya was merely the latest commander-in-chief with a penchant for throwing around America's military might.

The dangers presented by neofascism, which should serve as a rallying cry for the Left and a call to the righteous indignation of the American people, are best exemplified by the Bush administration's most outrageous moves since September 11: thumbing its nose at the Geneva Conventions, endangering American soldiers in future wars; applying Gestapo tactics of retaliation, apartheid, and repression in occupied Iraq; and using a military base in Cuba to deny basic rights to Muslim prisoners of war captured in Afghanistan.

AMERICA'S CONCENTRATION CAMP AT GITMO
Nothing says fascism like a concentration camp.

Beginning with the launch of the War on Terrorism during autumn 2001, the United States began shipping hundreds of detainees—in order to deny them the rights guaranteed them under international law, American officials refuse to dignify their charges as "prisoners"—to the U.S. naval base at Guantánamo Bay, Cuba. What began as the primitive Camp X-Ray tent city built to accommodate Taliban and al Qaeda soldiers captured in Afghanistan has expanded into a semi-permanent facility dubbed Camp Delta. Camp Delta is used to hold more than six hundred people from forty-two countries—including Saudi Arabia (at about one hundred fifty the biggest group), Yemen, Pakistan, Algeria, and even such Western nations as Great Britain, Canada, and Sweden.

An additional facility, Camp Iguana, was built to hold child prisoners—some Gitmo detainees were as young as twelve when they arrived—though U.S. officials say these children are not children. Afghan children are "not children," says Rumsfeld, because they're "very, very dangerous." "Teenagers younger than 16 being held at Guantánamo Bay are 'not children' and pose a lethal threat that justifies detention, U.S. military chiefs insisted," the English newspaper the *Guardian* reported.

One hardly knows where to begin when cataloguing the ways in which the Guantánamo Bay concentration camp offends basic human rights, soils

America's international reputation, and establishes a terrifying precedent for the world's most important democracy.

The primary reason that the Bush Administration selected Gitmo as the site of its detention camp was to place its prisoners in a Kafkaesque legal limbo. A bit of residual war booty from the Spanish-American War of 1898, Guantánamo is claimed by Bushie legal experts to fall neither fully under American nor Cuban jurisdiction. It's not America, it's not Cuba, it's nowhere. Therefore Muslim inmates held there cannot, as two U.S. federal courts have affirmed, file cases in the courts of either nation. They may not receive visits from attorneys, reporters, or family members; appeal for consular representation by their home nations; or demand to be tried for their crimes. Based on Gitmo's supposed unique status as legal no-man's-land and the inmates' classification as "enemy combatants," we're denying them all of the rights and privileges guaranteed to prisoners of war under the 1949 Geneva Conventions.

Most of the suspects were captured on Afghan battlefields, arrested based on powers claimed by equating the War on Terrorism with a real military conflict. Some were detained with no more evidence that they had been affiliated with the Taliban or al Qaeda militias than the word of an allied local warlord. (These Afghan suspects, it turns out, were sold by warlords to the United States for cash or in order to take vengeance on a rival clan.) Some inmates, reported CBS News in July 2003, "have been there over 500 days without being charged with a crime, without the right to a lawyer, and without knowing if they will be tried."

Setting aside for the moment the frightening moral implications of the establishment of a concentration camp under United States control, the Administration's two central legalistic justifications—that Guantánamo, like Antarctica, is not part of a recognized nation-state and that its POWs can be denied legal redress by declaring them "unlawful combatants"—fall apart upon cursory examination. As Pamela Falk, a member of the Council for Foreign Relations, notes, American authorities treat Gitmo as part of Cuba: "Curiously, I flew into the base directly from Fort Lauderdale with Defense Department clearance on their authorized charter, Fandango Airlines. Today, reporters who travel to Guantánamo fly from Puerto Rico on a military plane and pass though customs on return—a certain change that appears to acknowledge that the base is on foreign territory." Anyway, if Gitmo isn't subject to U.S. or Cuban law, wouldn't that mean that its residents could commit any crime, including murder, without facing charges? Of course not.

Soldiers fall under the jurisdiction of the Uniform Code of Military Justice, but no one expects Pakistani or Yemeni detainees to get their own judge advocate general anytime soon. As for the second point, Falk says, there is no precedent for unilaterally denying Geneva protections to captured enemy soldiers: "After bringing the prisoners to Guantánamo, the Defense Department (along with several other government agencies including the FBI, the State Department and the CIA) had to create what are known under the Geneva Conventions as Article 5 tribunals to determine which prisoners are given POW status. Not mentioned in the Geneva Conventions, an 'unprivileged' or 'unlawful combatant' is defined in the Hague Conventions, dating back to 1907 but not U.S. law until the Supreme Court case, Ex Parte Quirin. The clearest distinction between acts, such as murder, committed lawfully by soldiers in battle, and unlawfully by civilians, is stated in that case, where 'a soldier in uniform who commits the acts mentioned would be entitled to treatment as a prisoner of war; it is the absence of uniform that renders the offender liable to trial for violation of the laws of war.'" Incredibly, the Bush argument for indefinite detention is largely sartorial. As a Defense Department attaché who interrogates ("Okay, tortures," his fourth beer loosened him up enough to concede) Gitmo prisoners argued, "The Taliban didn't wear uniforms the way we wear uniforms. They're a militia, and militias aren't covered by Geneva."

Rewind to September 10, 2001. The World Trade Center still stood. The Taliban government controlled 95 percent of Afghanistan and enjoyed diplomatic recognition by three nations, which all had full relations with the United States. Bush and other top officials had met with leading Talibs in February 2001 to discuss building an oil and natural gas pipeline across Afghanistan. Negotiations on the Trans-Afghanistan Pipeline had stalled during July, but no one expected war. The Taliban were widely expected to deliver a knockout blow to the Northern Alliance during the coming summer of 2002. Like them or not—and I didn't—the Taliban were the de facto government of Afghanistan. Their troops didn't wear Western style outfits, that's true, but somehow I doubt that the administration would have declared them POWs under Geneva if they had. And they did wear recognizable clothing. Their long-tail turbans were so distinctive that Pentagon operators of remote-control Predator drone planes assumed that anyone wearing one was a Talib to be targeted by missile fire.

Even as it starts to build a death chamber for inmates to be executed after anticipated military tribunals, the Pentagon claims that Gitmo concentration camp—soon death camp—inmates are being well treated. "Each cell," the *New York Times* wrote in April 2003, "has a metal bed stenciled with a bright yellow arrow pointed to Mecca . . . There have been no credible reports of abuse or substantial complaints about the physical conditions of the detainees." Still, not everything comes up sweetness and light in the dog cages on the sea: "There is some dispute as to the cause of some 25 suicide attempts at the camp and the fact that more than five percent of the detainees are being treated with antidepressants."

UPI reporter Michael Kirkland wrote: "The majority of prisoners at Guantánamo's 'Camp Delta' are kept in solitary confinement in cells measuring six feet eight inches by eight feet, except for 30 minutes of shackled exercise on a small concrete slab . . . Lights are kept on 24 hours a day." By contrast prisoners in most maximum-security penitentiaries have cellmates, cells twice as large, and work and exercise several hours per day outside their cells.

By October 2003 there had been seven more suicide attempts at Gitmo and the Zoloft was flying off the shelf at the camp infirmary. After initial attempts to quietly improve the conditions of inmates by refraining from public criticism and working through official channels, the senior representative of the International Committee of the Red Cross had had enough. The worst form of torture being used against Gitmo inmates, Christophe Girod said, was the legal limbo used to justify their indefinite detention. "One cannot keep these detainees in this pattern, this situation, indefinitely."

Most of the detainees had languished in custody for more than a year. But Army Major General Geoffrey Miller, commander of the task force that administers Camp Delta and oversees inmate interrogations, insisted that he still needed more time with the prisoners. "There is intelligence of enormous value to the nation that is received every day," he told the *New York Times*.

From twelve—now thirteen—year-old kids?

On December 4, 2003, twenty-eight-year-old Australian detainee David Hicks became the first Gitmo inmate allowed to see a lawyer after a months-long hunger strike made him a cause celèbre Down Under. But Pentagon officials took pain to emphasize that they were rewarding Hicks for talking to his interrogators rather than liberalizing the conditions of incarceration. (Two days earlier, Yasser Hamdi, a U.S. citizen captured in Afghanistan and deprived of his legal rights after Bush classified him as an "enemy combatant," was permitted to see a lawyer—subject to Pentagon restrictions at the U.S. Navy brig in Charleston, South Carolina—for the first time in nineteen months of captivity.) Bush administration officials emphasized that they had granted him this "privilege" of their own volition, continuing to maintain their stance that neither he, nor his six hundred–odd fellows, was entitled to legal representation.

OPERATION IRAQI FREEDOM BECOMES OCCUPATION ISRAELI STYLE

They toppled Saddam's statue during a Baghdad spring. The subsequent revelation that the dictator's effigy was pulled down by U.S. marines rather than Iraqis, to a cheering crowd comprising 150 preselected associates of Iraqi National Congress leader Ahmed Chalabi (Rumsfeld's choice to lead postwar Iraq's puppet government) hinted at what would follow. A full-scale guerilla war against former Baathist troops, Islamist guerillas, and a new nationalistic resistance created so much mayhem, and inflicted so many serious casualties, that the United States turned its wrath from Saddam Hussein to his former victims.

After eighty-one U.S. soldiers were killed in November alone, U.S. Central Command began resorting to the sort of tactics TV news junkies are accustomed to watching the Israeli army apply on the West Bank and Gaza in its brutal campaign against the Palestinian intifada: cordoning off entire villages, demolishing homes, retaliatory air strikes, assassinations of political officials. These Gestapo methods debase those who employ them. Moreover, they arouse so much anger among fence-sitters that they radicalize people who previously espoused moderate positions vis-à-vis the U.S. They launch more attacks, which accelerates the cycle of attack-retaliation-attack into a vortex of spiraling violence.

"In selective cases," the *New York Times* reported on December 7, 2003, "American soldiers are demolishing buildings thought to be used by Iraqi attackers. They have begun imprisoning the relatives of suspected guerillas, in hopes of pressing the insurgents to turn themselves in." For the first time, the *Times* confirmed, Israeli advisers were tagging along with U.S. forces to share their "success" in dealing with the Palestinians.

I have to take issue with using the adjective "American" to describe armed thugs who kidnap innocent people to coerce their relatives to submit themselves to arrest. Few self-styled gangsters, after all, would sink as low. People who commit these crimes are stormtroopers, not Americans.

"In Abu Hishma, encased in a razor-wire fence [that stretches for five miles] after repeated attacks on American troops, Iraqi civilians line up to go in and out, filing through an American-guarded checkpoint, each carrying an identification card printed in English only," reported the *Times*. "I see no difference between us and the Palestinians," a villager named Tariq told the paper. "We didn't expect anything like this after Saddam fell."

Not to worry, though: it's all done out of love. "With a heavy dose of fear and violence, and a lot of money for projects, I think we can convince these people that we are here to help them," said Colonel Nathan Sassaman, who the *Times* noted, "is feared by many of Abu Hishma's villagers."

There are positive benefits of being feared. Although he had initiated talks prior to the Iraq war, part of the reason Libyan leader Colonel Muammar Khaddafi notified U.S. officials that his country had attempted to develop chemical and other "unconventional" weapons in March 2003 was his fear of becoming a U.S. military target. Libya promised to unilaterally disarm and submit to international arms inspections, and "decided of its own free will to get rid of these materials, equipment and programs, and to become totally free of internationally banned weapons." But for every country and for every man we successfully cow into submission, many more will react with vengeance fueled by contempt. North Korean leader Kim Jong Il has drawn a different lesson from Bush's preemption policy: the best protection against U.S. invasion is a large stockpile of nuclear weapons.

TIME TO STAND UP

Every schoolchild learns that evil triumphs when good people remain silent. Too many "good Germans" stood by while the government of their modern, civilized nation was corrupted by evil, and the result became the clichéd twentieth-century case study of the dangers of political and social apathy. The U.S. government's military and diplomatic organs are out of control, manipulated by a clique of ill-intentioned and misguided men whose baseless policies exist solely for the benefit of a tiny group of greedy individuals and businesses. They've endangered our international reputation and our relationships with allies and would-be friends; squandered thousands of precious lives and hundreds of billions of dollars that are desperately needed to solve our many problems; embarked on a reckless campaign of pointless military expansionism; and undermined fundamental principles of moral human behavior, law, and civility. Bush and his gang are not Americans, at least not America as you and I know it. If these psychotic neofascists succeed in creating some new bastardized America from their warped visions of

American triumphantalism and exceptionalism, "America" will no longer be worth defending—or living in.

The world is watching and it doesn't like what it sees. "There is no rule of law in Guantánamo; that is the whole idea," John Steyn, one of Great Britain's most celebrated jurists, scolded in an address in Ottawa. "Guantánamo Bay must be one of the lowest points in the distinguished story of United States jurisprudence. What must authoritarian regimes, or countries with dubious human rights records, make of the example set by the most powerful of all democracies?" He's right. We should be ashamed. More than that, we must do something about it.

This is a moment of crisis. Everything hangs in the balance. What kind of country, and world, do we want to live in? With luck we'll pull back from the brink in time to avoid disaster, but that won't happen unless everyone who cares about our country, liberal and conservative alike, stands up for our dearly held principles.

It so happens that, as occurred during the 1950s under the dark spell of McCarthyism, the forces of reaction are so closely entangled with Bush's gangsters that it's more difficult than ever for idealistic Republicans to step forward and retake control of their party. Liberals, on the other hand, have nothing to lose by taking on the GOP and everything to gain.

So far, mainstream liberal leaders have kept their lips zipped in the face of the Bush administration's most flagrant demonstrations of neofascist proclivities. None have decried the use of goon-squad tactics by U.S. occupation forces in Iraq. On our Cuban concentration camp, Senator John Kerry's wife Theresa Heinz Kerry said that the Gitmo prisoners "should have the rights that other prisoners of war have had," but that's about it. Kerry himself has remained silent. "I'm concerned by what we're doing over there [in Cuba]," Arizona Senator John McCain, who spent five years as a POW in North Vietnam, confided to a columnist for the *Arizona Republic*. "I'm concerned when we take people prisoner and keep them in this camp like this." But McCain's guilty conscience, while admirable, is a far cry from speaking out on the floor of the Senate. He has not done so.

Other presidential candidates knew that the attack on Iraq was wrong, but they sat on their hands for fear of drawing administration criticism. (Fear of retaliation is one of the most effective tools in the arsenal of neofascists.) Howard Dean, on the other hand, spoke out early and shot from political oblivion to the front of the Democratic pack. Liberals need to take a cue from Dean's willingness to take the heat: speaking truth to power works. Democrats ought to call press conferences to talk about Guantánamo Bay and Iraq. They ought to call Bush, Cheney, Rumsfeld, and their accomplices what they are: neo-Nazi scum. They should demand impeachment proceedings for the whole lot. Anything less won't get the attention of the media or the people, anything less won't stop these horrific abuses, and anything less won't save what's left of our honor.

Who knows? It might even encourage some "Republicans" to come back home to the Democratic Party.

chapter 6

MISTAKES WERE MADE

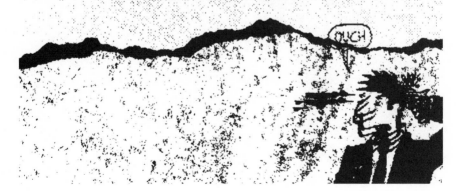

OUCH

Love me, I'm a liberal.
——Phil Ochs

Liberalism's recent high-profile disasters demonstrate with brutal clarity the idiotic tactics and wussy attitudes that have brought the Left to its present state of crisis. Progressives, if the popularity of beliefs and values were the sole determinant factor in politics, would dominate the Democratic Party—and Democrats would win nearly every election. But politics is more than the struggle of a society to identify its core principles. It's a military campaign where pollsters are generals in command of scattered platoons of pamphleteers and phone-bank dialers. Speeches and dollar bills are its artillery; sound-bite bon mots and bumper-sticker slogans are the random factors that can allow a small guerilla force to defeat a vast army. As military historian John Keegan asserts, when all things are equal in battle superior armaments defeat inferior ones—but things are rarely equal.

In recent years, a Republican Party with minority voter registration and fringe intrinsic political appeal has been trouncing the Democrats. This recent string of GOP victories came as the result of effective strategizing, not merely, as they claim, from pushing good ideas. Brilliant Republican tacticians like Karl Rove and Tom DeLay sized up the mood and composition of the electorate and manipulated both to obtain their desired results. Conversely, Democrats invited defeats that they might have suffered even at the hands of stupider opponents. Not to take anything away from Rove & Company—they earned their keep—but liberals made one bad decision after another. Their penchant for repeatedly failing to understand situations, predicaments, and public moods allowed the insurgent Right, led by a singularly uncharismatic "president," to drive them to one shameful rout after another.

A look at recent key battles between the forces of liberalism and conservatism demonstrates that no single factor determined the final outcome. Defeat came as the result of what airplane crash investigators call "cascade failure."

In a cascade failure, catastrophe results from a succession of contributing causes. Without any one of these factors, disaster would have been averted. A few years ago, French investigators believe, a small piece of metal fell off a Continental Airlines DC-10 just before it took off from a runway at Paris' Charles de Gaulle airport. The Continental flight arrived safely at its destination, but the left tire of the next plane in line for takeoff, the supersonic Concorde, struck the object. The spinning tire of the Concorde exploded and flung chunks of rubber into the plane's high-speed engine, causing it to catch fire. The fire disabled wing flaps that would have allowed the plane to return for an emergency landing as it began to lose altitude, and it crashed into a field a few miles away, killing everyone aboard. The age of supersonic civilian aviation came to an end.

No single factor brought down the Concorde. Had the Continental flight been properly maintained, the accident wouldn't have happened. Had the runway been swept between flights, it wouldn't have mattered that the piece of metal had fallen off the first plane. And had the engine been designed differently, neither a lack of maintenance nor absence of runway cleaning would have caused the crash. Built and managed as they are with redundant safety systems, planes rarely crash as a result of a single problem. Aviation disasters are typically caused by cascade failure.

Most Democratic Party debacles, coming at the expense of an organization enjoying sizable advantages of voter membership and inherent ideological compatibility with the citizenry, also result from cascade failure. These crucial battles are lost because they are, in an endless series of bad calls and inappropriate reactions to obstacles and challenges, thrown just as effectively as the 1919 World Series. Political disaster could have been averted at any point. All that had to happen was for one person to pull his head out of his ass long enough to realize what was really happening, explain it to his comrades, and resolve the situation. Whether the trouble was caused by flaws of personnel, personality, tactics or all three, the ramifications of the resulting ignominy remain with them years later: increased Republican voter registration, difficulty raising money to fund campaigns, liberal defeatism.

Nothing can be done about the past, but the all-American tendency to "just move on" leads to more of the same. Studying the great Democratic losses of the last few years paints a grim tableau of shame to be avoided. More usefully, these case studies demonstrate the anatomy of catastrophe, almost always more death-by-a-thousand-cuts than Hiroshima.

It's almost enough to make you wonder whether Dems lose on purpose.

CLINTON: THE WASTED YEARS

"The paradox is that a politician of extraordinary talent missed the opportunity to be an extraordinary president," the conservative pundit E. J. Dionne mused about Bill Clinton. It's true that, by every objective standard, Clinton had everything going for him. Elected by a public hungry to replace his predecessor's old-school paternalism with exactly his brand of energetic populism, his presidency coincided with an Internet explosion that, before it petered out in 2000, fueled the biggest and longest period of economic expansion in American history.

In the film version of *The World According to Garp*, Robin Williams's character watches a small airplane crash into a house he's thinking of buying. "I'll take it!" he shouts excitedly at the surprised real estate agent as smoke and flames billow from the roof of his home-to be. Garp figures that the odds of something terrible happening twice at the same address are astronomical. What more could go wrong? "It's predisastered!" Garp exclaims giddily. Clinton's presidency was predisastered by 1992 revelations that he had cheated on Hillary with Gennifer Flowers, a dalliance that he confessed to as his wife sat next to him on *60 Minutes*. Hey, if Hillary didn't care that the guy was a hound, why should we? When the Monica Lewinsky scandal broke six years later, most Americans reacted like the long-suffering sibling of a ne'er-do-well alcoholic. They may have been disappointed that he'd fallen off the fidelity wagon, but they couldn't claim to have been surprised. If the American people didn't know how Clinton was going to behave once he became president, they should have known. They knew that they were enablers, and enablers feel guilty for the sins they help facilitate. Clinton survived impeachment because, as the consummate con artist, he inculpated voters with a sense of shared responsibility for his sins.

As Dionne explains, Clinton ought to have completed his second term as one of the most productive and successful Democratic presidents since FDR. The expanding economy provided his administration with the financial flexibility to enact expensive government programs like socialized medicine, national and regional mass transit, initiatives that would have borne his name forever—had he made them priorities. He could have reversed many of the devastating cuts in social spending that had taken place under Presidents Reagan and Bush. Some conservative analysts claimed that Clinton's 1992 victory by a plurality rather than a full-fledged majority denied him a genuine mandate for change, but Clinton could easily have made the case that the election of a small-time Arkansas governor over an incumbent president, coupled with the support of one out of six Americans for third-party insurgent Ross Perot, signaled that the electorate wanted someone to lead them in a new, more liberal direction after twelve years of Reagan-Bush. Clinton enjoyed a mandate for change if he wanted to claim it, and—thanks to the dot-com boom—the tax revenues to do great things.

Eight years after an auspicious beginning, the biggest accomplishments of Clinton's presidency had been to balance the federal budget and begin paying down the national debt. He had succeeded where other presidents—*Republican* presidents—had failed. Echoing the traditional, conservative nature of his approach toward spending, the Man from Hope's major legislative triumphs were limited to wrapping up the unfinished business from prior Republican administrations: NAFTA, "welfare reform" that threw millions of needy families into the streets without providing job training, and a right-wing-style crackdown on illegal immigrants. Clinton turned right on foreign policy too, commencing with a sloppy intervention in Somalia and culminating with his 1998 cruise missile attacks against an aspirin plant in Sudan and abandoned al Qaeda training camps in Afghanistan. (A year after that strike, a Taliban official operating with the permission of the Musharraf regime in the Pakistani-controlled sector of Kashmir warned me that vengeance for the attacks—"Clinton didn't even apologize for Sudan," he spat—would soon take place on American soil, when radical Islamists planned to "bring the war home." The September 11 attacks followed two years later.)

Clinton was a liberal president when it didn't count, and then only concerning relatively minor issues. Robert Kuttner, writing for the *American Prospect*, summarized Clinton's compulsive involvement in inane media circuses to the detriment of matters that really counted: "Clinton did take some risks for unpopular causes, as in the Elián González case. By doing so, he sometimes made them popular. He defended affirmative action for blacks when it would have been easy to abandon it. He backed tolerance for gays. He went out of his way to find talented women and minorities for senior jobs." Certainly, Clinton deserves leftie praise for standing up for blacks, women, and gays. But one percent of one percent of a GOP-backed blockbuster like NAFTA easily overshadows those tiny liberal deeds.

A former Vietnam War protester grows up, marries a no-nonsense leftie lawyer—a lawyer who specializes in children's rights, for Christ's sake—and becomes president of the United States despite being tarred as a womanizer during the election. He goes on to win a landslide reelection victory. How did eight years that could and should have been remembered as Camelot 2.0 become a case study in missed opportunity for liberalism?

First of all, it's important to recall that Clinton rose through party ranks as a centrist "New Democrat," not an old-style liberal. During the 1980s he helped found the Democratic Leadership Council, which advocated what the group described as a moderate "third way" between traditional liberalism and conservatism. In practice, however, DLC "moderation" tipped more towards accommodating Republican positions than revitalizing old-school liberalism with the best that conservatism had to offer.

The truth about Clinton became obvious right away. During his first days as president-elect he decided to signal his devotion to "moderation" by appointing not merely centrist or conservative Democrats, but outright registered Republicans to his economic team. "The economic team he put together was remarkable for a Democrat because it was dominated by fiscal conservatives with close ties to the Washington establishment and to Wall Street," commented Chris Bury of PBS's *Frontline*. Forget any big liberal programs, they told him—we don't have the money. "The trouble for Clinton was that the government's fiscal house was in worse shape than anyone on his team knew at the time."

Liberal Democrats had convinced themselves throughout the campaign that their party's young nominee was a lot leftier than a Jimmy Carter retread. If I'd had a hundred dollars for every drunken Democrat who assured me in the Madison Square Garden pressroom at the '92 convention "not to worry, he just talks that way for the campaign . . . Clinton's *really* a liberal," I could have paid off the deficit myself. As Clinton's transition team filled with veterans of Republican administrations who issued statements that the country couldn't afford new programs, I wondered what those self-deluded saps were thinking about their Trojan Horse liberal theory then.

Everyone agreed that money would be tight if Clinton's campaign pledge to reduce the Reagan-Bush deficit was to be undertaken in a serious way. Labor Secretary Robert Reich, the administration's token unrepentant liberal (finding himself politically impotent, he later resigned to write a brilliant tell-all book titled *Locked in the Cabinet*), crunched the government's numbers during November 1992. Reich later recalled: "The president was not happy when he heard that the projected deficit was much larger than we had assumed, larger than we had been told, larger than the [first] Bush administration had told the public. It meant—and he knew that it meant—that we couldn't do everything that he wanted to do, everything that he had promised the public."

Clinton hadn't taken the oath of office yet, but he had already fallen for a typical Republican ploy. Reagan and Bush I had run up over a trillion dollars of federal debt during the eighties, blowing the people's dough on every bloated defense contract and tax giveaway to the rich and powerful they could think of. A key tenet of Reaganite "trickle down economics" was that leaving incoming Democratic administrations with high deficits would prevent them from funding the social programs that Republicans despised. "The fundamental fact is that Congress will spend as much as the tax system will raise plus as much more as it can get away with in the form of a deficit," argued right-wing economist Milton Friedman, the godfather of supply-side doctrine. "Cutting taxes [to max out the deficit] is the only effective way to restrain spending." The new president knew that he'd been scammed, but he refused to take to the airwaves to lambaste his spendthrift predecessors. As a self-defined fiscal conservative Clinton believed that the past-due bills he found on his desk required tightening the nation's belt until they were completely paid off.

In life as in politics, however, there's *always* a choice. Clinton had to have understood what his Republican predecessors had done and why. He could have delayed dealing with the deficit. He could have gone directly to the people and denounced the Republicans for their recklessness and dishonesty. Deficit reduction, he could have said three years before he would have to run for reelection, is off the table. Instead, he decided to scale down his most ambitiously pricey idea, which would have promised free healthcare to every American, by scaling it down to a national medical plan that was so convoluted and dedicated to preserving insurance industry profits that it found allies neither on the right or the left.

The same pattern of backing down in the face of adversity kept recurring during Clinton's first term in the White House. Days after taking the oath of office, he withdrew his nomination of Kimba Wood, and then of Zoë Baird, for the position of attorney general after both women came under fire because they had failed to pay Social Security taxes for their nannies. (Few wealthy people do.) He watered down his campaign pledge to sign an executive order allowing gays to serve in the armed services, instead coming up with a ridiculous "don't ask, don't tell" policy that lets them stay as long as they lie about their sexual orientation. The press and the Republicans had tested Clinton's resolve, and he had come up short. Worst of all, the public felt that Clinton had let them down on the main reason they had fired George Bush: the 1989–93 recession. Communications director George Stephanopoulos remembered, "We had lost the first week of the White House to an issue that most of the country looked up and said, 'What are these people doing?' They got elected to fix the economy, and nobody heard a thing about the economy." Clinton was flailing.

Not even a month after his inauguration, on February 15, 1993, the Man from Hope gave it up. "I had hoped to invest in your future by creating jobs, expanding education, reforming health care and reducing the debt without asking more of you," he told the nation in a televised address. "And I've worked harder than I've ever worked in my life to meet that goal, but I can't because the deficit has increased so much." That was the end of Clinton's twenty-three day attempt to construct a dynamic legacy. The remainder of his tenure was characterized by insult after insult piled onto that primordial injury.

The "centrist" president raced further to the right. Insecure people tend to look to their enemies for inspiration, and that's what Clinton did. He appointed a right-wing Republican, *U.S. News & World Report* writer David Gergen, as key political adviser. "The thing that struck me most forcefully when I first got to the White House was the fact that Bill Clinton had lost his way, and most importantly, he'd lost his self-confidence," Gergen later remembered. Gergen worked hard to take advantage of his boss's confusion.

By the end of 1993, things had gotten so bad that the Clintonistas considered Congress's mere approval of their first federal budget—usually a rubber-stamp affair—a major legislative victory. The healthcare plan went down in flames. Then, in 1994, Republicans surprised the political establishment by making higher than expected midterm electoral gains in the House (the party out of power normally picks up seats in the off-years) and taking control of the Senate. The outspoken new speaker of the House, Newt Gingrich, declared the election a mandate for a "Republican Revolution" and unveiled a thereto-invisible "Contract with America" that attempted to elevate the GOP legislative wish list to the level of a direct mandate for radical change from the American people.

The claim that presidential elections express mandates for change is dubious at best. They certainly don't result from midterm races. When the citizens of Ohio choose between Democratic and Republican candidates for Congress and the Senate, they do not act in concert with the citizens of

Hawaii. Ohioans weigh different concerns than Hawaiians; Clevelanders' issues are dissimilar from those of the citizens of Cincinnati. Moreover, although ideology enters the equation, personality becomes increasingly important as you go from the national to state to local-level races. (Although New Yorkers voted Democratic in national and state races—Al Gore carried 91 percent of the citywide vote in 2000—they've sent Republicans to the mayor's mansion for three consecutive terms. Rudolph Giuliani's personality, not his party affiliation, was the deciding factor in the last three campaigns.)

Anyone who claims that midterm Congressional races, with their distinct regional dynamics, form a unified statement about the national mindset is either lying or full of shit. But that's exactly what Newt did—and the media, then the Democrats, fell for it.

"There was no way to interpret it as anything but a repudiation of the Clinton administration, and that's how we saw it," says Reich. (Sure there was. Trapped in the White House and drowning in exaggerated editorials in the nation's newspapers, they just couldn't see that talk of a GOP mandate was empty bluster. Moreover, had the role of the parties been reversed, even if the population had spoken in one loud voice, besieged Republicans would have shrugged off the election as anomalous. No one can oppress you without your cooperation; a mandate becomes real only when it's accepted by its most fervent opponents.) "It was a dismal day. Everybody was devastated." The year of the bizarre "copresidency" followed when Bill Clinton tacitly agreed to share executive power with Newt Gingrich. In Clinton's 1996 reelection bid, Bury said, "Clinton campaigned that year on safe, middle-of-the-road proposals that [presidential Svengali] Dick Morris had validated in his polling: V-chips, school uniforms, curbs on teen smoking. And after anguished soul-searching in the West Wing, he adopted the Republican plan to reform the nation's welfare system." Then he declared the death of liberalism.

"The era of big government," Clinton told the country, "is over."

Clinton had finally embraced his outer Republican. But he didn't do it by choice. He was bullied and bullshitted into facilitating a faux rightward shift that reflected absolutely nothing true in the body politic. When Republicans claimed a mandate that they couldn't possibly have, a more self-assured president would have laughed them off. Possibly due to his traumatic early political experience in Arkansas, where he was turned out of the governor's mansion after his first term, Clinton never trusted that the Democrats who nominated him and elected him twice to the highest office in the land would stick by him. Perhaps he was so isolated by the trappings of the modern presidency—the Starr Report paints a pathetic picture of a lonely man reduced to ordering second-rate pizza because he didn't have the clout to order the White House chef to work nights—that he had no way to take the pulse of the people. For whatever reason, Clinton failed a test of wills. To his credit, he was no worse in this respect than most other Democratic politicians. To his eternal shame, he was smart enough to know better.

The lost opportunities of Clintonism represent a classic case of cascade failure. Clinton might have saved his legacy at any point during his presidency. He could have staked out strong ideological ground with epic legislation; instead, he created internal gridlock by balancing his cabinet between liberals and conservatives. Had he refused to fall for a GOP-constructed fiscal austerity trap, had he abandoned his balanced-budget pledge—a promise that every previous president had made and broken—voters would have forgiven him. Then he could have funded a real healthcare plan, one that would have borne his imprint for decades to come. He was repeatedly cowed—on gays in the military, on Zoë Baird, on Newt Gingrich's ersatz revolution—thus whittling away the mandate the voters had conferred upon him yet he had never claimed. He could have kept his hands off Monica Lewinsky or, if he couldn't resist her charms, admitted the truth when confronted. If nothing else, he would have avoided impeachment.

Clinton's sole legacy—the balanced budget—was frittered away by his succesor months after he moved to Chappaqua, New York.

Even after he committed all of these tactical errors, Clinton still had a chance to leave on an up note: rather than prolong his nation's and party's pain by fighting impeachment, he should have resigned. Vice President Gore would have entered the 2000 race with two years of incumbency under his belt, which would have enhanced his chances in what turned into one of the tightest elections in the annals of Western democracy. More importantly, and Democrats should accept this, *Clinton deserved to be impeached*. This was not, despite the liberal spin, just about sex . . . or even lying about it.

Democratic Party officials and politicians ought to have cut Clinton loose as soon as it became evident that he had perjured himself in the Paula Jones deposition. The point wasn't that he had lied about sex or that he had cheated on his wife; the point was that he had lied under oath and he had lied to us, his employers. Who could, after he stared us in the glassy eye of the TV camera to swear he had not had sex "with that woman, Monica

Lewinsky," trust him to obey his sacred pledge of January 20, 1993, to defend the Constitution of the United States? Closing ranks behind Clinton put the Democratic Party in the position of standing by their man instead of their country. This blatant parochial hypocrisy contributed to the stinging defeat of 2000.

Clinton accommodated his enemies, compromised with them, and invited them to share power. In the end, he became them. Democrats continue to pay the price of his mistakes. They're also repeating them.

THE 2000 ELECTION DEBACLE

It should come as little surprise that Clinton's vice president lost his own test of self-confidence and political integrity for many of the same reasons that Clinton blew his chance to make history: he too defeated himself after being bamboozled by Republican bullying and bluster. In the ultimate illustration of snatching defeat from the jaws of victory, Al Gore won a presidential election but lost the subsequent decisive test of wits over who got to claim the prize.

The seven weeks that passed between election day and Gore's December 13, 2000, concession speech witnessed a long series of tactical errors, half-assed legal gambits, and garden-variety witlessness impressive for their grand scale and predictability. Cascade failure again—Gore would have won by doing any one thing right.

America got its first glimpse of what Gore was made of hours after the polls closed. News outlets declared the pivotal state of Florida, along with the 271 electoral votes needed to become elected president, in Gore's favor at about 8 P.M. East Coast time. The call was based on sophisticated exit polling data that had proven correct in every state in recent elections.

(It was also accurate in Florida in 2000, as the next summer's unofficial recounts conducted by the *New York Times* and the *Miami Herald* were to prove. Had a statewide recount been completed, Gore would have won Florida by at least two hundred votes. Other factors, including absentee voter fraud, ballot tampering, and intimidation of minority voters, bring top estimates of Gore's victory in Florida to a margin of tens of thousands of votes.)

Minutes after talking heads began bandying about the phrase "President-Elect Gore," Bush campaign staffers and influential Republican politicians deluged news executives at the television networks with angry phone calls. Florida governor Jeb Bush, it seems, had telephoned his brother

Dubya to tell him to hang tight. Florida, he promised, would fall into the Bush column one way or another.

Based solely on calls from Republican campaign officials, nervous TV execs ordered their news anchors to place Florida back into the still-in-play category. As the night dragged on, graphics of the state flipped from blue to gray and finally to red. Gore, committing his first tactical error of the crisis, called Bush to concede. Why the rush? It was the middle of the night; even the most fanatic news hounds were long fast asleep. Gore could easily have waited a few more hours to see how things shook out. An hour after he called, he realized his mistake. He called Bush back to say that wanted to unconcede. "Let me make sure I understand," *Time* magazine quoted an incredulous Governor Bush. "You're calling me back to retract your concession." Bush then told Gore that his brother Jeb had "guaranteed" him that he had won the state. "Your younger brother is not the ultimate authority on this," Gore shot back with appropriate pique, but the Bushies smelled blood. Gore had been too eager to give up too quickly. If he could be spooked once, they might able to do it again. The Bush campaign, following the dictum that the condemned man remains in play until the second that the noose tightens around his neck, decided to dig in and wait for an opportunity to turn things around.

On November 9, the Gore campaign committed a second, far more damaging, tactical error. Gore's lawyers filed a recount petition for only four of the most heavily Democratic counties in Florida: Palm Beach, Dade, Broward, and Volusia. Democratic counties tend to be dominated by Democratic precinct and election workers; these people are naturally inclined to give their own party the benefit of the doubt when they analyze ballots whose chads haven't been completely punched through or double-marked. If Gore's team had been better analysts of statistical probability, they would have targeted a selective recount effort at Republican counties where workers would have tended to be biased against possible Democratic votes. Better yet, why not request a *statewide* recount? Had the Democratic posture from the outset been what Gore later claimed, that all the votes should be counted, their simple argument (fits on a bumper sticker!) would have appealed to Americans' sense of basic fair play. We live in a democracy. Of course all the votes should be counted. And, as it turned out, Gore would have won fair and square—something he might have guessed based on the initial exit poll projections. But former Secretary of State Warren Christopher, head of the Gore recount team, didn't know that at the time.

He wanted to hedge his bets. Christopher's timidity, coupled with his apparent unwillingness to count all the votes and abide by whatever result ensued, created an opening for the Republicans to exploit. "You're trolling for votes here because it's clear that you can't win this election," GOP lawyer William Sherer snapped. That wasn't strictly true—some Democratic analysts suspected that the exit poll data had been right all along—but that's what it looked like to the public.

After a month of similar invective, the Florida State Supreme Court voted along party lines, four to three, to order manual recounts in all the state's counties, not just the ones requested by the Gore campaign, which had substantial numbers of "undervotes." (Undervotes were punch-card ballots that for whatever reason—insufficient pressure applied by a stylus, for example—had chads only partly punched through.) A December 12 deadline for appointing Florida's representatives to the federal Electoral College was approaching—just enough time, according to state officials, to conduct the court-ordered recount.

Then Bush appealed to the U.S. Supreme Court to ask that the recount be suspended and that the partial count, which had him ahead, be ratified as it then stood. That afternoon I called several attorneys to ask them what they thought would happen next. "It's a no-brainer," replied a pal who is also a leading constitutional scholar. "The Supremes can't take the case because they don't have jurisdiction. Elections are a state, not federal, matter. The Florida Supreme Court is the highest authority in this dispute; its ruling can't be overturned. They'll refuse to hear it; they don't have a choice." Other lawyers agreed with his analysis.

Al Gore should have gone on the air on the evening of Bush's appeal to say that the Florida state recount should be allowed to continue as ordered by the Florida Supreme Court and that, in accordance with American constitutional law, the U.S. Supreme Court should respect "states' rights"—still a bugaboo in the South—by refusing to hear it. Instead, Gore watched along with the rest of us as the nine federal judges not only illegally agreed to *hear* the case, but then ruled five to four along party lines to halt the statewide manual recounts while it considered the matter. Their reasoning: the recount violated "Bush's rights" under the equal protection clause. (Apparently Bush's rights trumped our right to live under a president elected by all the votes it was possible to count.)

Four days passed without word from the Supremes. While Rehnquist and the other justices ultimately conceded that the Florida Supreme Court

THE STEALING OF THE PRESIDENCY, 2000

Democratic politicians often reference the fact that Al Gore won the national popular vote over George W. Bush. What most won't say is that Gore also won the state of Florida. By suspending the recount then underway in Florida, the United States Supreme Court effectively handed Bush a majority of the electoral vote; because the high court's decision to hear *Bush v. Gore* violated the jurisdictional separation of powers under the U.S. Constitution, which assigns the final say on election matters to state supreme courts, whoever was declared the winner by the U.S. Supreme Court became the de facto loser.

The *Miami Herald, New York Times, Boston Globe,* and other newspapers conducted their own recount during 2001 to determine who would have won Florida had the recount been permitted to continue. Al Gore, it turns out, won the electoral vote as well as the popular vote. Here's how the numbers break down:

1. Media Consortium Statewide Count of "Undervotes" and "Overvotes" Proves Gore Won Under ANY Standard

The Media Consortium hired the National Opinion Research Center to examine 175,010 ballots that were *never* counted in Florida. The investigation took eight months and cost $900,000. No matter what standard for judging ballots is applied, Gore wins.

	Gore Gain	Net Gore Lead
Certified by Katherine Harris		−537
Valid votes found after certification	+59	−478
Correctly marked paper ballots	+493	+15
Full punches	+100	+115
Poorly marked paper ballot	+309	+424

	Gore Gain	Net Gore Lead
3-corner chads	−208	+216
2-corner chads	−111	+105
Dimples with sunlight	+88	+148
Dimples	−47	+107

2. Miami Herald Statewide Count of "Undervotes" and "Overvotes" Proves Gore Won by 662

Without counting a single hanging or dimpled chad, Gore won by 662, according to the *Miami Herald*. The votes below were crystal clear votes as determined by the *Herald*'s accounting firm, BDO Seidman. Under Florida law, *all of these ballots should have been counted by election officials on election day*. Their failure to do so is official misconduct, not "voter error."

	Gore Gain	Net Gore Lead
Certified by Katherine Harris		−537
Clear "Undervotes" (optical scan)	+319	−218
Clear "Undervotes" (punch card)	+198	−20
Clear "Overvotes"	+682	+662

3. Other Media Counts Lead to the Same Conclusion

Date	Event	Gore Gain	Net Gore Lead
11/27/00	Certified by Katherine Harris		−537
12/8/00	Florida Supreme Court ruling	+383	−154

Date	Event	Gore Gain	Net Gore Lead
12/18/00	Lake County (Orlando Sentinel)	+130	−24
12/19/00	Broward County (Palm Beach Post)	+164	+140
12/29/00	Hernando County (Hernando Today)	+4	+144
12/30/00	Hillsborough County (Tampa Tribune)	+120	+264
1/3/01	Gadsden County (Democrats.com)	+40	+304
1/14/01	Miami-Dade #1 (Palm Beach Post) —minus prior recount included in 12/8	−6 +11 −209	+100
1/20/01	Collier County (Naples News)	−226	−126
1/27/01	Palm Beach #1 (Palm Beach Post)	+682	+556
1/28/01	15 County (Orlando Sentinel) —minus prior recounts in Lake and Gadsden	+366 −170	+752
2/10/01	Orange County (Orlando Sentinel)	+203	+955
2/15/01	Seminole County (Orlando Sentinel)	+13	+968
2/26/01	Miami-Dade #2 (Miami Herald)	+49	+1,017

Date	Event	Gore Gain	Net Gore Lead
3/8/01	Osceola County (Orlando Sentinel)	+25	+1,042
3/10/01	Palm Beach #2 (Palm Beach Post)	+102	+1,144
3/10/01	Martin, St. Lucie (Palm Beach Post)	+92	+1,236
Total Gore Gain from Recounts			**+1,773**

4. Overvote Analysis: Gore's True Margin of Victory

If every county in Florida—not just the Republican ones—had state-of-the-art voting machines that allowed voters to correct their mistakes, Al Gore would have *won by 46,466.*

Date	Event	Gore Gain	Net Gore Lead
1/28/01	Analysis of overvotes in 8 counties by the Washington Post	+28,510	+28,510
1/28/01	Analysis of overvotes in 15 counties by the Orlando Sun-Sentinel	+944	+29,454
2/8/01	Gore-Libertarian overvotes in 16 counties by Orlando Sun-Sentinel	+797	+30,257

Date	Event	Gore Gain	Net Gore
3/10/01	Analysis of overvotes in Palm Beach County by the Palm Beach Post (overlaps Washington Post analysis above)	+6,607	
5/11/01	Analysis of overvotes statewide by the Miami Herald (overlaps with all of the above)		+46,466

5. Disputed Votes

There are several categories of votes that have been widely disputed. Unlike the votes above, these disputed votes could not have been resolved by county canvassing boards, either on election night or during the subsequent recounts.

It is impossible to quantify most of these categories, but we can try to give our best estimates.

Categories favoring Gore

Absentee ballots cast statewide by Republican voters following the illegal solicitation of absentee ballots by the Florida Republican Party: 50,000?

Absentee ballots that could not be read by voting machines, but were illegally "duplicated" by county election officials: 10,000 (60% Bush?)

Legal voters who were disenfranchised by Katherine Harris through the criminally inaccurate purge of "felons": 1,100 (90% Gore)

Absentee ballots cast in Seminole and Martin counties by Republican voters following the criminal alteration of defective ballot applications by Republican operatives: 5,000 (99% Bush)

Votes meant for Gore but cast for Buchanan because of the "butterfly ballot" in Palm Beach: 3,000 (100% Gore)

Voters who went to the polls but were unable to cast a vote because of language problems (and no translators) or physical disability: (70% Gore)

Registrations submitted from black colleges but not processed: (90% Gore)

Overseas military ballots that were not legal, but were counted because of massive pressure from the Bush campaign: 680 (71% Bush)

Police checkpoints near black precincts: 0

Categories favoring Bush

Illegal votes by felons: 5,600 (90% Gore?)

Premature network projections for Gore ten minutes before polls closed in the Panhandle: 10 (60% Bush?)

The above overview of the statistics behind the counts and recounts in Florida is provided courtesy of Democrats.com.

enjoyed "the right to establish uniform standards" to complete the recount, they dallied from December 8 at 10 A.M. to 10 P.M. on the twelfth, two hours before the Electoral College deadline, before ordering them to do just that. (Because the eighth fell on a Saturday, the discussion began on Monday the tenth. Florida recount officials had notified the court that they were prepared to work over the weekend should they be ordered and/or permitted to do so. That offer was rejected.)

In their high-stakes gambit of running out the clock, the U.S. Supreme Court finally allowed that it would have authorized a full statewide recount—but now, alas, there was only two hours left to conduct it. Since the court's own delay had made a recount impossible, the Florida tally would have to remain as it was before the counting stopped, with Bush ahead by 537 votes. (To add to the controversy, the Electoral College "deadline" was flexible. Inauguration Day was still more than a month away.)

Had Gore requested a full statewide recount a month earlier, Bush's case against Gore couldn't have relied on the equal protection argument. There also would have been ample time to complete the recount before Bush's litigation wound its way to Washington. As we know now, Gore would have won that recount, but that's not the point. If a full recount had still led to a Bush victory—a legitimate one—Democrats would have gone on record as democratic purists. Gore would also have placed himself in a better position to fight a 2004 rematch against Bush.

Finally, Democrats compounded their long list of tactical mistakes by accepting the U.S. Supreme Court's most overtly illegal decision since *Dred Scott.* Even if Gore no longer cared whether or not he moved into 1600 Pennsylvania Avenue, he owed it to the nation to defend its fundamental constitutional precepts. He should have resisted Bush's judicial coup d'état. He ought to have denouced Bush for what he was: an illegal usurper with no more legitimacy than such tin-pot dictators as Saddam Hussein and Idi Amin.

George W. Bush, Gore ought to have shouted, is not our president.

If anything, that incendiary phrase—coup d'état, a couplet that implies backroom shenanigans more appropriate to banana republics than the world's sole remaining superpower—understates the truth. Bush pulled on a half-dozen strings to "win" the presidency: his brother Jeb Bush, the governor of Florida; Katherine Harris, the Florida secretary of state rumored to have carried on an affair with him; two Supreme Court justices who had expressed their desire to retire under a Republican president; and Bush's cousin at Fox News, the first media personality to begin calling the election for Bush. Harvey Wasserman wrote for *Columbus Alive* weekly: "Black citizens were removed from the voter rolls en masse by false charges that they were felons, a move choreographed by a sophisticated computer firm hired with state money to do just that. African-Americans were stopped from reaching the polls by police who demanded various forms of impossible identification. African-Americans were booted from actual voting stations by phony requirements reminiscent of the old poll taxes and other scams used by the descendants of John Ashcroft's beloved Confederacy. Voting machines in black and Jewish districts conveniently malfunctioned and made a mockery of democracy."

If this shabby scene had occurred anywhere else, the United Nations would have sent in peacekeeping troops.

Across the United States tens of millions of Democrats watched as the Republicans instigated their slow-motion seizure of power one day at a time. William Sheridan Allen chronicled a similar series of events in his seminal text *The Nazi Seizure of Power: The Experience of a Single German Town 1922–1945*. The citizens of Northeim, most of whom were socialists, knew that the Nazis' next move after Hitler assumed the chancellorship in Berlin would be to install his stooges into Germany's city halls. Determined to prevent the national right-wing coup from coming to their town, Northeim's socialist party activists waited for a call from their national party headquarters in Berlin. At a moment's notice, leftist militiamen were prepared to take to the streets to stop the Nazis from taking over their district. The call, bewildered socialists remembered, never came. No one knows why. In any event, the planned protests never occurred and we know how things worked out for Germany. In December of 2000, the United States was taken over by an unelected right-wing demagogue. Democrats waited for someone to do something, to say something, to express their rage and frustration at a process that was disenfranchising them, but that call never came. Democracy is more fragile than we think. Opposition politicians are often its first line of defense.

At a time of crisis, Americans couldn't count on Gore or the Democrats to stand up for them. People remember that.

(An aside: You may not believe that Bush stole the 2000 election. That is a legitimate viewpoint. The legal and political issues involved are convoluted and complicated. You may believe that the race was so tight—a statistical dead heat—that the U.S. Supreme Court had no choice but to step in and declare a winner in order to avoid a prolonged succession crisis. Even so, if you think that the election was too close to call, fair-mindedness requires you to accept that the Republicans had no more obvious *right* to the presidency than did the Democrats. Yet, every step of the way, the Republicans behaved as if an outcome favorable to the Republican side was inevitable. Their posturing proved pivotal, creating as it did an atmosphere of spin conducive to the subsequent corruption of the U.S. Supreme Court.)

Former Secretary of State James Baker III, Warren Christopher's counterpart on the Bush side, flew down to Florida to coordinate the first Republican legal filing. Appearing on PBS's *NewsHour with Jim Lehrer*, Baker laid out a line of argument that every Republican legislator and pundit within reach of a microphone would repeat during the coming weeks. Whether or not he won a recount, Bush would become president:

"Let me begin by saying that the American people voted on November 7," Baker said. "Governor George W. Bush won 31 states with a total of 271 electoral votes. The vote here in Florida was very close, but when it was counted, Governor Bush was the winner. Now three days later, the vote in Florida has been recounted. Over two-thirds of the state election supervisors overseeing that recount are Democrats. At the end of this recount, Governor Bush is still the winner, subject only to counting the overseas ballots, which traditionally have favored the Republican candidates. No evidence of vote fraud, either in the original vote or in the recount, has been presented. Now the Gore campaign is calling for yet another recount. In selective and predominantly Democratic counties, where there were large unexplained vote swings in their favor in the recount, it appears that the Gore campaign is attempting to unduly prolong the country's national presidential election through endless challenges to the results of the vote here in Florida. Furthermore, the more often ballots are recounted, especially by hand, the more likely it is that human errors, like lost ballots and other risks, will be introduced."

Baker was lying. No one, not even Katherine Harris, had declared Florida for Bush. Much of the recount was being conducted by local, not state, officials—and many of them were Republicans. There had been plenty of reports of voter fraud. And his argument that a recount *itself* would create human error in a recount—well, that's circular logic at its finest. But you have to admire his panache. It made all the difference when he went head to head against the genteel Warren Christopher.

Baker then went on to issue an ominous warning. Should the crisis continue, he implied, Republicans might be "forced" to take power by force:

"It is important, ladies and gentlemen, that there be some finality to the election process. What if we insisted on recounts in other states that today are very, very close; for example, in Wisconsin or in Iowa, or if we should happen to lose it in New Mexico? If we keep going down the path we're on, if we keep being put in the position of having to respond to recount after recount after recount of the same ballots, then we just can't sit on our hands, and we will be forced to do what might be in our best personal interest—but not—it would not be in the best interest of our wonderful country. And what's happening now, if I may say so, is not in the best interest of our country. And there is a way to stop that. There's a way to bring this thing back before it spirals totally out of control."

We just can't sit on our hands . . . we will be forced to do what might be in our best personal interest . . . there is a way to stop that . . . there's a way to bring this thing back. Baker was threatening a coup.

At a bare minimum, the Dems should have demanded that Bush fire Baker for daring to talk treason. Given an opportunity to point out what kind of people the Bushies were, they sat on their hands—blowing another chance to forestall a slow-motion train wreck.

By November 15, Baker was still claiming that the recount process had to end—with Bush declared the winner—this time in order to calm roiling financial markets. Again, Democrats failed to react to this absurd provocation. On November 27, two weeks before the Supremes issued their ruling, Bush declared himself the winner. In the finest tradition of self-appointed rulers, he announced the formation of his transition team. "The election was close," Bush told the country, "but tonight, after a count, a recount and yet another manual recount, Secretary Cheney and I are honored to have won the state of Florida, which gives us the needed electoral votes to win the election." It was a brilliant move. The GOP gambled that Democrats wouldn't stand in the way if they seized the initiative, and they were right. The Democrats didn't wallow in the politics of bluster, nor did they scream bloody murder when the Republicans did. In the final analysis, that made all the difference.

Two sub-stories buried in the lunacy of Florida 2000 perfectly epitomized the difference between a party gleefully resorting to the basest gutter tactics and one that tried, for the most part, to stick to the moral high road. One was the Attack of the Jocks. The other was the sordid tale of the absentee military ballots.

The controversy over whether or not to count the ballots of Florida residents serving in the military, which had been postmarked after the legal deadline, established an eerie precedent for the way George W. Bush would fetishize the American military to promote his political and personal agenda after September 11. The issue heated up on November 20, when Bush spokesperson Karen Hughes accused Gore of attempting to disenfranchise America's valiant men and women in uniform: "We are concerned that a targeted effort by the Democratic Party sought to throw out as many as a third of the overseas absentee ballots received since election day. No one who aspires to commander-in-chief should seek to unfairly deny the votes of the men and women he would seek to command."

It seemed kind of petty, but in a race that then hinged on a margin of roughly one hundred fifty votes, the twenty-three hundred votes that had been cast via absentee ballot in 1996 could have determined the outcome of the election. Florida absentee votes, which mainly included soldiers serving abroad and people living in Israel, had skewed Republican since 1980.

Florida law required absentee votes to be postmarked prior to election day, November 7, 2000, and to be received by November 17. Three thousand seven hundred thirty-three votes fulfilled these requirements, but thousands more were discarded because they were postmarked late, arrived late, or failed to have been stamped with a postmark at all.

The Gore campaign thought the law ought to be bent in favor of military personnel whose ballots were dated, if not postmarked, before the seventh. Bush's henchmen, as Republicans always do, pushed the pedal to the metal. They filed lawsuits in numerous Florida counties to demand that *all* military ballots be counted—even those that were *both dated and postmarked* after the seventh. There were several credible reports that GOP operatives had asked Republican soldiers who hadn't voted on time to send in their absentee ballots after election day. Now they tried to use the legal process to ratify these post facto "votes." "No serviceman on the front line overseas can go get his ballot postmarked," Bush campaign press secretary Mindy Tucker claimed. "I don't think it's reasonable for us to think that we should force him to do that or (we will) not count his ballot."

As the military newspaper *Stars and Stripes* reported on June 23, 2001, Mindy Tucker had lied. "Military postal regulations require all first-class mail to bear postmarks, according to Navy Captain Eugene DeCom, deputy director of the Military Postal Service Agency," the paper wrote.

No matter. Bush partisans played on emotions to get what the legal system wouldn't give them. Fred Tarrant, a Republican member of the Naples City Council, told the Collier County canvassing board: "If they [soldiers] catch a bullet, or fragment from a terrorist bomb, that fragment does not have any postmark or registration of any kind." What the hell did that have to do with anything? Gore campaign officials, again erring on the side of timidity, had decided that the public would think that they were bashing the military if they tried to explain the truth behind the Bush's attempt to arouse patriotic sentimentality.

A *New York Times* study published in July 2001 concluded that the pressure tactics worked: 680 illegal absentee ballots were counted as legit in Florida, more than Bush's 537-vote declared margin of victory.

Now on to the jocks. On November 22 approximately one hundred fifty beefy young white men with buzz haircuts burst into Miami's County Hall and began rioting outside the offices of the Miami-Dade County canvassing board, which had convened to examine about ten thousand undervotes. Scenes reminiscent of Berlin in the 1930s flashed across American television screens as Bush Youth goons shouted obscenities at canvassing board workers, screamed threats and attempted to break down the doors and windows of the board's nineteenth floor office, where the count was underway. They also beat and punched Democratic representatives attending the recount as witnesses. The "demonstration," television reporters explained to the folks back home, had been a spontaneous expression by conservative Floridians frustrated by a painful process that "sore loser" Democrats were trying to "drag out."

Five days later, however, the *Wall Street Journal* confirmed suspicions that the young thugs had in fact been "Capitol Hill aides on all-expenses paid trips, courtesy of the Bush campaign"—in the parlance of an earlier time in the South, out-of-state agitators. According to the *Journal*, the office of Congressional Whip Tom DeLay "took charge of the effort on Capitol Hill, passing on an offer many staffers couldn't refuse: free air fare, accommodations and food in the Sunshine State—all paid for by the Bush campaign." In *Salon*, John Lantigua wrote: "London *Sunday Times* correspondent Tom Rhodes, who was present during the protest, says he overheard one GOP protester on a cellphone in the midst of that political mosh pit bragging that he had tipped off Bush campaign strategist Karl Rove about the rally. 'I just told Rove,' Rhodes overheard."

Identified among the 150 Miami mooks led by Representative John Sweeney of New York were a National Republican Congressional Committee staffer, a House Republican Conference analyst, the Majority (Republican) Chief Counsel, and aides to Republican Congressmen Van Hilleary, Tom DeLay, John DeMint, Jim Ross Lightfoot, Fred Thompson, and Don Young.

Joe Geller, chairman of the Miami-Dade county Democratic Party, was evacuated from the building under police escort. "These were brown-shirt tactics," he said.

The marauding thugs worked their magic. Terrorized Miami-Dade officials suspended their court-ordered recount, leaving 10,750 ballots that would have surely tipped the final count Gore's way (Miami-Dade is an overwhelmingly Democratic county), uncounted. The Associated Press reported that about a quarter of the Miami-Dade votes had been analyzed at the point when the recount was suspended due to DeLay's gangsters, giving Gore a 157-vote lead over Bush. A rough extrapolation leads to Gore winning some 600 votes, which by themselves would have handed him Florida's determinant 25 electoral votes.

So what did Al Gore have to say about this reprehensible attempt to stifle the democratic process, not to mention deny him his life's ambition? "In one county," Gore noted a few days later, "election officials brought the count to a premature end in the face of organized intimidation."

That's it. He didn't call for the rioters to be arrested. He didn't ask for a state investigation into Tom DeLay's third world–style assault on the hapless bureaucrats of Miami-Dade County. He let the issue, and his bid for the presidency, die on the altar of dignity and reserve.

Here's the speech I would have written for Vice President Gore in the face of this outrage:

"My fellow Americans," Gore would have led off, "our great nation is under attack by the enemies of democracy. Shockingly, those foes of our basic values come not from overseas, from the distant lands of those who hate us, but from right here at home in the U.S. This afternoon top officials of the Republican Party and the Republican-controlled House of Representatives orchestrated a carefully coordinated attack by hired thugs to intimidate and threaten officials of one of the Florida counties currently conducting the recount ordered by the state's Supreme Court. As the world watched with disgust, these Nazi-style goons assaulted a Democratic Party official at the instructions of Republican officials. Terrified of further violence, county elections officials were prompted to stop a recount that would have helped to resolve the current impasse.

"I hereby call on Governor George W. Bush to condemn in the strongest terms the men and women on his staff and in his party who planned and participated in this banana republic–style attack on American democracy. I demand that everyone involved be forever prohibited from holding any posts in the Republican Party. I request that the police investigate and prosecute those responsible for any laws that may have been broken. And I will not rest until the process interrupted today is resumed, whether by court order or otherwise.

"In Germany during the 1930s, good men and women stood silently as their freedom was taken away. After the end of a terrible war sparked by evil leaders who took that silence as tacit consent, in which tens of millions of innocent people lost their lives, people of conscience swore that they would never again let would-be tyrants lead them down a similar path. Never again, they said. Well, today we have another chance to stand up and be counted. Free people are once again under attack by people who feel nothing but contempt for the right of Americans to have their votes counted freely and fairly in an election free of intimidation. I say, never again—and I urge Governor Bush to join me. Should he refuse, he is unworthy of holding any position of public service, much less that of President of the United States. Good night."

I know, I know—it's a ludicrous fantasy. The slow, passion-impaired vice president possessed neither the guts nor the political temperament to issue such a fiery repost to the Attack of the Jocks. But those votes were his votes. The aborted recount sealed his fate. And he let it go; he refused to stand up for himself or the democratic process. When Republicans push hard, Democrats fall flat on their faces. But if Democrats hope to be taken seriously, both by their opponents and a public that watches an awful lot of action movies, that has got to change.

To be sure, Republicans bent and frequently broke the rules during the 2000 election fiasco. They lied, spun furiously, and sunk to gutter tactics. Democrats owed it to themselves and to their constituents to fight back, and yes, to lower themselves to the Republicans' level.

They should have explained to the American public that there was no rush whatsoever—they had a president in the form of Bill Clinton and the

December 12, 2000, deadline for selecting electors to the Electoral College was purely arbitrary. They should have told them, over and over, that the recount needed to be thorough and complete so that whoever ultimately emerged as the winner wouldn't have his presidency tarnished by the specter of illegitimacy. There was no hurry, and Democrats and their allies in the media should have repeatedly made this part of their talking points. The Gore campaign should have raised hell over the fact that white police officers throughout the state turned away, and even arrested, African-Americans who attempted to vote.

Democrats should have scrambled their *own* street warriors to counter the assault by the Republican jocks at the Miami-Dade canvassing board office, insisted that military ballots sent in after election day be nullified, and demanded that the men who originated them be prosecuted for election fraud. They ought to have refused to accept any decision—even if it favored Gore—that emanated from U.S. Supreme Court, because elections are a state matter and not a federal one, and it therefore had no jurisdiction in *Bush v. Gore.*

ATTACK OF THE MILITANT MODERATES

Bush's side made clear that they would do anything—up to and including a coup d'état—to ensure that their man won. Gore's side wasn't willing to do the same—and their man lost it all.

Now the same Democratic Leadership Council that engineered Clinton's sit-on-your-hands centrism and Gore's strategy of passive defense is at it again. As Howard Dean's insurgent presidential candidacy began to appear more viable during the summer of 2003, DLC honchos met at a confab in Philadelphia to discuss the future of their party. "We have an important choice to make," said Senator Evan Bayh of Indiana. "The [Bush] administration is being run by the far right. The Democratic Party is in danger of being taken over by the far left."

The fact that Dean was anything but "far left" is beside the point. (As governor of Vermont, Dean had sided with ski resort operators over environmentalists and made balancing the state budget his number one priority.) The point is that the DLC doesn't get it. A tepid approach won't energize the party's downtrodden, depressed faithful, motivate apathetic non-voters to participate in the system, or attract liberals so in denial that they vote Republican. (At least Al Gore gets it now. Breaking ranks with the DLC, the ex-vice president and sitting President-in-Exile shocked the liberal establishment by endorsing Dean. Pundits attributed cynical motives to the move, but picking a likely winner—Dean seemed to have a lock on the nomination and polls said he had the best chance of beating Bush in the fall—was probably Gore's sole rationale for his statement.)

A good precedent for defeated Democrats to study for inspiration is the shattered Republican Party of the seventies. Brutalized at the polls in the wake of Richard Nixon's resignation, the party's national committee asked pollster Robert Teeter to study voter perceptions and find out what they were doing wrong. "We are no longer a minority party," he responded in a strongly worded report to the RNC. "We have achieved the status of a minor party." Teeter's survey showed that just 18 percent of Americans still called themselves Republicans, while 42 percent said they were Democrats. (Bear in mind that party affiliation is a different question than voter regis- tration. Most people register as members of one party or as an independent, but may consistently vote differently from their official affiliation. To add to the complexity of this matter, some people tell pollsters that they vote one way when in fact they vote the opposite or not at all.)

Sixty-one percent of respondents to Teeter's poll said they disapproved of the fact that Republicans were so closely aligned with the interests of the wealthy. (Interestingly this perception hasn't changed much. Rather than work to improve that aspect of their image, Republicans have preferred to redirect people's attention on other issues.) "While the Democrats are seen as being somewhat too much for labor and blacks," Teeter wrote, "they are also seen as being the most patriotic, having the greatest belief in hard work and the value of hard work, and by a very large margin the most open to new people, the most concerned for 'people like you' and having the strongest belief in the value of helping others."

Had a Republican equivalent of the DLC been in charge of the party back then, it would have moved towards the center, to the left. Compromising with liberals would have been a way to attract swing voters. But it wasn't and they didn't. Instead, GOP powerbrokers worked behind the scenes for the 1980 nomination of Ronald Reagan, a right-wing conser- vative who, as governor of California, had ordered police to shoot unarmed protesters at Berkeley during the Vietnam War–related disturbances. The party's shift to the right accelerated with the 1994 "Republican Revolution" that brought the GOP control of the House for the first time since 1955. They've kept the House since then, according to the *New York Times*' Adam Clymer, via "intense discipline, dedicated candidate recruitment and heavy spending, and much more forceful House leadership than Democrats ever managed. Their narrow majorities have held them together better than the Democrats' past big margins . . . Republicans are more cohesive than Democrats and have a few core beliefs—lower taxes, less bureaucracy, more military spending—that unite them more than social issues divide them."

Party discipline. Money. Interesting candidates. A narrow focus. These are key components to any party's rise to power. Their absence from the Democratic arsenal is critical to understanding why Al Gore, who by all rights should have swept to the White House on a landslide, lost an election that he won.

Enforcing discipline within the ranks is tough business, but without it a party is reduced to the status of a debate society. You'd think that Congressional Democrats would understand that the right has declared a jihad on them. After all, the Republican chairman of the House Ways and Means Committee even ordered the police to arrest Democratic Congressmen after they walked out of a hearing in 2003! Yet "Democrats" still wander across the aisle to vote with the other side. *Democrats who don't vote Democratic aren't Democrats.* When a politician goes to the Democratic caucus and requests leave to cross party lines, permission should be granted only if and when turning him down would cause him to lose the next election. Such papal dispensations ought to be a rarity; Democrats ought to be able to summon up the same, or higher, percentage of party-line votes in representative bodies as the Republicans.

Raising money is equally difficult; it involves arm-twisting and cutting deals with shady characters in business and elsewhere. Staying clean while the other side is rolling in the mud, however, isn't an option if you care about winning. Republicans collected $441 million in federally reported contributions to national party organizations in 2001–02; Democrats had just $217 million. Twice as much money means twice as many television commercials, twice as many paid staffers, twice as many stamps to send out mailers for more donations. Ideas don't matter unless you can spin and broadcast them with wide dissemination.

The recruitment of exciting candidates may require going outside the ranks of those, such as Al Gore, who have worked their way up the party echelon. Republicans didn't initially back Arnold Schwarzenegger's bid for the California gubernatorial recall election in 2003 because state GOP leaders thought he was too liberal. Yet they embraced him once it became clear he was catching on with voters. Democrats, on the other hand, considered

Howard Dean's rising popularity a threat rather than an opportunity. This tunnel-vision attitude of stiff-arming insurgents, if allowed to dominate thinking within the party, can only plant the seeds for future fiascos.

A BAD REPUTATION WITHOUT THE FUN OF EARNING ONE

Finally there are mistakes endemic to the party, errors of strategy that create negative perceptions. Democrats need to focus on a few stupid taglines and stick to them.

Clymer's *Times* analysis asked ordinary people why they vote Republican. "I feel that [Bush] is putting pressure on the Congress to really come to task and be responsible in their social spending," replied Tim Chrysler of Minnesota. "Because of the budget deficit, I feel that the Republicans are the best party to be able to bring a balanced budget back to the United States."

Mr. Fox, welcome to Consolidated Henhouse Corp. We're sure you'll do a wonderful job here as a security guard.

That someone smart enough to work as a computer consultant could believe that Bush is tough on Congress, not to mention a deficit hawk, is incredible. Bush, after all, ran up the largest budget deficit in the history of the U.S.—in fact, in the history of any country that has ever existed. And it's not like the House or Senate is giving Bush any trouble; they're controlled by the same brand of Republicans as he is.

Republicans are now the real big spenders; they have been for the last few decades. Bruce Bartlett, a conservative economist who worked for Presidents Reagan and Bush I, conceded the irony of Republicans getting credit for fiscal conservatism during an appearance before Congress to defend Bush's huge income tax cut, which came at a time when the nation was fighting two wars and a recession. "Year after year," Bartlett conceded, "I heard my party's leaders attacking your party for running up deficits, which exacerbated inflation, raised interest rates, caused premature balding, brought on postnasal drip and all manners of social evils, they said. Republicans have a hard time explaining why spending is bad, so they seized on the deficit as a proxy." Newt Gingrich, who pushed the House to pass a balanced budget amendment as part of his "Contract with America," also defended the GOP's budget-buster tax cuts: "You're in a period when you want to stimulate investment and consumption in the U.S. to ensure you don't end up in real deflation." Uh-huh.

Cato Institute chairman William Niskanen, a famed deficit hawk, says: "The Bush Administration has been associated with unusually rapid spending growth even before the war [against Iraq]. There's been no significant spending restraint anywhere in the budget." Indeed, House Majority Leader Tom DeLay said a few minutes before the tax cut vote, "Our budget says we're going to have $1.3 trillion in tax cuts, and you bet we're coming back for more."

So why does Mr. Chrysler, the computer consultant, still think Republicans are better than Democrats when it comes to balancing the budget? I don't think he's dumb. He's just busy, so much so that he doesn't have time to read the latest quarterly report issued by the Cato Institute. For decades Republicans have hammered away at Democrats with their assertions that they're the party of fiscal responsibility, that they favor a balanced budget amendment to the Constitution, that Democrats are terrible tax-and-spenders. We're looking out for your money, they say, and we want to give it back to you. We're cutting expensive bleeding-heart liberal do-gooder bullshit. Coke adds life, Pepsi is the drink of a new generation, 7-Up is the Uncola. Say anything over and over and over again, and people who don't have the time or inclination to check out the facts for themselves will believe you. Republicans create an information vacuum and fill it with propaganda. Maybe it's too late to take the fiscal responsibility line away from Republicans; I don't know. What's interesting is that that voter perception—that Republicans are more fiscally responsible than Democrats—is so far removed from reality. Choose a slogan and stick to it. Accuracy is immaterial. Forty years from now, everyone will believe it.

John Nicholas of Gentrysville, Indiana, answered the *Times'* query about why he was a Republican as follows: "Republicans believe in the sovereignty of our country . . . The Republicans are for smaller government."

Republicans, of course, are even more enthusiastic backers of NAFTA and the WTO than Democrats. Those free trade agreements, as Pat Buchanan tells anyone who will listen and many who won't, have done more to abridge national sovereignty than any participation in U.N. peacekeeping operations ever could. Bush found that out last year, when his imposition of tariffs on imported steel, an attempt to buy off the support of the steelworkers union in his reelection effort, got overturned by the WTO. As for the smaller government trope, how does Nicholas explain the creation of the new Department of Homeland Security, which employs 120,000 federal employees? (DHS was originally a Democratic proposal, but was shelved until the GOP dragged it out and rebranded it after September 11.) I'm guessing that he heard Bush's famous soundbite opposing "nation building" from 2000 a lot more often than he heard liberals make snide passing comments about how we're doing exactly that in Afghanistan, Iraq, and now Haiti (again). Ditto with Homeland Security; maybe because it was originally their baby, or more likely because they didn't want to appear unpatriotic, Democrats failed to call Bush what he was: the creator of the largest new federal bureaucracy since the 1970s and a true believer in big-ass government.

Mssrs. Chrysler and Nicholas are among the middle-class white men— "angry white males," pundits called them in the nineties—who've switched to the Republican Party in recent years. Although they continue to enjoy a demographic advantage, "We're at a postwar historic low of Democratic Party membership," Democratic pollster Mark Penn says. Most of the R-to-D switcheroos have occurred among white males, only 22 percent of whom now call themselves Democrats. Penn says that white guys, particularly those who earn more than $20,000 a year, believe that Democrats "stand for big government, want to raise taxes too high, are too liberal and are beholden to special interest groups."

For the most part, this perception stems from a historical hangover nursed by years of Republican attack ads. Democrats, after all, haven't created a new "big government" program since the Beatles first appeared on the *Ed Sullivan Show*. Most of the tax increases suffered by these middle-income working stiffs happened at the hands of the GOP, which had to get the money elsewhere as it eased the burden on the wealthiest Americans.

It takes a long time for perception to catch up with reality, especially when your opponents are doing everything they can to spread the bad word about you. Democratic leaders don't want to jump on the anti-tax bandwagon because they want to look "responsible." What if the need for an increase occurs under their watch? They won't get elected, however, unless they define the Democrats as the party of lower taxes for most people and lower taxes for you personally. Yes, they should admit, we're going to soak the hell out of millionaires, billionaires, and giant corporations, but what the hey—they can afford it!

"Year after year," I can imagine the first of a blizzard of Democratic ads intoning, "Republicans increase taxes on people like you and me. They *talk* about big tax cuts, but you get squat. Meanwhile the millionaire across town gets enough to buy his spoiled prep-school son a couple of Ferraris. Real tax cuts. For real Americans. Vote Democratic." And don't just run them during the campaigns. Run them during the off-season so they become part of the nation's subliminal perception.

It will be harder to shake the longstanding impression that Democrats kowtow to special interest groups. Every time you turn around, you see Democrats sucking up to labor unions, feminist groups, and the NAACP. They try to defend themselves by pointing out that Republicans have their own special interests—big business, the NRA, the Christian Right—and that the organizations with which they form alliances aren't nearly as unsavory as those. True enough, but Democrats don't keep harping on that point. The GOP sop about "Democrats and their special interests" still sticks, partly because it's true but mostly because it works for the Right. A couple of chapters ahead, we'll get into what Democrats should do to transform themselves into the party of all of the people, all of the time. Freeing themselves of parochial interest groups, however, is a long-term strategy. Hitting the Republicans twice as hard as they hit them needs to happen right now.

chapter 7

DUM DUM DUM DEMS

Neither party has a monopoly on wisdom, and if Democrats have valid improvements to proffer then they should step forward.
—Conservative pundit John Perry, January 31, 2002

Victory generates its own momentum. Losing is similarly circular: the more you become accustomed to failure, the more you come to expect it. Eventually, like a version of Pavlov's dog that never receives a reward for its efforts, you stop trying entirely. Trapped in a rut of self-defeatism and defensiveness, Democrats began viewing original thought as a luxury. Hobbled by a lack of self-confidence, they lost the can-do attitude one needs to look, feel, and act like a winner. Paradoxically, Democrats need to make themselves feel even worse about themselves before they can begin to win: only taking a hard look at the wimpy attitudes that got them into their present fix can provoke enough self-loathing to force them to decide to just . . . stop . . . being . . . pussies.

Eight years of Ronald Reagan's presidency were drawing to a close when I walked into Michael Dukakis's New York campaign headquarters. I was twenty-five, old enough to have acquired some good campaign experience and young enough to be optimistic. In 1984 I'd served as a regional coordinator for George McGovern's primary campaign, going to work for Walter Mondale during the run-up to November. I'd designed posters, buttons, and literature, set up Mondale for President organizations on college campuses and brainstormed with strategists about attracting the youth (under twenty-five) vote. I had a lot to offer. Most importantly, I felt optimistic about Dukakis's chances. The eighties faux boom economy had left most Americans behind, then–Vice President Bush possessed little charisma and the Iran-Contra scandals had sent top Reagan-Bush officials to prison. American voters, I thought, were ready for a change. With a little luck and a lot of hard work, I believed, Dukakis could win.

I was soon disabused of this belief.

Dukakis for President headquarters was a hideous case study of high-speed disorganization: people walking to and fro, phones ringing, papers all over the floor, nothing getting done. When you paid attention, it became obvious that the phone was ringing because nobody ever answered it. The high-energy campaign workers were jittery from refilling their free cups of union-donated coffee. They weren't accomplishing a damn thing, yet they were moving at the speed of light.

"I'm here to volunteer for the campaig—" I tried to tell one person after another as they brushed by, but no one paid attention to me. After several minutes, an irritated lady who looked like she worked at the dreaded DMV—who, I later learned, *did* work at the DMV—graced me with her majestic presence. She gave me the once-over, evidently deciding that I didn't deserve the standard "thanks for coming in" speech. She propped her hands on her hips. "Go over there"—she pointed at a long table lined with empty chairs, each facing a huge dot-matrix printout of phone numbers of registered Democrats—"and work the phones."

There's nothing wrong with making telephone solicitations to registered Democrats. I'd dialed for Dems in '76, '80, and '84. But I was a youth strategist now. My specialized knowledge and experience, I thought, could be better applied to motivating increasingly apathetic young Democrats than to working the phone bank. I told her that I wanted a more challenging assignment.

"Go over there"—this time she glared for emphasis while she pointed—"and work the *phones*." I was accustomed to being mistreated by my employers. I didn't have much self-respect left.

But this woman expected me to be abused for free?

I walked out the door. Thinking that I might hook up with the campaign on a national level instead, I kept in touch with some old Mondale-era buddies who'd ended up working for Dukakis's main campaign HQ in Boston. My friends' tales of incompetence and stupidity, even more extreme than the horror stories reported in the media, sent shivers of nausea coursing through my veins. Every time the Republicans attacked, Dukakis's wrongheaded strategy was to bend over and take it like a gentleman. They didn't want to hear from anyone who urged a more aggressive approach.

I haven't worked for a political campaign since.

Was I a snot-nosed punk? Sure. But manpower is the most precious resource a candidate has. Well-organized campaign offices post a friendly "greeter" at their front desk to sign up volunteers, quiz them about their skills and, if the only work they have for them to do is excruciatingly tedious (say, working the phone bank), explain to them why their labor is important to the cause and thank them for contributing their services, yadayadayada. This is particularly true if you're running as a Democrat, since the Democrats don't pay their low-level staffers.

The most committed, hardcore political partisans may not be deterred by a lack of pay, disorganization, and depressing working conditions. But most folks are more easily discouraged or disgusted. Just as no army can spare a single soldier in time of war, no political party or campaign can spare a person willing to dial phones, stuff envelopes, or run around town nailing up signs. Dukakis's DMV lady lost me to him and the party, and it wouldn't have taken much to avoid that. It isn't much of a stretch to assume that similar scenes took place in that office, and others like it around the country, throughout the summer and fall of 1988.

Republicans, on the other hand, understand how to motivate people. Walk into GOP headquarters in any major city in America, say hi, and pick up a few buttons. Then go visit the Democrats. In Dayton, where I grew up, Republican headquarters was in a second-floor office directly across the street from Courthouse Square, notable locally as the site of a speech by President Abraham Lincoln and the center of downtown. A crisply designed sign in the office's big windows urged passing drivers to vote for the Republican *candidat du jour*. Inside, the office was furnished with modern equipment, and wall-to-wall carpeting (a pleasant royal blue). The front desk was manned by a friendly older receptionist.

The Dems held court only a few blocks away on Wilkinson Street, though they might as well have been in another country. Wilkinson marked the edge of the sprawling West Side ghetto. The Party of Roosevelt operated out of a fetid little fake-brick dump indistinguishable from the dollar-a-drink gin mill dedicated to the slow self-destruction of laid-off General Motors workers. The décor was Depression-era floor tiling trimmed with more cheesy wood paneling than a Veterans of Foreign Wars tavern. Two decrepit secretaries engaged in comical fights over the single electric typewriter. "I can't *type* on that thing!" one would yelp, referring to an ancient manual Underwood. "You could if you changed the *goddamned ribbon*!" the other would retort. Completing the air of desperation was the fact that campaign materials were always in short supply. "Now where exactly are you going to take these stickers?" you'd be asked, as if they weren't to be given to *just anybody*.

"How do these people ever win?" I remember asking myself.

SHOW US THE MONEY

A huge money gap between the two major parties is obviously a contributing factor to the defeat of Democrats. The 2004 Democratic nominee for president, John Kerry, will probably have roughly $100 million to spend against George W. Bush's $250 million during the general election. It's a massive difference—one of the major reasons the minority Republicans challenge, and beat, majority Democrats—and it's nothing new. In the 1994 midterm elections that brought us Newt's "Contract with America," Republican Congressional candidates outspent Democrats $185 million to $111 million. "Republicans will always have more money and the fervor of right-wing ideas," President Clinton admitted in 2002. But, as Clinton said in the same breath, "The most important thing we have to do is to get our ideas out there. I still believe ideas and results matter when people hear evidence over ideology."

He's right. Ideas matter. But ideas don't just mean new political platform planks. They mean new, more efficient ways of reaching voters using limited resources, working harder to raise more money, and adopting a tough attitude in its expenditure.

On the first point, strong enforcement of party unity would bring about substantial cost savings. With Democrats routinely being outspent by 150 to 500 percent, they can't afford to squander precious campaign donations by beating each other up in frivolous primaries.

In the 2004 primaries, nine Democratic candidates spent over $100 million vying for the presidential nomination. Most of these guys were doomed to failure the day they declared their candidacies, yet the three most viable contenders—Howard Dean, Dick Gephardt and John Kerry—spent millions to fight them off, as well as one another. Had the race been limited to these three, it still would have included two too many. The important threat came from George W. Bush, but the campaign against him couldn't commence until the nomination was secured on Super Tuesday.

Had party leaders possessed an ounce of common sense, they would have issued a *diktat* that the Democratic nominee would be selected in advance, in the style of the smoke-filled rooms of early-twentieth-century conventions. Their pre-approved nominee could then have gone head-to-head against Bush (who, thanks to smart GOP leaders enforcing strict party unity, ran unopposed for the Republican nomination) over $100 million richer, with months of additional attention and exposure. There still would have been a money gap, but $250 million to $200 million isn't nearly as bad.

Instead, as Republican consultant Scott Reed predicted, "[Democrats] will be flat on their backs, tired from an exhausting primary campaign, still at each other's throats and completely broke." Leave it to a Republican to tell Democrats what's wrong, and to Democrats to ignore him.

The Republicans' decision not to allow anyone to challenge Bush in primaries—and it *was* a decision—saved Bush a lot of money. "Because Mr. Bush faces no rivals for nomination," the *New York Times* reported in October 2003, "he was able to establish his campaign organization much later than most of the Democrats seeking his job. His campaign has been deliberately slow to hire staff members and put them on the payroll; its payroll expenses of $1.8 million since it began operations last May are half of the $3.5 million since the beginning of [2003] for Senator John Kerry's campaign, which got a much earlier start." And he saved tens of millions of dollars on television advertising.

Republicans ignore conservative principles when it comes to the federal budget but know how to squeeze pennies from their campaigns. "To keep expenses down," says the *Times*, "staff members often travel on discount airlines like Southwest, even when that means driving an hour to Baltimore-Washington International Airport instead of using nearby Reagan National."

Democrats also need to work harder to cultivate individual and corporate contributors with deep pockets. It made sense for Bill Clinton to thank Barbra Streisand for her contributions to his campaign with a free night in the Lincoln bedroom while he held the keys to the White House, but fundraising requires more imaginative means of quid pro quo when one's party is out of power. Democratic Party officials should reach out to corporate America, not with inducements that compromise core party principles like advocating unfettered free trade agreements or welfare reform, but by educating them about the true relationship between economic growth and the party in power. Since World War II, one of American politics' greatest untold secrets is the fact that Republicans have driven us into recession while Democrats have presided over periods of expansion. If corporate America can be convinced to abandon its obsession with short-term quarterly earnings reports in favor of long-term profitability, it will see that it makes more money with Democrats in charge.

WAKE UP, CORPORATE AMERICA! YOU'RE DEMOCRATS!

Corporate America believes that Republicans put more money in its pockets. Pro-business individuals think the economy does better under conservative rule. History belies that notion. In fact, every major indicator shows that, since World War II, Democrats do better than Republicans when it comes to the economy. Democrats create more jobs, run up fewer debts and generate higher productivity—and they should remind CEOs and big corporate campaign contributors of that.

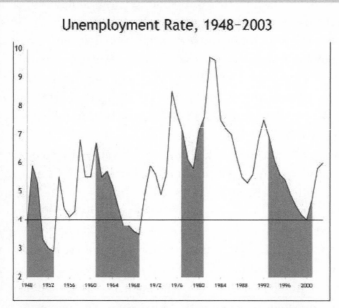

Unemployment Rate, 1948–2003

Democratic administrations (shaded periods) preside over rising or even employment. The opposite prevails under Republican presidents.

Source: U.S. Department of Labor Statistics

Federal Budget Surplus, 1948-2004

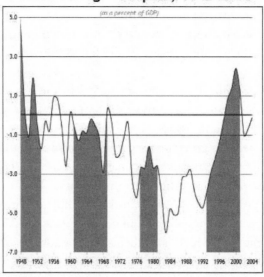

(as a percent of GDP)

Republicans consistently outspend Democrats (shaded periods).

Source: U.S. Office of Management and Budget

Annual Change in GDP, 1944-2004

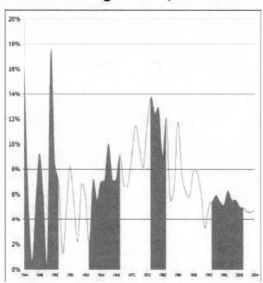

Democratic administrations (shaded periods) feature periods of accelerating or steady rates of increase of GDP; Republicans slow down the economy.

Source: Executive Office of the President of the United States

AGGRESSION AND CONSISTENCY: RINSE, LATHER, REPEAT

At the risk of sounding like Krishnamurti, the Big Problem for Dems is their mindset: they're not as serious, determined or vicious as their right-wing counterparts about remaking the country in their own image. One example of this problem is the way progressive causes fail to cultivate ideological allies in the media.

Roughly 80 percent of working journalists in the print and broadcast media in the United States vote Democratic or identify themselves with "liberal" positions on various issues. This isn't surprising, since most well informed people tend to gravitate towards politicians who understand that social justice is morally righteous and a linchpin of peaceful stability. (Rightist pundits cite this statistic as prima facie proof of a "liberal media." Most *reporters* are liberal, or more precisely, moderate liberals. But most of them work for newspapers, radio stations, and television networks that are owned by large corporations, which are themselves managed and owned by Republican executives. There is no liberal media. What's really going on is that a lot of liberal lite journalists are working for right-wing conservative bosses. Just as the boss at your company has the final say-so on its press releases and public image, most of what the American public reads and sees is largely tinged with a right-of-center viewpoint—with a little liberalism mixed in whenever the boss isn't paying attention.)

Sympathetic producers, radio personalities, and television anchorpeople ought to be targets of press releases, study results, and all matter of propaganda by the Democratic Party and progressive-minded political groups, but they're not.

Without having asked for it—trust me on this—I receive regular mailings, e-mails, and review copies of books from the Republican-controlled Ways and Means Committee of the House of Representatives, the Christian Coalition, and the Heritage Foundation, just to name a few of the many groups aligned with the GOP that I hear from daily. I have written my syndicated opinion column for nearly a decade, yet I can count the total number of communiqués I receive from environmental, racial justice, and other leftie organizations on the fingers of one partially mutilated hand. When I pointed this out to a friend who works at one of the nation's biggest environmental groups, she promised (threatened?) to add me to her organization's mailing list for information about global warming and similar subjects. What has she sent me? Nada. When I followed up (three times!), she admitted that "we're not set up for that" yet. How can you claim to be serious about protecting the environment if you don't bother to keep in touch with journalists? This shoulder-shrugging attitude is so discouraging it's almost enough to make one turn right. Repblicans are mean and evil and wrong, but at least they're organized.

TALK THE TALK

If you spend a day channel surfing between CNN, MSNBC, and Fox News, you'll see "talking points" in action. Members of Congress meet in closed-session party caucuses in order to discuss and determine their sound-bites in reaction to the big political story of the day. Then, counting on the fact that with more than a hundred channels few Americans will hear any of them say anything more than once, they file out to face the cameras. You'll hear a lot of similar phrasing and identical points being repeated by each party's legislators. As Gannett's Carl Weiser wrote in advance of the 2003 State of the Union address, "On Wednesday morning, as local readers digest the reaction—members of the President's party invariably 'applaud' the speech and call it a 'home run' or say they would give it 'an A'—the president himself joins the marketing effort." It's a predictable pattern, but it works.

Unlike their Democratic foes, Republicans don't limit their talking points to politicians. When the war in Iraq began to go badly, Republicans began positing the outlandish argument that far from being dismayed at the fact that U.S. occupation troops were becoming the targets of Islamist militants from around the Muslim world, George W. Bush had *planned* this brilliant scheme. They claimed that Bush was luring terrorists to Iraq in order to kill them more efficiently: "one-stop shopping," in the parlance of the GOP. Spin doesn't get much sillier, but journalists who should have known better took the "terrorist flypaper" justification seriously. The terrorist flypaper argument became so ubiquitous that it couldn't be ignored. It appeared simultaneously on Rush Limbaugh's syndicated radio show, in the mouths of numerous Fox News anchors, and flowing from the pens of syndicated Republican columnists. When "terrorist flypaper" failed to stem Bush's drop in the polls, it vanished from the talking points—and a lazy media addicted to journalism-by-press-release failed to notice or follow up.

These aren't cases of great minds thinking stupid thoughts alike, but rather of carefully coordinated propaganda attacks across a broad spectrum of media.

"The media is kind of weird these days on politics, and there are some major institutional voices that are, truthfully speaking, part and parcel of the Republican Party," Al Gore remarked in a controversial (but accurate) 2002 speech. "Fox News Network, the *Washington Times*, Rush Limbaugh—there's a bunch of them, and some of them are financed by wealthy ultra-conservative billionaires who make political deals with Republican administrations and the rest of the media. Most of the media [has] been slow to recognize the pervasive impact of this fifth column in their ranks. That is, day after day, injecting the daily Republican talking points into the definition of what's objective."

Interestingly, Rush Limbaugh, speaking to a friendly reporter at Fox News, tacitly admitted Gore's assertion that he and other right-wing media personalities received daily GOP talking points. His response was notable for what he didn't say: "[Democrats] don't refute the issues that we stand for. They don't refute the points we make. They just attack us personally, and now Fox and all this other media [sic], they get challenged. They had a free run for all those years with the mainstream press just parroting whatever they said, and those days are over." Listen to what we say, Limbaugh said. Please don't pay attention to how we broadcast it.

Perhaps Democratic officials believe that their liberal media allies would find bullet-pointed lists of Democratic talking points offensive and overly manipulative. Maybe they just don't have the wherewithal to get their shit together. Whatever the reason, the lack of widely distributed liberal talking points is a major tactical omission from the liberal battle plan. The American people are barraged by hundreds of television channels and thousands of websites, all competing for their attention. When you're surrounded by people screaming at you, you're only likely to remember the arguments you've heard the most often. David Shenk's *Data Smog* estimates that the average American is deluged with three thousand "messages"—e-mails, phone calls, meetings, conversations—every day. Six hundred of these demands for attention come in the form of advertising. People are busy, stressed and overwhelmed—*Fast Company* magazine reports that the average businessperson faces a backlog of two to three hundred hours of work at any given time. If Democrats want to be heard over the din, they'd better start shouting. Spin, blather, repeat.

RECOGNIZING AND SEIZING OPPORTUNITIES

Republicans understand the problem of overwork. (Maybe it's because their anti-vacation and longer workday policies helped create it.) For months during the build-up to and the immediate aftermath of the attack against Iraq, Republican politicians and their media allies took advantage of the American public's unwillingness or inability to read between the lines of official spin by repeatedly mentioning Saddam Hussein and the September 11 attacks in the same breath—while taking care not to explicitly state that there was a direct link between al Qaeda and Iraq. "I remember the Twin Towers falling," one Republican leader said typically. "That's why it's important to end the threat posed by Saddam Hussein." Of course, their logic was idiotic: I remember my cat vomiting on my carpet; that's why it's important to throw a flowerpot at my brother-in-law. The linkage was inferred—you couldn't find a single administration quote where Saddam was directly blamed for September 11—but never before had such false implication been pushed so far by top government officials.

The Bush administration's media disinformation campaign was so successful that at one point 70 percent of Americans told pollsters that Iraq—rather than Osama bin Laden—had carried out the attacks. Finally, key media outlets accused Bush of "misleading" the public. In order to inoculate himself from charges that he had lied both about weapons of mass destruction and an Iraqi connection to Islamist terrorists to gain support for the war, Bush issued a statement "clarifying" the fact that there was no such link. (These revised talking points were parroted by Dick Cheney, National Security Advisor Condoleezza Rice, and GOP media allies. No-link rhetoric was repeated just enough to sate an uncharacteristically questioning media, but not enough to dissuade most of the "misled" 70 percent of the public that Iraq was part of the war on terrorism. A month later, the Bushies reverted to pro-link sound niblets, and 57 percent of the public had been "respun" by the end of 2003.) Josef Goebbels would have envied their mastery of propaganda.

Democrats, on the other hand, seem allergic to staying on message. One Congressman attacks the Iraq war for its cost, another for deaths caused by faulty equipment, another for the failure to plan for the occupation. One liberal pundit argues that angering the international community was the war's principal mistake; others call Bush to task for lying about weapons of mass destruction. Throwing a lot of shit at the wall in the hopes that some of it will stick is a natural tendency and it's particularly tempting when one's opponents provide so much ammunition, but it rarely works. When I was starting out as a cartoonist, my editor Jean Arnold used to take me to task for drawing "kitchen sink cartoons," in which I incorporated as many facets of my opinion on an issue as I could. "You tried to get three ideas for the price of one here," she'd say, "but I can't tell what the hell it's about. Stick to one point." It took years for me to apply her wisdom: one idea per cartoon, one aspect of one argument at a time. Obviously, there are lots of things to say about any given subject, especially something like Gulf War II. Life is complex, politics more so. But only a few thousand wonks have the time to focus on the ins and outs of, say, the war in Iraq. While one could attack Republican policy on a number of grounds—poor planning, morality, legality, insufficient troop strength—picking one point and sticking to it is the way to go.

By far the most potent weapon Democrats could have deployed against Republicans in the war debate was the failure to find weapons of mass destruction (WMD) in Iraq.

On October 2, 2003, chief CIA weapons inspector David Kay told Congress that the fourteen hundred members of his Iraq Survey Group "have not yet found stocks of weapons." Kay's report, the *New York Times* said, "left the door open to a possibility that many government officials now describe as increasingly likely: that Iraq destroyed its illicit weapons after the 1991 war, as it has claimed, and that what it was hiding was not weapons but evidence of arrangements to rebuild them."

Before the war, the Bush administration had claimed that the U.S. had to invade Iraq to prevent an "imminent threat" from proscribed nuclear, biological, and chemical weapons. Secretary of Defense Rumsfeld even claimed to know the exact locations of these weapons caches—he named them at a press conference. But when Bush launched his preemptive attack, it turned out that those weapons didn't exist in the first place. Rumsfeld couldn't have "known" where the WMDs were because, as far as U.S. intelligence agencies were aware, there weren't any. Despite the overwhelming evidence to the contrary, Bush continued to stonewall. "One thing is for certain," Bush said when the report came out, "terrorist groups will not ever be able to get weapons of mass destruction in Iraq because Saddam Hussein is no more." (This was at the time he began reasserting a link between Iraq and terrorism.) Still, this was hot stuff. Phone calls and e-mails shot around the journalistic and political communities: impeachment, many believed, was a strong possibility.

Gulf War II, according to the Pentagon, will cost at least $500 billion over its first five years. Should present casualty rates continue, thousands of American soldiers will be killed and tens of thousands more wounded in Iraq. Their sacrifice will have done nothing to protect American national security, spread democracy, or fight terrorism. And it will have been based on a lie.

Democrats were handed George W. Bush's head on a plastic tray when WMDs failed to turn up in Iraq. Their lackluster response to this offering reveals that the party is divvied up between those who can't recognize a good thing and those who can but can't figure out how to exploit it. "This [lack of WMDs in Iraq] presents the president with a huge problem," stated former Democratic Congressman Lee Hamilton of Indiana. "It's extraordinary," said Senator John D. Rockefeller IV of West Virginia, "that a decision was made to go to war, and that we were told by our highest policymakers that there was an imminent threat."

And those were the tough remarks.

Dems, a dismaying number of whom had voted for Bush's pro-invasion resolution—there's the fear factor again—pulled their punches or threw none at all. The issue made the rounds of the cable news talking head shows for a few months—the fact that it lasted that long was a tribute to those "liberal" reporters—before dying for lack of additional fuel. To be fair, liberals politely asked ranking committee Republicans to pretty-please consider opening an investigation. Others said that they supported staying in Iraq despite Bush's "misleading" statements because a premature withdrawal might spread anarchy through an already unstable Middle East. But no leading Democrat or left-of-center media personality said out loud what needed to be said:

Bush lied. Thousands of Americans and Iraqis died as a result. He had increased the one danger America didn't need after September 11: anti-Americanism. At bare minimum Bush merited impeachment and removal from office. Prosecuting him for waging an illegal war should have been seriously considered.

Republicans guessed that flighty Democrats wouldn't be able to stay focused on the WMD issue, and they were right. A story about a lack of something only becomes more interesting if that something is found, thus ending the story. The scandal of the missing WMDs should have *grown* by the day; it faded away instead.

Democrats and a unified Left should have seen passing time as a way to increase pressure on the administration. They should have prefaced every public appearance, regardless of its subject, with the following line: "It has now been *x* days since the beginning of the occupation of Iraq. We still haven't found any weapons of mass destruction. Why did you lie to us, Mr. Bush?"

The Left will reap the political fallout for their failure to challenge Bush on the WMD issue in unexpected ways. Bedrock liberals who opposed the war as imperialism at worst or dangerous adventurism at best feel betrayed by their party. "We needed to stand up for what's right," a pal in the Texas Democratic Party confided. "If not us, who?" Pro-war conservatives, on the other hand, understood the leftie refusal to seize an opportunity to build political capital, a telling sign of weakness. "You guys are afraid when you should be making *us* afraid," a Republican TV personality wrote in an e-mail. "If your guys had played this right, we'd be out of power for the next 50 years."

That may be overstating the scale of this particular lost opportunity. But we'll never know either way, because the Democrats never even tried.

REINVENTING RULES

Robert F. Kennedy famously said, "There are those that look at things the way they are, and ask: 'why?' I dream of things that never were, and ask 'why not?'" Kennedy is dead. Now the Right uses its vivid imagination to change old rules to its liking. A recent battle over the seemingly mundane matter of Congressional redistricting in Texas demonstrates how the GOP reinvents the rules to suit itself.

Bush political advisor Karl Rove and House Majority Leader Tom DeLay, the Bush administration's "wet ops" fixers, noticed an opportunity presented by recent population shifts in Texas. If they played their cards correctly, Texas voting districts could be remapped to yield a net increase of the number of Republican seats from Texas and thus in the United States House of Representatives. Traditional practice had had leaders of the two parties in the Texas State House negotiate the borders of the state's Congressional districts every ten years after the results of the new U.S. census were released. Since this had last been done in 2001, after the 2000 census, Republicans would have normally had to wait until 2011 to pick up those extra seats. DeLay noted, however, that the ten-year cycle was but a "gentlemen's agreement." It didn't have the force of law, and neither Rove or DeLay were gentlemen. Texas's State House had a Republican majority, one that could be trusted to follow orders from the big boys in Washington. The two men met with Texas Republicans and asked them to break tradition by pushing for immediate redistricting.

Aware that they would be defeated on the redistricting question in a straight party-line vote, Democrats in the Texas state legislature decided to break some tradition themselves. They chartered a flight to Albuquerque, New Mexico, where they holed up in cheap hotel rooms in order to deny the State House a quorum. Republicans had the votes for redistricting but no way to ram it through.

The "runaway Democrats" would probably have gotten away with their gambit had their nerve held up. But the Bushies—all along, this was a matter orchestrated by the national Republican Party—played hardball. Incredibly, they requested the Department of Homeland Security to track the Democrat state representatives' plane with a view to forcing it to return to Texas. (HomeSec refused.) GOP leaders even considered having the runaway Democrats arrested, though no one could invent a charge for their offense. In the end, an order came down from national Democratic headquarters: go back home. Spooked by Republican accusations that the scrappy runaway Democrats were creating government gridlock—a joke considering Republicans' willingness to shut down the government while blocking a Clinton budget package—the Washington wusses worried their way out of victory. Rove and DeLay got their extra seats.

Even after being repeatedly victimized by other such beyond-the-pale maneuvers, the thinking of liberal Democrats remains: what's good for the Republican goose is too hardcore for us wimpy Democratic ganders. Democrats bitterly threaten to unleash the same nasty tactics that Republicans deploy against them, but when push comes to shove they rarely follow through. Whether they lack heart, guts, or the belief that breaking the rules is right, they obey customs and regulations that their opponents routinely ignore.

Creative strategizing isn't always about pushing your weight around. Smart tacticians like Rove take a fresh look at a situation and employ legal strategies that no one previously considered. Too often Democrats fail to appreciate new possibilities.

Officials of Al Gore's presidential campaign began to understand the potential danger posed by Ralph Nader's candidacy early in the summer of 2000. As the English newspaper the *Guardian* presciently pointed out that

June, "With George W. Bush and Al Gore neck and neck, the seven percent showing for Mr. Nader has provoked a debate on the left about whether supporting him may leach away some Democratic support and help Mr. Bush and the Republicans." To some pundits the obvious solution was to take a page from European-style parliamentary politics. Why not, they suggested, offer Nader a post in a future Gore administration in exchange for dropping out of the race? Joel Schechter mused that Nader would make an excellent secretary of transportation or energy in a piece entitled "A Modest Proposal" for the *San Francisco Examiner*.

The thing is, it would have worked. As the count stood when the U.S. Supreme Court suspended Florida's vote tally, Nader received more than 97,000 ballots, most of which would have otherwise gone to Gore. Since Bush was declared the victor by fewer than 600 votes in that crucial state, bringing Nader in from the cold—personally I think he would have been happier as secretary of labor—would have handed Gore a decisive victory.

Monday morning quarterbacking aside, most analysts believed that Nader might cost the election months before November. So why didn't Gore's campaign try to neutralize him?

In their own ham-fisted way, they did. Gore was largely responsible for getting Nader tossed out of the presidential debates, which he tried to enter *as a spectator*. If anything, Gore's hostility increased Nader's visibility and caused liberals choosing between Nader and Gore to become disgusted by the latter. But the Gore campaign limited its response to Nader to hostility. Coopting the *Unsafe at Any Speed* legend never arose as a serious possibility within the campaign heirarchy. "This isn't Europe," a campaign insider told me at the time. "We don't cut deals with nobodies for cabinet seats. It's better to lose than to be beholden to a guy like Nader." I trust that the Goreites' scorn keeps them warm at night.

RECOGNIZE WHEN YOU'VE WON

Republicans have declared war on everyone to the left of Dick Cheney, but Democrats are still acting like they're working a college debate class, where the participants follow the rules or face dire consequences. Not only must Democrats fight a multipronged war against their hostile adversaries on the right, they must compensate for the time they've lost failing to understand the truth of the situation. If they do both, they'll start winning again. But winning won't mean anything if, like Bill Clinton, you continue to act like the other guys are still in charge after you win. Unless they adopt a harsher attitude, the next major Democratic victory will look like the movie *Revenge of the Nerds*. What's the point of beating the jocks if you don't get to humiliate them and steal their girlfriends? A winning strategy for Democrats means acting like you've won when you have won.

Consider the example of George W. Bush: "During his campaign . . . Bush told us that he was a 'compassionate conservative' and a 'different kind of Republican,'" Al From, leader of the centrist Democratic Leadership Council, wrote three months after Bush took the presidential oath of office, "but as the Bush Administration completes its first hundred days, a starkly different picture is emerging. He is governing as a conventional conservative whose ideology is to the right of recent Republican presidents, including Ronald Reagan."

"When we prevailed," From continued, "our party was very different, standing for economic growth and opportunity, not just redistribution; for fiscal responsibility, not 'tax and spend'; for work, not welfare; for preventing crime and punishing criminals, not explaining away their behavior; for empowering, not bureaucratic, government; and for fostering a new sense of community and an ethic of mutual responsibility by asking citizens to give something back to their country."

Poor, sad man; the irony was lost on him. Republicans run moderate campaigns before governing to the right; Democrats do the opposite—thus ensuring that the legacy of their rule won't long outlast their tenure. Had Clinton passed a mondo national health plan when he had the chance, subsequent Republican administrations might have tried to roll it back. But they could never have eliminated it. At worst, they might have nibbled away at its edges, as they're perpetually attempting to do to Social Security and Medicare with privatization schemes. Clinton's healthcare program would have outlived him.

Upon taking office, Clinton sent signals designed to demonstrate his commitment to bipartisanship. In other words, he acted like a man with an imposter complex rather than a president enjoying the people's mandate for change. Unsure of himself and his policies, Clinton appointed a Republican, William Cohen, as secretary of defense, and a Republican-friendly southern Democrat, Richard Riley, as secretary of education. His first hundred days saw the announcement of a deficit-reduction package designed to appeal to fiscal conservatives, a health-care plan dedicated to protecting the profits of large insurers, and a half-assed attempt to permit gays and lesbians to serve openly in the military. The message was clear: I ran as a Democrat but on the big issues, you can count on me to make concessions to the other side.

Clinton was continuing a trend. Jimmy Carter, who ran a maverick "outsider's" campaign against Watergate-crippled incumbent Gerald Ford, was widely expected to clean house when he arrived in Washington during the brutal winter of 1977. But Carter too took pains to send signals that he planned to govern as president of all of the people—which meant making compromises with the party he had defeated at the polls. Inviting your ideological enemies into your cabinet, however, depresses your supporters. And it will never, ever sate your opponents, who are forever laying the grounds for your destruction.

L. R. Morris asked in *Harper's* magazine later that year, "What body of Jimmy Carter's 'outsiders' has 11 heads, about 70 cumulative years on the public payroll, some 30 corporate directorships, and an average 1976 income of $211,000? Answer: the cabinet of the United States." Not only were Carter's cabinet secretaries wealthy; some were Republicans. Analogous to Clinton's gays in the military opening salvo, Carter made a quick gesture to liberal party loyalists on January 21 by issuing a blanket amnesty to Vietnam draft dodgers hiding in Canada. But Carter's first *major* policy initiatives were to pledge a commitment to a balanced budget and increased military spending. Even before taking office, *Time* reported, he "gave Congressional leaders the distinct impression last month that he would not be pushing for expensive new programs in his first year, a prospect that cheered the conservatives and dismayed the liberals." Yale historian C. Vann Woodward sighed: "It is still too early for pessimism, but it is already too late for optimism."

Carter is now regarded as one of our best-liked and least effective presidents.

Recent Republican presidents, by contrast, haven't pretended to be interested in bipartisanship. They had won the White House, and by God they were going to act like it. Neither George W. Bush, nor his father, nor Ronald Reagan, invited a Democrat to serve on their cabinet. (John Connally Jr., the former Texas governor who had been shot along with JFK in 1963, is the sole exception. Nixon's defense secretary from 1971 to 1972, he changed his party affiliation to Republican in 1973.)

Since World War II, no Republican president has deviated substantially from his party's platform during his first months in office. George Herbert Walker Bush spent early 1989 pushing for a reduction in the capital gains tax, a brazen concession to wealthy investors. Reagan pushed for an expanded defense build-up; Nixon continued fighting the war in Vietnam that he had promised to end.

Democrats consider what they'd like to get, think about what they'd settle for, and come to the bargaining table with the lower sum in hope of receiving credit for seeming reasonable. Clinton wanted a true national health insurance plan but, figuring that such a radical proposal wouldn't be well received by Congress, instead presented a compromise favorable to the insurance companies. Of course, whatever you request in a negotiation inevitably gets watered down as offer meets counteroffer; what's left is a hollow shell of a once grand intent. Republicans, on the other hand, know from haggling. Few of them have bargained in a Middle Eastern souk but like any businessperson worth her salt, they know to ask for more than they hope to get. When Bush wanted a $350 billion tax cut bill, he asked Congress for $726 billion. "Some in Congress say the plan is too big," Bush told workers at a tank plant in Lima, Ohio, wearing his trademark sneer. "Well, it seems like to me they might have some explaining to do. If they agree that tax relief creates jobs, then why are they for a little bitty tax relief package?"

Bush later "settled" for what he'd wanted all along.

Attempting to appease your enemy is an endeavor inherently doomed to failure. You anger your base; your opponents see you as weak and indecisive. When Democrats finally win, they ought to strive to make a profound ideological impression. They should claim a mandate, demand enormous reforms, ask for twice as much as they want, pretend that their victory proves that their opponents have been consigned to the dustbin of history. Burn the crops, salt the fields, melt down their art and use the metal to raise a statue in your own honor.

POLITICS IS NOT A TEA PARTY

When Dems win, they ought to appoint top officials exclusively from their own party. They should rule as if they enjoy a 100 percent mandate for radical change, then settle for something less—but only slightly less. This advice is, of course, less than charitable. It would be a far better world if victors were generous, allowing losers to keep a modicum of dignity.

Politics, however, is not a tea party. It's Genghis Khan leading a million horses across the steppe, surrounding the city of Samarkand, and slaughtering its entire population over the weekend, using nothing more than knives and swords.

Rightists give no quarter when they take power. They show no mercy. To the victors go the spoils, say they, and vengeance isn't the only reason they act the way they do. They understand the necessity of rewarding your own long-suffering supporters, of reversing policies that disgusted you and yours, of cowing your enemies in preparation for future engagements. Mostly it's about achieving your goals. In the short run, favorable policies and personalities must be promoted. In the long run, preparations must be made to mitigate the effect of future defeats—a fact of life since history became cyclical. "Keep your eye on the prize," admonished Martin Luther King Jr. Stay focused. Too often, Democratic and liberal leaders allow themselves to be distracted by petty, battles over inconsequential issues like flag burning, posting the Ten Commandments in public schools, and all matter of silliness that have nothing to do with big-ticket issues like social and economic justice. They worry about the next election rather than harvesting the fruits of recent victory. They get bogged down in scandal, defending their personalities from persecution when what matters is the cause, not the person. Staying focused means recognizing when you've won, and taking full advantage of that victory.

What's a good first move when you win? For Charles de Gaulle, leader of the Free French resistance movement exiled in London and Algiers during World War II, it meant erasing his enemies from history.

The early 1940s were a time of great bitterness and disappointment for the exiled resistance leader. After searching in vain for someone of higher rank and prestige to lead the anti-Nazi resistance in France, General de Gaulle almost single-handedly coordinated the disparate groups that emerged to fight the Germans. The United States, however, refused to have anything to do with him. Roosevelt continued to grant diplomatic recognition to the collaborationist Vichy regime run by Marshall Philippe Pétain, a puppet government that sentenced de Gaulle to death for treason should he ever have set foot on the French mainland. FDR, planning to bypass de Gaulle in favor of direct Allied Military Government of France, even refused to give de Gaulle advance notice of the D-Day landings. In the end, the Free French fought a behind-the-scenes civil war in order to seize power village by village from U.S. military governors.

Upon assuming the reins of the Provisional Government of the French Republic in August 1944, with little thanks owed to the U.S., de Gaulle faced the dilemma of the conqueror. Pressured by the Americans to show mercy to Vichy officials and other collaborators, De Gaulle instead turned a blind eye to what would become known as the bloody *épuration*. An estimated ten thousand Vichy sympathizers, war profiteers, and related unlucky *mecs* were summarily executed by drumhead tribunals. But even that purge wasn't enough for de Gaulle.

To drive home the point that the Vichy regime had been an illegitimate interruption of legal rule between the Third and Fourth French republics, de Gaulle's first legislative act as president was to invalidate every law, rule and regulation passed by Vichy from 1940 to 1944. Many such rules involved matters bureaucratic and apolitical—funding for dams, fines for jumping turnstiles in the Paris metro. These had to be reissued under the Fourth Republic, but the symbolism of de Gaulle's edict was lost on no one. Pétain's face doesn't appear in official lists of French rulers. A French court condemned Pétain to death, but de Gaulle, refusing to give his supporters the gift of a martyr, commuted his sentence to life in prison. Pétain died in 1951 but de Gaulle killed him in 1944.

The next Democratic president may want to consider an analogous measure relative to the years 2001–05. George W. Bush was, after all, installed extraconstitutionally by a rogue Supreme Court. His "victory" came as the result of a suspended recount that, had it been permitted to continue, would have handed the state of Florida and the presidency to Al Gore. If, as most Americans believe, Bush's regime was installed illegitimately, all laws and rules propagated under his tenure are by definition invalid and should be overturned. Perhaps such a radical approach would be too dramatic. Alternatively, the future Democratic president could make the case to the public that, given the disputed nature of the 2000 election and the extremist policies that followed September 11, reversing Bush's more extreme post-attack policies—the USA-Patriot Act, tax cuts and doctrine of preemption—would be a prudent exercise in moderation: a way to bring the political system back into pre–September 11 equilibrium. At bare minimum the lowlights of the Bush interregnum should be abolished.

Would Republicans undertake such measures if the situations of the two parties were reversed? What do *you* think?

REINCARNATING THE ORGANIZATION MAN

Identifying a problem is essential to solving it, but it's only a start. Coming up with a solution is equally important, but a solution isn't any good unless it's realistic. It has been suggested, for example, that what most ails the American Left is the Great Right-Wing Conspiracy—the thousand-plus radio stations owned by Clear Channel Communications, a company that carefully coordinated pro-Iraq war rallies on behalf of the Bush adminis-tration, Rush Limbaugh's syndicated radio group, the Fox News Channel, and to a lesser extent the Gannett newspaper corporation.

One would be a fool to deny the facts. These right-wing media con-glomerates are extremely effective at spreading their extremist message across the airwaves. Eric Alterman's book *What Liberal Media?* does an exceptional job at documenting how and why Republican-affiliated media works the way it does, but you don't have to buy the thesis that the Right owns the media from some whiny liberal. Paul Weyrich, known as "the godfather of the conservative movement" for co-founding the Heritage Foundation in 1973, brags: "There are more than 1,500 conservative radio talk show hosts. You have Fox News. You have the Internet, where all the successful sites are conservative. The ability to reach people with our point of view is like nothing we have ever seen before!"

You can almost hear him cackling.

And while there are non-conservative media outlets—National Public Radio, PBS, the *New York Times*—their editorial vantage point isn't so much liberal as nonconservative.

The answer to right-wing media hegemony, argue some liberals, is left-wing media hegemony. The most well-publicized attempt to address this perceived imbalance in the world of pseudojournalistic propaganda is an outfit formerly called AnShell Media, a ten-million-dollar Chicago-based start-up that announced its hopes to take on Clear Channel with its own net-work of liberal Democratic talk radio stations. If my experience with this organization is any indication, though, it's a safe bet that it won't be giving the Excellence in Broadcasting network (Rush Limbaugh's syndication company) a run for its money any time soon.

AnShell enjoyed a lot of hype, including front-page coverage in the *New York Times*, when it announced its intention to create a chain of liberal talk radio stations to counter those on the right. My career history caused me to be intrigued.

In 1998, visionary program director David Hall, renowned for discov-ering conservative advice guru Dr. Laura Schlessinger, signed me to host a weekend talk show on KFI-AM in Los Angeles, a fifty-thousand-watt powerhouse that can reach fifteen Western states on nights when the iono-sphere cooperates. It took me about a year to find my stride, but everyone, including David, agreed that in radio I had found what I was meant to do.

Producing cartoons and columns is a ceaseless struggle for me. It's hard work. Talking about the issues and arguing about them came naturally. My take on the format, which relied on my eclectic mix of comedy routines, interviews, and regular features like "Dial a Dump" (unhappy lovers asked me to shit can their unsuspecting significant others on the air), "Stan Watch: Breaking News from Central Asia," and "Brooklyn Traffic" (I called author Dave Eggers to ask him whether his block three time zones away from Los Angeles was congested or moving smoothly) proved popular, being simulcast by both National Public Radio and the British Broadcasting Corporation. I broadcast the first live talk show from Cuba and in September 1999 broke news from Pakistan-controlled Kashmir that the Taliban had crossed the Line of Control to fight India. I took twenty-two listeners on a proto-*Survivor* bus trip across Central Asia ("Stan Trek 2000"), reporting my traveling companion's latest misadventures live from Turkmenistan, Uzbekistan, Kyrgyzstan, and Kazakhstan. My ratings were highest among partisans on the left and the right; opinionated listeners liked the fact that I let people finish their thoughts rather than dumping them thirty seconds into their call— a talk radio "rule." As my ratings rose, so did my star at KFI. I moved from midnight to dinner to mid-afternoons, from once a week to all weekend, sometimes filling in during the week.

When I joined KFI, the station was owned by Cox Communications. Cox sold it to a company called AM/FM, which was itself acquired, in 2000, by Clear Channel. When David called me to let me know he was firing me in favor of former O.J. prosecutor—or rather, former *failed* O.J. prosecutor—Marcia Clark, something told me that he wasn't being totally straight. Only after Clear Channel's corporate offices organized pro–Bush administration "Rallies for America" around the country did the truth become clear: unlike traditional radio entrepreneurs, Clear Channel was driven less by profits than by ideology. "Talk radio," a Clear Channel exec (not David) told me, "is intrinsically conservative." When I asked him how that model explained my ratings, he responded with a bit of sophistry that remains one of my favorite lines of all time: "Your ratings would have been *even higher* had you been Republican."

Clark, whose ratings paled next to mine, lasted fewer than six months.

So naturally I was thrilled when I heard about AnShell. I'd been ahead of my time, doing aggressive, politically incorrect liberal talk radio from 1998 to 2000 when nobody cared. I'd spent hundreds of hours talking about how the Middle East was yesterday's news and arguing that the big problems that were going to affect American foreign policy were going to come out of Central Asia, and Afghanistan in particular. Here, finally, were people—Anita and Sheldon Drobny, the founders of AnShell—who understood the untapped potential of liberal radio.

There's no doubt that building leftie talk radio would be a challenge. "According to the Senate Democratic Policy Committee, the top five radio station owners currently control 45 powerful, 50,000-watt or better, radio stations," writes Joe Bevilacqua for TomPaine.com. "On those stations, on any given Monday through Friday, you can find 310 hours of nationally syndicated right-wing talk. As for liberal talk, you'll find a total of five hours, three of which feature the moderate Alan Colmes as part of conservative Sean Hannity's show." Driving across the United States is to take a trip through the Rush zone: as one Rush AM station fades out, fiddling with the dial finds you another.

Talk radio distributes conservative talking points to baseline activists, ordinary like-minded individuals. Bevilacqua quotes Bob Borosage of the Campaign for America's Future: "It's not that the corporate media is so conservative, but there is no liberal equivalent that helps liberals, that arms liberals with how to make their argument. You've got now [Rush] Limbaugh and Clear Channel and places that enormously, effectively train conservatives in how to make their case. So if you're a conservative, you can go a hundred places on the dial and you can find somebody who basically is giving you pure message. They're telling you, 'Here's how you make your case against liberals on the war, on the economy, on tax cuts, on this, on that, etc.' And they're doing it in kind of pure unvarnished fashion and they're doing it again and again and again. So if you're a conservative over the fence or in the bar when you're talking to your buddies, you're very confident you can make your argument. You've heard it before. You've heard people that you respect say it. You've got one-liners you've learned. You've got stories you're telling and you're sharing an e-mail with your friends."

Rush Limbaugh, in other words, is a force that gives Republicans' lives meaning. Is there a similar force of personality on the left, on the majority side of American politics? Obviously not.

To hear the AnShell people tell it—and I agree with them—the left-wing vacuum on AM radio presents not just a need for equivalent propaganda, but a business opportunity. "I've never seen anything that doesn't exist get so much press," marvels Michael Harrison of the *Talkers* trade magazine. The problem is, AnShell—now called Air America—seems para-lyzed by that old virus, Liberal Disorganization Syndrome.

After reading the *Times* piece about the new venture, I dropped a sam-pler tape of my KFI show into the mail to AnShell. A month passed, and I didn't hear anything (whatever happened to the good old days, when com-panies were courteous enough to send out rejection letters?). When I called, however, the person who answered had no idea who I was. She brusquely informed me that they'd eventually get back to all the wannabe talk hosts. Okay, so I'm not Michael Moore. Still, in the rarified world of the liberal media, people know who I am. Given that I was one of the few talk radio hosts in the country with a liberal political bent to have achieved success, AnShell should have already had me on their short list. This was not a good sign.

As it turned out, they *had* heard of me. About six months later, one of the AnShell mucketymucks called me from Illinois to feel out my interest in doing an early-morning drive show, either alone or teamed up with stand-up comic and actress Janeane Garofalo. (AnShell had a thing about comedians; Al Franken was going to be their headliner, going up against Rush hour by hour.) As our conversation progressed, however, two things became clear. First, they had no idea how much their proposed venture was going to cost. Second, they didn't read their mail. ("Could you send me an aircheck tape?" the guy asked.)

It doesn't take a seasoned CEO to know that a company that doesn't read its mail may suffer problems. What if a big check comes in? It might sit there in the pile, yellowing in its envelope until it expires! Furthermore, taking on Clear Channel wasn't going to cost $1 million or $10 million. Buying up, say, five hundred stations in the top markets would require Fortune 500-level financing. To their credit, they realized this—and by August were able to announce a modest seven-city affiliation agreement. It was a start, but a small start—and it's not going to give Clear Channel any grief, much less give listeners a Democratic alternative to the vast ocean of right-wing swill that dominates the AM dial.

By the way, I haven't heard anything back from Air America. Maybe they're still interested; probably not. I heard that they'd been bought out by some rather straight-sounding dudes led by former America Online execu-tive and Democratic National Committee member Mark Walsh. The upscale new management team could be an improvement. Or their corpo-rate approach may kill the idea's central anti–Clear Channel precept—

something that Walsh's bland comment about making the company "centrist, with a hint of liberalism" would tend to confirm. Either way, the deafening silence is unprofessional.

Keep your eye on the prize. Even outside of politics, it's a good way to run your life. It's absolutely essential if you're trying to change the world. I was discussing AnShell with an executive at XM Satellite Radio, a rapidly growing subscription radio provider. "I don't think they have what it takes," one guy told me, "but not because they have a bad idea. Quite the contrary; there's an opening for a company that figures out how to get liberal programming on the air and keep it there long enough for listeners to catch on that things have changed. They just don't seem to have their shit together."

Failing to read your mail, courting talent and not following up, flailing around when one's original vision fails to catch on with potential investors—they're all classic symptoms of that intangible problem that everyone recognizes when they encounter it. It's a big Democratic problem: lack of organization, lack of vision, lack of energy, lack of guts, lack of follow-through. The progressive political message is potentially the most potent around. If you can get the American people to pay attention, you can convince them that most of what they believe falls closer to the left than to the right. But no one will listen unless you seem secure in your message, organized in your approach, and dedicated to fighting the war for the long run.

chapter 8

THE CASE FOR DIRTY POLITICS

We're up against an enemy, a conspiracy. They're using any means. We are going to use any means. Is that clear?
—President Richard Nixon, 1972

I think the American people are tired of this kind of "gotcha politics." They're tired of this kind of last-minute dirty tricks and I think the Democrats owe the American people an explanation.
—Bush campaign manager Karen Hughes, November 2000

"The intelligent left," mourns columnist Nicholas Kristof, "is dumbing down and showing signs of slipping into a cesspool of outraged incoherence" in its reaction to the depredations of the Bush Administration. "It's debasing and marginalizing itself by marshalling epithets rather than arguments."

Kristof cites several examples of what he calls "the latest leftist silliness." The heretofore solemn Citizens for Legitimate Government sends out a press release with the headline "We have an idiot usurping lying weasel for a president." Liberal websites ponder the possibility that Minnesota's late Senator Paul Wellstone was murdered in order to assure a GOP-dominated Senate. Kristof's Bush-bashing columns—he's a moderate liberal in the Clintonian vein—spark "torrents of e-mail in terms so strident that they appall" him. "Dick Cheney is a maggot feeding on the decaying flesh of human misery" is an example of these vexing missives.

If Kristof's opinion that progressives are "debasing and marginalizing" themselves by expressing their anger is correct, they're making their already grim situation still worse. Fortunately for us, he's mistaken.

For the first time since the 1960s, Democrats are enraged. They're furious at the stolen 2000 election and the media's determination to sweep the scandal under the rug of national discourse. They're disgusted that the Bush Administration, which promised an epoch of moderate "compassionate conservatism," used September 11 as an excuse to turn hard right. They despise the war in Iraq, and more so the lies Bush used to justify it. They fear a future burdened by a record national debt. They loathe Bush's politics, they look down on him intellectually, and they consider the people around him corporate fascists. They can't stand his crooked face, whiny voice, grade-school vocabulary or insistence on calling the United States "the homeland." If you're liberal or you know one, odds are that you've seen someone yell back at the TV whenever Smirky, the Chimp, or Piehole appears to announce more bad news.

When Sally Baron of Wisconsin and Gertrude Jones of Louisiana died, at ages seventy-one and eighty-one respectively, they hadn't met but they had something in common. Both of their obituaries asked that mourners send donations to any group working to oust Bush. "If Ronald Reagan was the Great Communicator," John Dickerson and Karen Tumulty wrote in *Time*, "Bush is proving to be the Great Polarizer. Reagan and then Bill Clinton ushered in the modern age of the acrimoniously divided electorate, but George [W.] Bush has cleaved the U.S. into two tenaciously divided camps . . . Bush is like a one-man Rorschach test for what kind of nation America wants to be and what kind of President Americans want to have." Responding to the magazine's request to describe Bush, most Republican poll respondents called him "decisive," "determined," and "strong." Democrats preferred "cocky," "arrogant," and "boneheaded."

Increasing polarization, *Time* points out, has resulted in a shrinking pool of fewer swing voters: "For years pollsters said America was a 40-40-20 country—that is, 40 percent Republican, 40 percent Democrat and 20 percent independent. Now, they say, it's a 45-45-10 nation—with even fewer than that 10 percent truly up for grabs." As was the case during the 1960s, shoring up your base—if you're the Democratic Party, that means targeting liberals—is the key to success in a politically polarized climate.

Anger, we have learned, is a potent motivator. Rage energizes. Left-of-center political organizations have seen donations and new memberships soar as resentment mounted throughout Bush's ersatz presidency. The over-the-top statements that Kristof deplores are a symptom of inchoate liberal rage at what they consider a rightist coup—rage that, if properly nurtured, can be channeled into potent political action.

Despite decades of evidence to the contrary, old-line liberals still believe that acting polite and deferential is the way to seduce hearts and minds. "The vitriol is bad for the country, by turning every policy fight into a zero-sum game," writes Kristof. His let's-be-reasonable crowd doesn't get it. Clinton's nineties accommodationism put the left wing of the Democratic Party to sleep. From their standpoint, Clinton's most appealing feature was not being

Republican. Because he never pushed for items on the leftie wish list, left-ies weren't vested in his success or failure. Then liberal activists saw their causes ignored or wounded by a president they couldn't attack because his Republican alternative would probably be worse. Extremists on the right, observing that mainline Dems weren't standing up for traditional liberal values, were emboldened to escalate their demands. When they got their chance, they finally led the charge to impeach the president. Conservatives, not liberals, started our current bout of no-holds-barred political warfare.

Republicans are usually the first out of the gate with dirty tricks and the most willing to cross ethical boundaries to win. They lie, smear, and slan-der relentlessly. And most of the time, lefties sit back and take it. "We don't want to become just like *them*," a correspondent wrote to take me to task for making some snide remark about Bush's IQ. They—the Right—are kicking our ass. It's about time that we used their tactics—but we should be more: meaner, more aggressive, and more willing to bend the rules to get our way.

They sure as hell don't play by any "rules." Why should we?

Flinging grade-school epithets at the president and vice president (or the men who play them on TV) won't get progressives elected or policies changed to our liking. But it's an important first step. I don't know whether he intended it or not, but Scott Adams created a politically radical comic strip in his office-cubicle saga *Dilbert*. Calling the boss stupid insinuates that he doesn't deserve respect. Without respect he doesn't enjoy the authority he needs in order to instill fear. He becomes powerless. That's revolutionary. Calling Bush an "idiot usurping lying weasel" is the first step towards stripping him of his carefully constructed air of majestic invincibil-ity. You can't beat your enemy without respecting his abilities, but you can't rally your troops without making fun of the other side.

Getting mean creates the barnstorming attitude that allows your side to regain its self-confidence. It has the happy side effect of spooking the oppo-sition. Basic components of pumping up your ass-kicking mojo are:

- *Disrespecting your opponent.* Starting in the seventies Republican officials up to and including the president have refused to call the Democratic Party by its proper name. They continue to refer to their adversary as the "Democrat Party." Dropping the "ic" is a subtle, inten-tional slur they use to annoy Democrats, causing their party name to sound awkward and slightly alien. Terms like "bleeding-heart liberal," "limousine liberal," and "lunatic left" convey loathing and disgust (inspired by Nixon speechwriter William Safire's classic "nattering nabobs of negativism," Republicans love their alliteration). They don't just insult liberal leaders. Ann Coulter called Howard Dean's young campaign workers "impotent nosepickers hoping to make some friends and unsuccessful auditioners for Gap commercials." When he had a TV program during the early Clinton administration, Rush Limbaugh opened each show with a sign stating the number of days in "captivity" that the U.S. had suffered under Clinton's presidency. Comparing the administration of a legitimately elected president to the humiliation of the Iran hostage crisis of 1979–81 sent a powerful message: we conservatives do not recognize Clinton as president.

- *Don't whine.* "Just get over it." "Stop whining." "Quit complaining." These are the lines people who screw over other people use to try to convince them to shut up. The sad truth is that such tactics are effective. So-called "conservatives"—see? I'm using the disrespect tactic already!—bludgeon Dems with these dismissive remarks whenever they make a cogent, well-thought-out point. When are liberals going to learn? People don't *care* about well-reasoned arguments. They like funny quips, like Ronald Reagan's "there you go again" and Walter Mondale's "where's the beef?" I appeared on HBO's *Real Time with Bill Maher* twice the same week. The first time I came armed with all sorts of relevant quotes and statistics that I used to bolster my arguments; I was a flop. The following show I shot down an insulting caller with the response "I've never heard such a stupid fucking question in my life." I was lauded as that episode's living reincarnation of Lenny Bruce. Constructive retorts come off as whining. Like it or not, cutting remarks and stupid zingers are more effective than logical argument.

- *Don't play by the rules.* Republicans did an end-run around the Constitution, even threatening a violent coup d'état, in order to end the Florida 2000 recount crisis and get George W. Bush installed as president. They broke standard practice in Texas to scam a few extra seats via Congressional redistricting. They planted bugs in George McGovern's campaign headquarters, asked a like-minded columnist to steal Jimmy Carter's strategy briefing book and dug up Bill Clinton's bimbos. Get real and accept it: these are the kinds of people we're dealing with. They're not about to change, but lefties must. Conflict inevitably reduces itself to its lowest common denominator: if the other guy in a street fight bites you, you have every right to chomp him back. In fact, once the other side starts to hit below the belt, you have the right to escalate, to bite twice as hard *and* kick them in the balls. There's a word for those who fight fair: loser.

The first step, disrespecting your opponent, is easy. The Left must brainstorm a bunch of ridiculous alliterative catchphrases with which to denigrate the Republican Right—hey! There's one! Radical Right, Republican Radicals, Repugs, Reprobates, Republotards, Ruplicants, Repulsicans . . . you get the idea. Pick one or two, issue them to the liberal faithful along with appropriate talking points, and *never ever stop using them*. Don't stop when people ask you to, don't stop when you get tired of using them, don't stop when that nice man Nicholas Kristof says that the "intelligent left" is making itself look foolish. Tom Daschle and Michael Moore and Janeane Garofalo and Al Gore and John Kerry and everyone who cares about helping ordinary people, saving the environment, and stopping the looting of America should make it their business to use the same nasty insults to refer to Republicans and their allies *for the rest of their lives*.

Next they have to do what Rush did to Clinton: delegitimize the Right, its partisans, their accomplishments, and everything they stand for. Because he wasn't elected, liberals refuse to call Bush "president." (You will note that, throughout this book, I have never referred to the Thief-in-Chief as "President Bush." It wasn't easy to for me to stay on track, but you nonetheless understood to whom I was referring.) I used it first, but liberal film director Michael Moore calls George W. Bush "Governor Bush." (He's welcome to it.) I coined the phrase Generalissimo El Busho (because, like General Augusto Pinochet of Chile, Bush came to power as, and rules like, a tinpot dictator), which has come into fairly wide currency (166 discrete hits on Google). Most of my friends, typically wearing a facial expression appropriate to a guy suffering the presence of a diseased toad in his mouth, refer to him as *That Man*. Recognizing that Bush isn't president—He Is Not My President, reads a popular button—and reminding people of this fact at every opportunity (as Moore did at the 2003 Academy Awards) is incredibly important. It keeps alive the issue of Bush's illegitimacy and it demonstrates a willingness to openly express contempt for a man who attempts to rule via intimidation. But what should lefties do if, God forbid, a Republican is legitimately elected?

The same exact thing. The radical Right (there I go again) claimed that Clinton wasn't a legit president because he didn't receive a majority of the popular vote in 1992. (Ross Perot's Reform Party run denied him 50 percent, but he still beat Bush.) Republicans claimed that Hillary had Vince Foster murdered. They even sold videotapes purporting to document the many innocent souls the First Couple had allegedly dispatched to an early grave. Clinton had his faults—I detailed many of them throughout eight of my years as a cartoonist and columnist—but conservatives weren't interested in criticizing the man or his policies. They were out to make the very *idea* of a Democratic president so distasteful in the mind of the American public that they would never again consider voting for one. It's high time that Democrats return the favor.

After three years of dutifully mouthing the oxymoron "President Bush," leading Democrats began seeing the light. At a December 2003 gathering of the major Democratic presidential candidates in Florida, most reflected the angry mood of party activists by finally remembering that Bush had lost the state and thus the national election, in 2000. "We are never going to let the United States Supreme Court choose the president of the United States again!" shouted the usually tepid Senator John Edwards of North Carolina.

Liberals must not, cannot, should not "move on." The Right, remember, never lets go. They're pit bulls. Once they get their teeth in your ass it takes a crowbar to pry them off.

Forgetting is the easiest thing in the world. During the nineties, when major sports teams began renaming their stadiums after corporations willing to pay for the privilege, fans swore never to accept the bogus new names. As corporate executives assumed would occur, however, time has passed. People have gotten bored with their own irritation, so they've stopped talking about it. The *San Francisco Chronicle*, which promised never to use any name but Candlestick after that city's baseball stadium was renamed for an obscure computer company, has since given in to referring to it as 3Com Stadium. Continental Airlines Arena will always be the Meadowlands to me, but not to those who tire of fighting the good fight. Remember when theaters began running Coke commercials before the movies? Everyone hissed. But theater owners kept showing the ads, and moviegoers got tired of hissing. Now there are as many as a half-dozen ads—someone recently hissed at *me* for talking during one of them. Life is a war of attrition, a perpetual battle where evil usually wins because it's more determined than good. Of course it's easier to call Bush "President Bush" than "Generalissimo El Busho" or even just "Bush." But that's an active decision, a choice. We can decide to change any time we want.

Now for the toughest part: we have to play rough. The Right doesn't take prisoners and neither should the Left. Liberals need to get down in the gutter and, in the words of *Boondocks* cartoonist Aaron McGruder, "lie and steal and murder with the best of them." Dirty tricks during elections, unfair smears of political opponents, wholesale slander of their entire ideology—all are essential if the Left ever hopes to have another chance at changing America.

It's time to get ferocious.

THEY STARTED IT

To hear Americans tell it, they like their politics clean and straightforward. Eighty-seven percent told a 1999 Institute for Global Ethics poll that they're against negative campaigning. "Voters are especially concerned about lying by candidates; the lack of debate about, and media coverage of, issues; negative campaigning; and the role of money in politics," summarized Celinda Lake, a Democratic pollster. Yet America's political consultants— the men and women who come up with the dirty tricks, sleazy TV ads and below-the-belt insults voters claim to deplore—"have clear consciences," says Andrew Kohut of the Pew Research Center. "Most [political consult- ants] do not think campaign practices that suppress turnout, use scare tac- tics and take facts out of context are unethical. They are nearly unani- mous—97 percent—in the belief that negative advertising is not wrong, and few blame themselves for public disillusionment with the political process." An overwhelming majority of campaign managers said it was okay to "focus primarily on criticizing one's opponent" or to "focus primarily on the kind of person a candidate is, rather than issues."

Why do pollsters, fundraisers, media consultants, and general political consultants consistently give the people what they repeatedly claim that they don't want? Because there's little-to-zero relationship between what people say they want and what they actually respond to.

If negative campaigning really turned voters off, it would hurt candidates who resorted to it. It doesn't. Quite the opposite: negative campaigning works, as the pros have learned from personal experience. The Pew survey found that 82 percent of political campaign workers rate "the quality of a candidate's message"—in other words, spin delivered through sound bytes and TV ads—as the single most important factor in determining the success of a candidacy for elected office. They rank the "amount of money available to a candidate" as number two. So much for integrity and experience.

Perhaps because many of us are ignorant of history, we labor under the naïve belief that politics used to be more genteel during the early days of our republic. True, Aaron Burr and Alexander Hamilton ultimately settled their differing views of federalism and the national banking system with dueling pistols in a New Jersey field. For the most part, though, contemporary Americans mistakenly believe that issues took precedence over personal attacks back then.

In truth, gutter attacks—negative ads, character smears, outright lies, and even ballot-box stuffing—date to the beginning of our republic. Benjamin Franklin Bache, editor of a Democratic-Republican Party newspaper called *The Aurora*, crossed the bridge from the eighteenth to the nineteenth centuries by referring to our second president as "old, querulous, bald, blind, crippled, toothless [John] Adams." Not to be outdone, Federalist pundits like Noah Webster spread rumors that Thomas Jefferson, founder of the Democratic-Republicans, was bonking his slave Sally Hemmings. (Two centuries later, that one turned out to be true.)

During the modern era neither political party has enjoyed a monopoly on the high road, but Democratic efforts at partisan mudslinging peaked around 1964 when President Johnson was forced to withdraw his notorious "daisy ad." In that commercial, which only ran once, a little girl sits in a field of flowers, counting, "One, two, three . . . " as she pulls the petals from a daisy. Then an announcer counts down, "Four, three, two, one," to a nuclear blast that reflects in her eyes. LBJ intones: "These are the stakes: to make a world in which all of God's children can live; or to go into the dark. We must either love each other or we must die." Rough stuff, and it exemplified Johnson's (ultimately effective) strategy of implying that Republican rival Barry Goldwater, if elected, would allow his anticommunist rhetoric to get so out of hand that he might provoke a nuclear war with the Soviet Union. Outraged *Democrats* deluged the White House with phone calls—even back then, liberals tended towards excessive timidity—and the ad was yanked immediately.

Since then a few Democrats have run hard-hitting campaigns on the state and local levels, but the party's national candidates have largely ceded such gutter tactics to the GOP.

In 1972 Nixon operatives sabotaged the campaign of Edmund Muskie, who was considered his most formidable potential Democratic challenger, by calling New Hampshire voters at three in the morning to "urge" them to vote for Muskie. A barrage of similar shenanigans literally reduced Muskie to tears on national television, marking the end of his presidential ambitions. Having thus obtained a weaker challenger in the form of George McGovern, Nixon's aptly acronymed CREEP (Committee to Re-Elect the President) broke into the office of a shrink who had treated McGovern's vice presidential running mate Thomas Eagleton and leaked his psychological records to the press. (Some years earlier, Eagleton had suffered a nervous breakdown and taken meds as part of a prescribed treatment. In the age of *Prozac Nation,* such a revelation might not affect a politician's career, but popular acceptance of psychiatry wasn't nearly as widespread in 1972 as it is today.) During the last few months before the November election, Nixon's campaign deluged television viewers with sinister ads implying that McGovern's proposal to guarantee medical care to anyone who needed it was "socialized medicine"— and the precursor to a communist revolution in America.

With the exception of a few sporadic snipes over the Watergate break-in carried out by Nixon operatives that spring, McGovern refused to react in kind. McGovern, unlike Nixon, couldn't or wouldn't lie or steal or murder with the best of them. He lost in a record landslide to a man who had cheated, lied, embezzled, and authorized several felonies—crimes that forced him to resign less than two years later. McGovern, whose insistence on playing nice would have pleased Nicholas Kristof, was the last liberal presidential nominee of the Democratic Party.

Even prior to the outrageous Republican dirty tricks of the disputed Florida recount, the 2000 contest between Al Gore and George W. Bush marked the greatest widening of the sleaze gap between the two major parties to date.

Bush's men were willing to do just about anything to get their man into the White House. During key Bible Belt primaries they spread false rumors that their chief threat, plain-talking Arizona Senator John McCain, had fathered an illegitimate African-American child. After securing the Repugnican nomination—*there I go again*—they ran TV attack ads that ignored the fact that Al Gore was the Democratic nominee. They acted as if Bill Clinton were running for a third term, implying that voting Democratic would prolong the "immorality" and lack of "dignity" that had characterized Clinton's tenancy of the white mansion across the street from the Ellipse.

By all accounts, Gore had always been faithful to his wife Tipper. Moreover, the vice president had been so angered by Clinton's reckless affair with Monica Lewinsky that he refrained from talking to him any more than he had to. He rejected Clinton's offers to campaign on his behalf. Only Gore knows whether his disgust was tactical or emotional; some advisers believed Clinton's presence would have been a liability. What's certain is that it was grotesquely unfair, given Gore's distancing of himself from Clinton and disparate personality, for Republicans to associate the two men's morality. Gore's presidency may or may not have been a disaster but he probably wouldn't have left semen stains on the Oval Office carpet.

The summer and fall of 2000 passed in a predictable pattern. Americans watched a blizzard of TV ads asserting that only the squeaky-clean George W. Bush could exorcise the stench of Clintonian debauchery from the nation's highest office. Gore ran comparatively few ads; none responded to Bush's harping on the morality smear. Gore's early lead—in late August he was expected to defeat Bush by a landslide 30 points—steadily eroded as election day drew closer.

Most likely because they bought into the usual voters-hate-negative-campaigning BS, Gore's strategists decided not to exploit three juicy opportunities to hit Bush: highly corroborated revelations that as a young man he had gone AWOL, and deserted, from the Texas Air National Guard from 1972 to 1974; tacitly admitted allegations that Bush had snorted cocaine and used other illegal drugs as a young man; and hard evidence that he had been arrested for drunk driving in Kennebunkport, Maine, on September 6, 1976, records of which he later attempted to have destroyed or covered up. (Bush dismissed this incident as a "youthful indiscretion." He was thirty at the time.) In addition, there were unsubstantiated reports that Bush had bought and sold marijuana.

Neither Gore's campaign nor Democratic political action committees ran a single ad exploiting the dirt on Bush's personal life.

George wasn't the only Bush with a spotty driving record. At seventeen, Laura Bush (then Laura Welch), ran a stop sign in Midland, Texas, on November 6, 1963, smashing into a Corvair driven by her high-school friend Michael Douglas. Douglas died, but no vehicular manslaughter charges were filed.

It doesn't stop there. Bush's running mate, Dick Cheney, was twice arrested in Wyoming within eight months for "operating a motor vehicle while intoxicated," in Cheyenne in November 1962 and Rock Springs in July 1963. He was found guilty both times, fined, and had his driver's license suspended.

Gore might have had a field day with these revelations. "Get these nuts off the nation's roads," one of his ads could have read, "and give them chauffeured limousines. Elect Bush-Cheney."

Our country's future was at stake. Gore's decision to stay positive led to an administration dedicated to policies of endless war, deficit spending, and a poisonous atmosphere in which dissenters are branded as unpatriotic and treasonous—a far cry from Bush's campaign pledge to be "a uniter, not a divider." Gore can tell his friends that he took the high road; he refused to wallow in "the politics of personal destruction," as Hillary Clinton likes to say. It's easy to argue that Bush's military inexperience wasn't pertinent to his suitability for high office; Reagan and Clinton didn't go to war either (though Reagan lied about it). Most Baby Boomers had experimented with drugs.

But it is relevant. Republicans have long argued, vehemently so during the Clinton impeachment crisis, that a man's personal life is indicative of his political morality as well as his susceptibility to corruption. GOP impeachment prosecutors, for example, pointed out that a priapic president like Clinton could be vulnerable to blackmail by foreign agents. National security, not just lying about sex, was at stake.

Of course Democrats didn't buy into this line of reasoning, but once the Republicans had stooped to personal attacks they no longer had a real choice but to do the same. It was a brawl. Republicans were poking eyes; Democrats ought to have bitten ears. A combatant who refrains from lowering himself to the same level as his opponent may earn the respect of the audience, but depriving himself of that tactic may also cause him to lose the match. For

PLAIN TALK DISTRESS:
How Bush Derailed the John McCain Juggernaut

All but forgotten by an electorate accustomed to "moving on," but well worth remembering nonetheless, is the sordid story behind George W. Bush's victory in the 2000 Republican presidential primaries. It's an early predictor of future behavior, sure. But it's also instructive in a more important way, as a reminder that in politics as in war, the victor writes history. And, of course, that politics *is* war.

After Arizona Senator John McCain's appeal to independent and liberal voters—creating the potential of the first Republican nominee with wide crossover appeal since Ike—caught Bush's RNC-approved campaign by surprise, it decided to resort to dirty tricks.

The first broadside, as these things go, wasn't that big a deal. Bush ran an ad claiming that McCain opposed funding for breast cancer research. Given that McCain's sister Sandy had survived breast cancer just two years earlier, insiders considered this a below-the-Beltway move.

Things really heated up during the South Carolina primary. "If we win here," McCain said, "I don't see how we can be stopped." Based on their behavior, Bush's forces obviously agreed with that assessment. Pro-Bush pamphleteers passed out leaflets referring to his wife Cindy's past battle with drug addiction. A professor at Bob Jones University, a racist institution that bans interracial dating and is well known for its virulent anti-Catholicism, spammed journalists with an e-mail claiming that McCain had fathered an illegitimate child with an African-American prostitute. The dark-skinned child in question, Bridget McCain, was actually Bangladeshi. Moreover, Bridget had been adopted by McCain and his wife. Nonetheless, South Carolinians reported receiving mysterious phone calls from phony pollsters asking "How would you feel about John McCain if you knew that he had fathered an illegitimate African-American child?" This was a case of "push polling," a dirty trick developed by Republican strategist Lee Atwater during the seventies. "Push pollsters" call voters with insinuating questions to make them believe that a scandal is about to break around a candidate.

Bush denied direct involvement with the attacks on McCain but refused to condemn them. Instead, top Bush strategist Karl Rove took the campaign on the offensive, implying that McCain's experience being tortured at the Hanoi Hilton had caused him to become mentally unbalanced, and bizarrely accusing the ex-POW of anti-anti-Catholic bigotry because he had criticized Bush's visit to Bob Jones.

McCain lost South Carolina and the nomination. GOP unity was preserved when McCain made good on his pledge to endorse and campaign enthusiastically for Bush in the general election against Al Gore.

That's unity for you.

decades, Republicans beat up Senator Edward Kennedy over his personal failings, successfully convincing the American people that he should never become president because of his behavior at Chappaquiddick. Democrats ought to have held Bush—who couldn't compensate for his dismal personal history with the intellect or articulateness on the of a Ted Kennedy—to a similar standard.

Scruples? Save 'em for your deathbed.

ATTACK, ATTACK, ATTACK

I collect propaganda posters, specializing in those from World War II. One of my favorites depicts wild-eyed American GIs charging, bayonets drawn, across a muddy field as fleets of bombers fly overhead. "Attack! Attack! Attack!" it reads. A copy of that poster should hang in every Democratic Party office in the country. It shows Americans doing what they do best when they did it best: relentlessly pursuing their objective in a manic style.

Power is force expended over a distance; political power is determination extended over time. Republicans have mastered political power. They have remained dedicated to their goal of remaking America in their image since getting their butts kicked during Watergate. For Dems to match the GOP's relentlessness or even overwhelm it, they must go on the attack over and over and over again. They must, like the Terminator, never ever stop until their enemies are (politically) dead.

Lord knows the Right provides plenty of openings for liberals to attack them. All you have to do is choose a recent outrage, broadcast a message that said outrage proves that Republicans despise mom, apple pie, the American way, and everything that's good, and keep laying it on thicker than even you can stand. At first they'll try to ignore you, but if you keep it up they won't be able to resist issuing a response. Naturally, that's when they're doomed. Anyone can make an assertion about someone; once that someone tries to defend himself from that assertion, a discussion is underway. The subject has become valid fodder for discourse. Your victim can't move his agenda forward. He's bogged down until he's disposed of your accusation. With luck, you'll have yet another attack ready with which you can keep him distracted.

It seems counterintuitive, but big-ticket controversies like Gulf War II are difficult to use against Bush and the Republicans precisely because they're wrong on so many levels. They're so complex that leftists have trouble agreeing about which evil is the worst or offers the most political potential. Some opposed the invasion of Iraq as pacifists; they oppose all violence. Other liberals focus on the administration's lies about Saddam's fictional weapons of mass destruction and supposed ties between Saddam Hussein and September 11. Some favored the war in theory but chide the Pentagon for failing to prepare for the anarchic period after the capture of Baghdad. Still others think Bush's main sin was to slight the international community by going in without U.N. approval. Americans heard these liberal factions go after Bush on all of these fronts; they canceled each other in a din of invective. The critics, it seemed, couldn't get their story straight.

Other would-be scandals remain stillborn because they can't be explained in a few words—a corallary of bumper sticker politics. In Iran Contra, President Reagan was accused of striking a secret deal with the nacent Islamic Republic of Iran wherein the Iranians promised to hold American hostages from the Tehran embassy until after the 1980 election so that Jimmy Carter would be denied an "October Surprise" that might have swept him to reelection. In addition, Reagan secretly sold arms to the Iranians to raise a slush fund for the benefit of anti-Sandinista right-wing "contra" fighters that Congress had proscribed the government from suporting. Part of the scheme involved money laundering through a bank account in the name of the Sultan of Brunei. According to the *San Jose Mercury-News*, the CIA may also have imported cocaine into inner-city America as part of Iran-Contra, sparking the 1980s crack epidemic that led to hundreds of murders on urban streets in order to supplement the Nicaraguan counterrevolution and prop up El Salvador's military dictatorship.

Confused yet? Most people were. That's why, aside from a few iconic Congressional hearings starring Oliver North and the delectable Fawn Hall—both of whom kept their "I was just following orders" defense simple, incidentally—Iran-Contra didn't catch fire.

The hottest scandals are easily comprehensible. They offer a resolution that's as obvious as it is damaging. From a GOP perspective, Monicagate fulfilled only the first qualification. "The married president had sex with an intern young enough to be his daughter" was gettable. That left the question of justice. Clinton deserved punishment, but people couldn't agree what form it should take. Most people thought impeachment was too severe and that doing nothing wasn't enough, but what form of rebuke would be just right? Censure, forced resignation, disbarment—we considered them all. Tales of snapping thongs and unorthodox cigar humidors notwithstanding, the scandal fizzled because Republicans couldn't agree which punishment to demand.

Democrats know that bigotry is Republicanism's dirty secret. Much of the GOP's right-wing base is composed of anti-Semites, racists, sexists, and homophobes attracted by a platform that explicitly scapegoats the disadvantaged and sends subtle signals designed to convey tacit support for extremists. The decision of Lousiana Republicans to allow former Klansman David Duke to serve on their state committee is one example. Bush's 2000 campaign speech at Bob Jones University, a brazenly racist and anti-Catholic institution, is another. "Don't you boys worry," Bush's wink-wink-nudge-nudge to his racist constituency said, "I'm one of you. I may have a few blacks in my cabinet, but that doesn't mean I like 'em."

Most of the time Republican bigwigs are smart enough to confine their anti-black and anti-gay remarks to one another over martinis in the privacy of their no-Jews-need-apply country clubs. Every now and then, however, one lets out a big honking brain fart in public. Such bigotry eruptions are inevitable, and Democrats rightly try to use them to get some political traction.

Rick Santorum, a Republican who afflicts the otherwise proud state of Pennsylvania as one of its two U.S. senators, let fly with such a boner in a 2003 interview with the Associated Press. Asked about a recent court ruling overturning anti-sodomy statutes, Santorum replied: "If the Supreme Court says that you have the right to consensual sex within your home, then you have the right to bigamy, you have the right to polygamy, you have the right to incest, you have the right to adultery." Homosexuals weren't pleased that the senator compared their acts of consensual sex with incest. Democrats barraged the media with statements deploring his "apparently" anti-gay remarks. To be fair, that's not what Santorum was getting at. He meant to make a legalistic slippery-slope argument, to claim that it would be dangerous for government to relinquish its "right" to regulate sexual activity simply because it occurred in a private dwelling. I suspect that his Democratic colleagues realized that and that's why they didn't go after him full-throttle.

The fact remains, however, that Santorum *is* anti-gay. His remark equating gay sex with incest doesn't explicitly prove it per se, but his votes in the Senate and other public statements create a pattern of homophobia that's unmistakable. Two lines later in the same interview, by the way, was a more telling yet less widely reported exchange. Homosexuality may not be as bad as "man on child, man on dog, or whatever the case may be," Santorum said. The man hates men who love men—that's all there is to it.

It's not just Santorum, described by the *New York Times* as "a new young face of the conservative movement of his party," who hates gays and lesbians. During a 2000 Republican primary debate, radical Right candidate Alan Keyes—who has literally called for me to be "shot" or "jailed" because I oppose Bush's aggressive, militaristic foreign agenda—decried "the radical homosexual agenda." Neither George W. Bush nor other Republican candidates, standing a few feet away on the same podium, stood up to disagree with him. With the overwhelming majority of Americans, including many Republicans, supporting gay rights, it would be fair—and more importantly, smart—for liberals to go after the GOP as homophobes and gay-bashers.

Santorum's remarks created an easily understood outrage: "Republican senator says gays are dog-fuckers." Appropriate censure was fairly obvious: if you said something like that at *your* job, you'd probably get fired. A mere apology—which, in any event, Santorum refused to issue—couldn't possibly have erased the ugliness of his words. They should have become a central talking point for Democrats as well as the centerpiece of a TV ad campaign to run in his home state demanding that he resign at once.

"Gay Pennsylvanians want the same things we all do," a DNC attack ad could have led off after showing the relevant quote. "Their own home. A chance to succeed. Like you and me, they want to be left alone to lead their lives. But when it comes to gays, Rick Santorum agrees with Hitler and the KKK." (Show black-and-white footage of a cross-burning.) "Rick Santorum hates gay and lesbian Pennsylvanians. Pennsylvania doesn't need Santorum's brand of bigotry. Call President Bush and demand Santorum's resignation."

"Washington is a town filled with cannibals," said Pennsylvania's other senator, Arlen Specter, at the peak of the Santorum buzz. "The cannibals devoured Trent Lott [the GOP Speaker of the House forced to resign after praising Strom Thurmond's segregationist 1948 presidential bid] without cause. If the cannibals are after you, you are in deep trouble. It depends on whether the cannibals are hungry. My guess is that it will blow over."

Specter guessed right. Democrats whiffed yet another perfect chance to stir up the capital's cannibals. Forcing Santorum to resign would have tipped the fifty-fifty Senate in their favor, deprived the GOP of one of its rising stars and forced them to make statements in favor of gays, alienating them from part of their homophobic contingent. It could have been a perfectly lovely scandal, if only Democrats had understood its full potential—and been willing to pursue it to its glorious end.

PAYING ATTENTION

Most promising scandals wither on the vine of the day's events without being recognized as potential fodder. News stories that could spark outrage across party lines, dash old allegiances and become a rival's ideological albatross for years to follow are frequently allowed to slip away unnoticed. Whether such oversights are caused by insufficient imagination, distraction by other battles, or flawed assessments of their value, there are more lost opportunities to inflict political damage in an average week than are attempted in a year.

I was astonished, for example, when Democrats dropped the ball on a shocking story that had the Bush administration suing Gulf War veterans.

In April of 2002, when Saddam Hussein was still in power, seventeen vets of the first Persian Gulf War and their families sued the government of Iraq in U.S. federal court under a 1996 law that allows plaintiffs to bring claims against foreign governments designated as state sponsors of terrorism. (Iraq was branded with this status due to charges that it funded the Hamas and Hezbollah organizations in occupied Palestine.) The former soldiers alleged that their Iraqi captors had physically and mentally abused them as prisoners of war in 1991. The Iraqis never sent a representative to court, dooming their defense. In July 2003, after Hussein's government was deposed, Judge Richard Roberts, ruling for the ex-prisoners, wrote that "only a very sizable award would be likely to deter the torture of American POWs by agencies of Iraq or other terrorist states in the future." He ordered that the former Baath Party regime pay almost $1 billion to the seventeen plaintiffs: $653 million in compensatory damages and $306 million in punitive damages. Fortunately, there was more than $1 billion sitting in Iraqi Baathist-era bank accounts in the United States. The veterans' lawyers slapped a lien on the dough, freezing it until a judge could cut checks to the war heroes.

"No amount of money can truly compensate these brave men and women for the suffering that they went through at the hands of a truly brutal regime," said White House spokesman Scott McClellan. He meant that literally. Bush's State and Justice Department lawyers filed motions intended to insure that the vets received "no amount of money." (Legal experts expect the administration to prevail.) Why didn't the Bushies want the vets to collect their judgment? "Those assets," McClellan said, "were resources required for the urgent nationals security needs of the rebuilding Iraq." Paul Bremer III, chief administrator of occupied Iraq, swore out an affidavit claiming that "restricting these funds as a result of this litigation would affect adversely the ability of the United States to achieve security and stability in the region."

At the time that Bremer signed his statement, U.S. forces in Iraq were suffering an average of thirty-five attacks from resistance forces, claiming an average of two deaths and twenty-five serious injuries, every day. And that was *with* the POW's extra billion bucks. Neither security nor stability were in great supply.

Despite Bremer's statement, denying the ex-POWs access to the money they won in court won't make much of difference in the long run. Relative to the minimum $500 billion total estimated cost of rebuilding and occupying Iraq over five years, of which more than $87 billion had been appropriated at the time, $1 billion was "just a drop in the bucket"— one-fifth of one percent—in the words of Colonel David Eberly, a pilot the Iraqis subjected to mock executions after his F-15 was shot down.

"It never occurred to me in my wildest dreams that I would see our government coming in on the side of Saddam Hussein and his regime to absolve them of responsibility for the brutal torture of Americans." Who said that: Hillary Clinton? Ted Kennedy? Dick Gephardt? It was John Norton Moore, professor of national security law at the University of Virginia and one of the POWs' lawyers, but it should have been a Democrat leading the charge against Bush.

"George Bush thinks a woman shouldn't get paid more than $250,000 if a doctor mistakenly removes one of her breasts," one can imagine an outraged Hillary on the evening news, "but this is taking tort reform too far. What kind of treasonous president sides with the enemy—a *defeated* enemy—against his own soldiers?"

Democrats should have arranged a press conference for the vets fiscally fragged by their own government. "I feel betrayed," Cynthia Acree, wife of a Marine colonel held by Iraq for forty-seven days, told the *Times*. Can you imagine the rage of the American public if they knew what "their" president was up to? But there was no press conference. There were no angry speeches on the floor of the Senate. There were no appearances on the Sunday morning political talk shows. Democrats did nothing, the vets got the shaft, and another chance to do good while getting even fell down the memory hole, reduced to faded newspaper clippings and expired URLs.

DIRTY POLITICS 101

The first rule of gutter politics is that anything goes. The second is that not everything is worth doing.

Going after Bush for his intellectual shortcomings, for example, might seem truthful and pertinent. Anyone who watches the man speak intuits that he's an idiot. It's hard to escape the obvious conclusion that we'd be better off with a smarter person as leader of the free world. But on this point everybody's opinions are already formulated. You can't draw attention to a fact that's common knowledge; people who think the man's a genius aren't about to change their minds. Pointing out Bush's lack of intelligence, reminding America that their commander-in-chief refuses to crack open a newspaper, would be a waste of energy.

Sleazy attacks on figures perceived as disadvantaged can backfire. The first President Bush's Willie Horton ads may have helped his campaign, but they harmed the Republican Party's efforts to recruit black voters and candidates. And implications that Senator Max Cleland—a decorated Vietnam War veteran who lost three limbs in the war—didn't care about defense were deemed to have gone too far.

Forget the stuff everyone already knows. It's usually more fruitful to draw the people's attention to a small, easily comprehensible revelation that's well sourced yet underreported. Bush's AWOL years during Vietnam are a good example. They reflect a flaw of personal character that few people knew about until recently. When I receive e-mail from irate members of the military demanding that I stop criticizing their hard-charging leader in the war on terrorism, I respond by sending them links to news stories that describe how Bush used family connections to ensure that he not be drafted and to land a safe spot in the Texas Air National Guard, from which he ultimately went AWOL and deserted. "I didn't know that" is a typical response, sometimes followed by "I'm going to tell the other guys." The Bush AWOL story, coupled with his willingness to wear military uniforms for political gain, is a great potential scandal. It undermines Bush's phony image as a pillar of strength ready and willing to fight any war to defend us, and it proves that he's a hypocrite. Had Bush addressed and put it to rest earlier ("I was young but now I regret that I didn't serve"), the

AWOL story would be dead. Instead, the fact that the desertion story has been buried actually increases its potency.

Beyond the truth lies more treacherous ground: insinuating *possible truth*. In this category lies stuff like stories that Bush did pot and coke. Currently there isn't any hard proof, but a whispering campaign (on liberal talk radio, perhaps?) might inspire someone to come forward with the goods. And there's always the possibility of taking things all the way, as Republicans do when the going gets tough, to outright lying. Examples: Bush was a cheerleader at Yale. Could he be gay or bisexual? Would that explain Laura's mannishness? Nobody believes Bush's story that he fell out of a chair while chewing on a pretzel. Is he back on the sauce? Why won't he submit to regular blood alcohol tests?

Timing attacks for maximum payoff is of paramount importance. Documentary proof of Bush's DWI arrest and subsequent cover-up didn't surface until a few days before November 7, 2000. It would have been better if the Gore campaign had released that information—information that could have been especially damaging to a "family values" candidate who promised to restore the rule of law, order and dignity to the White House—about three weeks earlier. Stories need time to percolate through media outlets, draw new witnesses and accusers to propel and expand upon them, until they result in a negative national consensus. Gore didn't do anything with this particular story. Even if he had, its timing wouldn't have been perfect. You have to strike when people are paying attention, early enough to generate some heat but late enough in the game that they're still thinking about it when they head to the polls.

AN ETHICAL LINE IN THE SAND

Last up is Advanced Dirty Tricks, the kind of stuff Nixon's henchmen excelled at. Wiretapping, blackballing, money laundering, bribe taking, ballot stuffing, voter intimidation up to and including violence are currently part and parcel of the Republican repertoire. They will always be part of the political process. My advice to Democrats is not to cross the line from the dastardly bastard zone to the mental place occupied by loathsome creatures like G. Gordon Liddy. If it would break the law, don't do it.

The liberal values that form the core ideology of the party, if properly advertised and defended—yes, with a strong offense—appeal to more Americans than not. If the Left promotes itself, it will win. Unless something happens that breaks precedent with all of recorded history, there will always be more poor and middle-income people than the wealthy folks whose interests the Republicans work so hard to defend.

The numbers are on our side. We need to cut corners and get aggressive to fend off the well-organized conservative minority, but we don't have to go *berzerker* in the lawbreaking department in order to win.

Beware, however, of the earnest liberal mantra that maintains that if we act like our enemies, we become them. We *want* to become like our enemies in one important respect—we want to defeat them. Republicans despised Franklin D. Roosevelt because he bullied Congress, unfairly smeared opponents, broke tradition to run for four terms, lied to con us into getting involved in World War II and even tried to stack the Supreme Court by amending the Constitution in order to add more justices—FDR-appointed justices. On the other hand, he used those vile tactics to create Social Security, end the Great Depression, fight a just war against fascism, and defend workers' rights. If we keep our eyes on the prize, the means we use to achieve victory needn't necessarily corrupt the ends.

chapter 9

GETTING THE LEFT TOGETHER

The inherent contradiction of a whole society banding together to assist tightly differentiated groups begs the question of "what's in it for me?"

—Derek Larson, College of Saint Benedict
and Saint John's University, 1994

Lefties are selfish. The problem is, they're never selfish in the right way. What on the surface appears to be a massive coalition of like-minded activists is in reality an unwieldy alliance of splinter groups, each pursuing its own narrowly focused short-term interest. "The very conservative wing [of the Democratic Party] has almost completely deserted to the Republican Party," writes Adam Clymer. "But the Democrats are still a coalition of interests, notably African-Americans, labor, feminists, and all-purpose liberals." Pro-abortion activists can't be counted upon to show up for the animal rights rally; anti–free traders give little more than lip service to the cause of gay and lesbian rights. And these interest groups are further subdivided into infinitely narrower shades that advocate particular approaches to their causes. Advocates for the rights of transgendered and bisexual people complain that mainline gay rights groups don't give them the time of day. Tribalism is the defining feature of the American Left.

Republican officials, on the other hand, vigorously enforce a "big tent" strategy. After they win an election, when they have finally obtained the power to promote an agenda, they ask their various constituencies to wait their turn while they work to achieve whatever they determine to be their top priority. They work tirelessly to ensure that the Right doesn't disintegrate into leftist-style balkanization. During the late nineties, when the GOP was gearing up for the 2000 presidential election, party honchos struggledto keep fundamentalist Christian groups under wraps. These zealous "family values" rightists, dedicated to their goals of outlawing abortion and eroding the constitutional separation between church and state, have the unfortunate tendency of drawing attention to themselves in untoward ways—but they do know how to get out the vote.

In order not to scare off swing voters, Republicans try to maintain their relationship with the Bible thumper set on the down low. Every now and again, however, the Christian Right tires of being treated like the party's ugly stepsister. In 1995 James Dobson, head of a Christian fundamentalist organization called Focus on the Family, threatened to leave the Republican Party and to take his two million members along with him unless GOP leaders began taking his group's concerns more seriously. Dobson told the Associated Press: "Republicans are taking a walk on moral issues such as abortions and gays in the military. If they continue to pursue a 'big tent' strategy that avoids taking a stand on moral issues in the interest of party unity, it will be conservative Christians who walk out in large enough numbers to insure a Democratic victory." Had a liberal group numbering two million people—more than enough to decide most elections—threatened to leave the Democratic Party, it's a safe bet that party leaders would have caved into their demands. Not the GOP. Republican leaders, figuring that Dobson was bluffing, refused to give an inch. Where else would he go? It's not like Focus on the Family voters were about to run off and join the Democrats. And a voter strike, sitting out elections in order to allow liberals to win, was an empty threat. It's even harder to ask activists to sit out an election than it is to convince them to change sides.

In the end, Dobson was silenced. He didn't call for a boycott. The Republicans kept the Christian Right.

After George W. Bush seized power in 2000, lobbyists for a host of right-wing special interests lined up at the trough, expecting to secure everything they had been hoping for during the Clinton years: the overturn of *Roe v. Wade*, elimination of tariffs, tax cuts, smaller government, you name it. But they were quickly disabused of their expectations. As one news story put it in 2002, "[The religious rightists and New Rightists] complain that Bush has increasingly chosen political expedience over principle: supporting campaign finance reform after promising to veto it, imposing tariffs on imported steel despite his free-trading rhetoric, expanding federal power in response to the threat of terrorism, and choosing moderates over conservatives in a few Republican Congressional primaries." Principle, the Bushies told them, would have to wait longer still.

"During the Reagan years," David Brooks wrote, "Republicans tried to cut the size of government and failed, then blamed the Democrats controlling Congress. In 1995, Republicans tried to reduce the size of government and failed, then blamed the Democrats controlling the White House. Now

Republicans control everything, and [since 2001] the size of government has *still* increased, not even counting the war on terror." (Emphasis is Brooks's.)

So why didn't the right-wing base revolt? A telling example of how Republicans keep their big tent from blowing over comes straight out of Texas.

The Lone Star State's Log Cabin Republicans, a group of gay and lesbian conservatives, became annoyed when, during the 2000 campaign, Texas GOP officials started moving against gay rights more aggressively than the national party. (Bush, leading his party's charge against homosexuals, had recently come out against gay marriage, saying that officially sanctioned betrothal should only be permitted between men and women.) Angry Texas Log Cabin Republicans resorted to attacking their own party. They issued a press release describing their state party leadership as "very extreme and out of touch with the mainstream voter and mainstream Republican in Texas . . . They think it's fine to discriminate against gay Republicans."

This volatile press release had the potential to expose a schism within the party in Bush's home state, which could have embarrassed the national party. In a nation that is becoming increasingly friendly to the proposition that gays and lesbians ought to be free to live their lives however they choose, the split-off might well have cost the national party votes among moderates and swing voters as well as conservative homosexuals. It was a geniune crisis, but you probably never heard of the imbroglio at the time. Here's why.

Steve Labinski, head of the Texas Log Cabin Republicans, can personally attest that GOP party discipline comes from the top. "The Bush campaign had nothing to do with the state party convention, but they have had everything to do with the national convention," he said after national officials had reached out to smooth his ruffled feathers. "I think that people are watching the national convention right now and seeing that the whole of them are outreaching to untraditional groups and talking to every voter. The Bush campaign has liaisons that meet with us. It's their job . . . Log Cabin and gay delegates in general are more involved and are being treated better than ever." After meeting with the Log Cabin Republicans, Bush campaign officials asked the Texas GOP to "soften and take out much of the anti-gay language as possible from the platform." This they did, Labinski & Co. dropped their crusade and all was well with the world.

As he often does, Bush welched in the long run. If anything he hardened his anti-gay stance after moving into the White House, making remarks that made the excised anti-homosexual sections of the Texas Republican platform pale by comparison. But he kept the Log Cabin Republicans happy enough, long enough, to garner their crucial votes during a tight election.

It's easy to see why a national political party must enforce unit cohesion. According to the Voter News Service, Bush received a surprisingly high 25 percent of the gay vote—in Florida, itcertainly amounted to more than his official 537-vote margin. But what do the interest groups get out of putting up and shutting up?

In the case of the Texas Log Cabin Republicans, not much. Bush appointed John Ashcroft, a staunch opponent of homosexual rights, as attorney general. He picked Gale Norton, who fought for an anti-gay rights initiative as attorney general of Colorado, as secretary of the interior. He maintained the Clinton-era "don't ask, don't tell" policy on gays serving in the military. His ballyhooed plan to fight AIDS in Africa turned out to be a bait-and-switch scheme in which no new funds were actually allocated. And he came out in favor of a constitutional amendment banning gay marriage. But Bush understood that his small gay constituency would have to be pushed hard—really, really hard—before it would defect to the Democrats. The Log Cabin types, you see, are Republicans who happen to be gay, not gays who happen to be Republican. Their loyalty was a given. They couldn't credibly threaten to barter it away or offer it up to the highest bidder.

From the standpoint of the various interest groups that compose a party, the big tent philosophy is a variation on European-style parliamentary democracy. Under the European system, small political parties form coalitions in order to create a ruling majority in parliament. The system only works so long as each member party of the coalition feels that its platform is adequately addressed in the form of legislation and other initiatives. If one feels ignored, it drops out or tries to form a coalition with another voting bloc. Either way, the government collapses. In a big tent coalition forming a single party, no single interest-driven segment can spark wholesale defeat, at least not overnight, so the challenge is subtle as well as daunting. If you allow too many adherents to slip away one day you wake up to find yourself in the minority. By then it's too late. Thus smart party leaders treat all of their coalition members as important partners, rewarding and entreating them, even as they ask each for patience and cooperation. One challenge for Democrats hoping to form a solid, loyal coalition to replace their current messy amalgamation of splinter groups is to force each group to wait its turn while simultaneously doling out rewards whenever it becomes feasible to do so.

COALESCING THE EXISTING LIBERAL COALITION

Republicans are working to lure away "traditional Democratic constituencies" such as Latinos, blacks, and Jews because, according to Bush pollster Matthew Dowd, "before Democrats can go after swing voters, they have to solidify their base." It is imperative that the Left not take the bait by obsessing on its base at the expense of efforts to attract new adherents. After all, increasing the number of Americans who think of themselves as Democratic is every bit as important as convincing them that liberalism is mainstream. But unlike Gerald Ford, we can walk and chew gum at the same time. Along with attracting moderates and conservatives, recapturing and energizing traditionally liberal voters must become a top priority for the Democratic Party.

Democrats got close to achieving reunification in 1992. As Jacob Weisberg wrote in *Slate*: "Bill Clinton touched all the party's erogenous zones, wooing each faction into the illusion that he loved it alone. After the inauguration, each awoke to the realization that the president was a policy polygamist. Disappointed by Clinton's too-sweeping healthcare reform plan and his failure to cut spending, the Democratic Leadership Council trashed him openly and, at one point, even considered breaking off from the party. Disenchanted by Clinton's pursuit of free trade expansion, labor largely sat out the 1994 midterm [election]. That election taught all of them that there are things worse than partial victory. In Newt Gingrich and the Republican radicals, Democrats new and old found the unifying force of a common enemy. Whether you wanted charter schools and tradable pollution credits or higher pay for teachers and EPA mandates, you didn't want the federal government to abdicate all responsibility for education and the environment. And with the President defending against an anti-government assault wave, there was no need to settle on a Democratic agenda. The question of what new programs to support would be a largely theoretical exercise, at least for a while."

"We're all on the same team." CEOs drop that line on employees whose salaries are 1/400th of their own; coaches use it to convince players who spend whole seasons warming the bench to show up to practice—just to sit on that stupid bench again. Of course it's a big lie, but much of politics is predicated on just that kind of falsehood. Clinton's technique, which extrapolated his charming habit of making whomever he was talking to at a given moment feel like she was the center of the world—"When he talks to you, he is 100 percent involved with you," gushed his friend Vinod Gupta—charmed everyone from the Audubon Society to the AFL-CIO. Where Clinton went wrong, and why he didn't have a unified party to pass on to Vice President Gore, is that he failed to pay off these groups with meaningful concessions.

"Don't worry, I won't forget you" works for a while but not forever. Stalling has a time limit. Eventually you have to reward your allies' patience or they'll drift away to a rival suitor. Ralph Nader cost Al Gore the presidency mainly by drawing away the votes of disenfranchised liberals who, had they been convinced that Gore planned to govern in occaisional accordance with their beliefs, would have voted Democratic. Most Naderites were dismayed by Clinton's Republican Lite approach to governance and expected Gore to follow suit. Liberals, and particularly young people, had voted for Clinton in high numbers in 1992; eight years later, they hadn't gotten anything for their trouble. Clinton appointed black judges but pushed for welfare reform—which disproportionately affected blacks. He named women to his cabinet but his biggest legislative sop to the second sex was a weak parental leave bill that forces employers to give workers *unpaid* time off so they can care for their newborn babies. Females and minorities voted Democratic in lesser numbers than usual.

Generation Xers, the demographic group most responsible for the Democrats' 1992 win, weren't rewarded with so much as a percentage point shaved off their student loan repayment rates. Young people began to drift across party lines. Gore said nothing during the 2000 campaign to indicate that he planned a more liberal presidency than Clinton's. (One complaint muttered by the MTV generation but never mentioned by mainstream political analysts was that Gore's wife Tipper had never apologized for her role as a 1980s music censor.) By 2003 a third of people under thirty called themselves Republicans, up from a quarter in 1983, an exact mirror reversal of the age distribution for Democrats. Democrats threw away the youth vote.

Prescription drug benefits for senior citizens, a patients' bill of rights, school uniforms—they were attempts to pass insignificant laws that, if enacted, would barely have improved the lives of relatively small segments of the population. Bigger ideas mean bigger payoffs to interest groups. When signed into law, they also buy more patience in the future.

BROADENING THE COALITION

Clinton's habit of ignoring or paying off his constituent groups with teensy-weensy favors blended the worst of both political worlds. Traditional liberal allies such as trade unionists and environmentalists only became slightly vested in him and his party. They didn't work as hard for him or his chosen successor. Meanwhile swing voters and open-minded Republicans—people who, if they paid attention to their paychecks or were targeted more effectively, could be convinced to reclassify themselves as liberals—were turned off. Only 11 percent of self-described white male conservatives (a record low) voted for Al Gore.

Kowtowing to a traditional ally can go too far. When Republicans proposed a ban on partial-birth abortion, Democrats rallied against it because they saw the bill for what it was: an attempt to incrementally roll back a woman's right to an abortion. Democratic lawmakers also knew what the public didn't: the GOP bill (which ultimately passed and became law) was so vaguely written that it prohibits a lot more than the gruesome eighth-month procedure described in news reports. If the results of a pregnant woman's amniocentesis determines that her fetus probably has Down's syndrome, aborting it is illegal under the partial-birth ban. This is because amniocentesis is usually performed in the second trimester, which necessitates the partial-birth procedure. If most Americans had known what the Republicans were really up to, they would have opposed this legislation.

As it happened, they didn't know jack. Rather than attempt to educate citizens about the implications of the new law (surely groups like NOW and NARAL Pro-Choice America might have run a few TV prime-time ads to inform the public), Democrats worked the incremental slippery-slope angle in public appearances: take away partial-birth now and all abortions will be banned later. The problem is that Americans don't know from slippery slope. They have next to no knowledge of history. They don't remember what happened when Reagan tried trickle-down or when Saddam was an American ally. They don't see the correlation between Bush's detention camps for Muslims and the Nuremberg laws. Every situation is new and nothing like what's going on now—whatever that is—has ever happened before. Francis Fukuyama declared December 25, 1991, the end of history, but he was wrong. In America, history never begins.

"The voters say they do not want partial-birth abortion," said Democratic pollster Celinda Lake. "On the other hand, they do not want anything that would interfere with saving the life or the health of the mother. They have a very hard time figuring out what is at stake here, and what is really the issue." Neither Democrats nor Republicans made it any clearer.

Ironically, when Dems stood up for a popular right—a woman's ability to obtain an abortion on demand—they ended up getting their butts kicked. They were perceived as defending a bizarre, unusual procedure on the outer edges of what most folks think to be abortion. More than 90 percent of the American public—most of whome favor abortion rights—sided with the Republicans on the partial-birth issue. To white males who had already drifted away to the right, the liberals—who were actually fighting off hard-right extremists—looked like radicals. Standing up for *basic* abortion rights, while pushing for a ban on third trimester abortions where the mother's health isn't endangered, would have been a smarter posture. Smarter still would be to concede, as few pro-choicers do, that life begins at conception. The abortion debate weighs the awful choice between murdering unborn children and forcing women into societal body slavery reminiscent of Margaret Atwood's *The Handmaid's Tale*. Given these grim options, liberals should argue, allowing women the right to kill their unborn babies is the lesser of two evils. The partial-birth debate pushes Democrats away from this ideal stance. Fighting for what pro-lifers presented as an exceptionally extreme version of those rights set off the average American's common-sense alarm. Even the venerable Democratic ex-senator from New York, Patrick Moynihan, mused that Democrats ought to have voted against partial-birth abortion.

BIG IDEAS

Democrats espouse majority principles but tend to assert them in ways designed to appeal to tiny minorities. They persist in this approach although recent electoral routs demonstrate that cobbling together liberal interests no longer works. "During the 35 years of dominance from FDR's New Deal through LBJ's Great Society," Matt Bai wrote in the *New York Times Magazine*, Democrats constructed what Gary Hart, the former senator and presidential candidate, calls an 'ideological cathedral': the GI Bill, welfare, Social Security, Medicare and Medicaid, voting rights. But . . . leading Democrats have fallen into the role of protecting their fathers' agenda from attack rather than inventing a vision of their own. 'There have been bits and pieces of an agenda,' Hart said recently. 'Somebody had an idea about healthcare. Somebody had an idea about education. But nobody's pulled it all together.'"

What do Americans want more than anything else? Peace, prosperity, a better life for themselves and their children. Not having to worry so much—about crime, losing their jobs, falling behind on their bills, getting blown up by a terrorist bomb. Basic stuff. They want their government to defend their borders, maintain an army, pave roads, teach kids. They want business to provide good jobs and the opportunity to let them make something of themselves. As long as they don't hurt anyone else, Americans believe that the government should leave them alone to do whatever they want.

Neither the Democrats nor the Republicans currently espouse a platform that looks anything like the above paragraph, and though both parties have their adherents, neither has captured fervent enthusiasm or devotion among the general public. Democrats think that white men deserve to lose out on jobs, raises, and slots in top colleges simply because some other white guys, usually not even related to them, enslaved blacks way back when. That's a major bummer if you're an average white guy trying to get ahead. Republicans say that your problem is just that: your problem. If you lose your job because some CEO stole the company's money and ran off to Tahiti, tough titties. Laissez-faire conservatives are not very good at making people worry less.

Since Republicans are currently on a roll, they're unlikely to accept my suggestion to adopt a platform that conforms to my description of what Amerincans want—a platform that I've expanded upon in the next and final chapter. Democrats, conversely, are desperately looking for answers. It so happens that their outlook is already closer to the model of an enlightened party whose ideas appeal to the broadest possible cross-section of the American public. Democrats would need to make fewer adjustments than Republicans to become the party of the overwhelming majority of Americans.

Nonetheless, the Democratic mindset still has a lot of ground to cover, especially when it comes to strategy. Liberals inside Washington are still spinning their wheels, scheming to replicate Grover Norquist's "K Street Project," which Paul Krugman reports "places Republican activists in high-level corporate and industry lobbyist jobs—and excludes Democrats." (To be sure, this back-channel co-option of corporate America is a dazzling bit of manipulation that effectively increases the number of Republican advocates in Congress through the back door. But if liberals are smart, they can ensure that the knife cuts both ways by forcing Republicans to increase their reliance on corporate backers.) Bai's *Times Magazine* article describes John Podesta's Center for American Progress and its groundbreaking attempt to sell the Democratic Party on a "big idea" agenda. So what exactly are these "big ideas" that will "reinvent the wheel of Democratic thought"?

First up, they say, is "a flatter tax." A flatter tax like Steve Forbes' old flat tax, but instead of taking a piece of your income it would also cover investment and capital gains income. Next comes "a solution to the three-fighter-jet problem in the military." Then there's "a project to address long-term challenges facing public education, relying on academics who *may* have innovative solutions." [my italics]

Yawwwwwwwwwwwn.

Taxes are important. So is military spending. But I've got news for Podesta's wonks: nobody *knows* that there is a three-fighter-jet problem and no one *cares*. Successful marketing of big ideas to the public requires simple, easy-to-describe descriptions. Otherwise they won't sell. Democrats' elusive bumper-sticker slogans will fail unless they kick serious ass: lower taxes for ordinary Americans. A little long, but it sure beats "a flatter tax," whatever the hell that is. Oh, and let's forget the boring education study. Until you have your solution to the education crisis ready in slogan format—Equal Education for All—it won't be ready for public consumption.

The strategic focus of Podesta and others considered by media and political insiders to be the nation's leading liberal thinkers is the rarified world they know best: the tiny circle of land encompassed by the Washington Beltway; "three hundredsquare miles surrounded by reality," Tom Clancy called it. Believe it or not, what America's Big Liberal Thinkers say American liberalism needs more than anything else is—hold your breath ten counts—a "think tank on steroids." If he can line up the money, Podesta says, his new organization would "recruit hundreds of fellows and scholars . . . to research new progressive policy ideas." They'd launch an "edgy website." They'd "book liberal thinkers on cable TV."

"[Republicans] have a dozen think tanks, and we have none," grouses House Minority Leader Tom Daschle.

A website? Yeah, that'll help. How very twentieth century. I'm sorry, but cable TV producers already know where to find liberals. Trust me on this: if you live in New York and you're good for a snappy witticism in a sixty-second segment, you'll get called. They'll even send a car to pick you up. The trouble is that that's all the guys from CNN, MSNBC, and Fox

News want: leftie foils for hosts whose ideological positions span the range from Giuliani to Genghis conservative. Creating a booking agency dedicated to liberal luminaries isn't going to change that.

Of course there's nothing wrong with the idea of a liberal think tank. (Just ask the Brookings Institute.) When Podesta points out that the right "built up institutions with a lot of influence, a lot of ideas" starting in the sixties, he's right to note their signifigance. But think tanks weren't critical to the rise of the American right in subsequent decades. Ideas, or more accurately the *perception of ideas*, were.

There were bumps along the way, but liberalism triumphed throughout most of the twentieth century. It tamed the excesses of the Industrial Revolution with labor laws and anti-trust legislation, exploited and cured the Depression by creating a social safety net, and led the charge to defeat the totalitarian Axis in World War II—a horror we'd still be living with had things been left to isolationist conservatives. The postwar period saw the expansion of individual rights. The sociopolitical status of ethnic minorities, women, homosexuals, and handicapped people was elevated closer to that of straight, able-bodied white males. We've come so far that "fat acceptance" is just about the final frontier of civil rights. Egalitarianism and liberalism have become synonymous.

American society wasn't perfect—not by a long shot. It still isn't. But as any seventy-year-old American woman can certify, the amount of social progress she has seen during her life has been breathtaking. She came of age in a nation where blacks weren't allowed to eat at the same restaurants as whites and abortion was illegal. Gays were jailed just for being gay; now they can walk down the street holding hands. Every president but one has been a white male Protestant (and even he was a white male Christian), but there's no denying that we've come a long way.

By 1980 liberals found themselves in a position not dissimilar to imperial Rome at the peak of its expansion: overextended, anxious to consolidate their gains, and wary of conquering new ground lest they lose what they had achieved. God knows there was plenty left to be done. All liberals had to do was look out their car windows during the drive from the Beltway to the Capitol, where they passed block after block of decrepit, violent slums. LBJ's War on Poverty created the welfare system—conservatives dubbed it "the nanny state"—but welfare wasn't helping America's vast and growing underclass. The trouble was, it was taboo, even among liberals, to think about class differentiation as the root cause of American poverty. Blacks, post-Vietnam liberals believed, were poor soley because they were victimized by racism. Women earned fifty-nine cents to every dollar collected by men because of sexism.

It was important to understand how discrimination translates to economic disadvantage. On average, blacks are poorer than whites, women poorer than men, children poorer than the elderly. But discrimination isn't destiny. Gays are richer than straights, Asians score higher on standardized tests than whites. The Democrats' obsession with identity politics drove the party into right into an intellectual wall. In his book *The Long Detour: The History and Future of the American Left*, historian and *In These Times* editor James Weinstein writes: "In the absence of a left based on universal principles, many little lefts for which the [1960s-era] New Left had acted as a catalyst survived and went their own ways." Moreover, Weinstein argues, feminist and gay groups alienated "a large working class constituency of 'Reagan Democrats' by slinging wacky slogans like 'smash monogamy' and 'destroy the nuclear family.' We needed to close the gap between rich and poor, regardless of how the gap had developed, but liberals refused to accept that they needed to reach out to white Appalachians with the same enthusiasm as urban blacks. The 'isms' caused poverty, they assumed, so they created programs to take on the 'isms.'"

Programs like affirmative action did help. Record numbers of African-Americans and Hispanics were admitted to colleges and universities and began climbing the corporate ladder. Since members of these minority groups had suffered disproportionately from poverty, the problem was partly ameliorated. But not everyone whose skin was dark was poor, and not everyone whose skin was white was rich. Millions remained behind.

When Reagan became president, liberals believed that they had done just about all they could to remake America in their image. Blinded to new ways of thinking about social needs and confidant that the gains they had won had become irremovable fixtures, they were taken by surprise when the Reagan "Revolution" (conservatives prefer the R-word to the real thing) attacked not only their minor initiatives but even the basic tenets of liberalism. The progressive tax code brought to life by Cordell Hull before World War I in order to reduce income disparity, Theodore Roosevelt's national park system, and even the Sherman Anti-Trust Act came under fire from rampaging conservatives.

Liberal legislators and interest groups manned their rhetorical Maginot Line to defend their ideological empire. The partnership between

Democrats and their allied constituent groups grew closer. A symbiotic relationship, Bai writes, degraded into dysfunction. "Got an idea to reform education? Not if it upsets the teachers' union. Figured out how to restructure Medicare? You'd better run it past the [American Association of Retired Persons]. 'There's just such an incredible timidity among Democrats,' says Ted Halstead [of the New America Foundation]. 'They dare not think outside the box for fear of being punished by one of their constituencies.'"

As Democrats and their liberal allies spoke up on behalf of their old victories, trying to spur the American people to action on matters they'd read about in high school history class, Reagan and the second Bush—Bush I was little more than a caretaker president—dazzled Americans with new ideas. Liberals talked about holding the line in Gaul. Forget that old crap, the right said. History is dead! Let's conquer new lands! Who's up for attacking Parthia?

Actually, most of the Republicans'"new ideas" were very old. School voucher plans transfer state and local taxpayers' funding for public schools to private and religious institutions, with the practical effect of undermining the nineteenth-century idea—successfully promulgated by liberals—that government owes its children a free education. More tax cuts to stimulate the economy are, well, just more of the same old tax cuts we saw under Reagan. The flat tax, wielded as a conservative foil in arguments to flatten the existing progressive income tax, was marketed as a way to "simplify" the tax code by making IRS forms less complicated to fill out. Once enacted, a flat tax would serve as a stepping stone for conservatives' real goal—getting rid of income taxes entirely, relying on sales and use taxes to collect government revenues. "Pay for what you buy" has a novel-sounding Puritan appeal, but it's just as ancient: the nineteenth-century robber barons grew rich and fat under the same regressive system. And both the national treasury and the average citizen were pauperized as a result.

Reagan's defense build-up was nothing new. It was merely a throwback to Eisenhower's military industrial complex. "Workfare" took a page from Dickensian England's debtors' prisons and workhouses for the dispossessed. Critics lambasted Bush II's doctrine of preemptive warfare, used to justify the invasion of Iraq, as "new" and without precedent. "Imagine establishing a precedent," Richard Falk wrote in the *Nation*, "that might be invoked by China to attack Taiwan preemptively, or India in relation to Kashmir." Right or wrong, preemptive warfare wasn't a new idea either.

Israel used it to justify bombing an Iraqi nuclear reactor two decades ago; Hitler said he had to invade Czechoslovakia to protect ethnic Germans in the Sudetenland. Hit-them-before-they-get-us-first augurs back to the days before Woodrow Wilson argued that peace would reign if every nation agrees not to attack first.

Taking advantage of Americans' ignorance of history, Republicans present their retrograde, reactionary, and antique agenda as new ideas.

On December 5, 2003, the *Washington Post* reported, Bush decided to ramp up a "big idea" strategy in preparation for the 2004 election. "Big works," an unnamed White House official told the paper. "Big grabs attention." Among the blockbusters Bush was considering were campaigns to increase human longevity, reduce hunger, or childhood diseases. The idea that first caught fire in the White House war room, however, was a mission to the moon—and when that failed, to Mars. Perhaps Bush forgot that we'd already been to the moon. Either that, or he's counting on the rest of us allowing Neil Armstrong to slip our minds.

Liberals can bemoan American ahistoricity all they like but whining won't change reality. Until our culture and educational system transform the American people into learned scholars of history, economics, and politics, those who work to defend "old ideas" will lose to those who claim to have a new plan.

What about protecting previous victories? Sometimes, in order to go after Britannia, you have to let Asia Minor go. The Social Security system, for example, is under such ferocious fiscal attack, squeezed between demographic problems related to Baby Boomer retirements and Republican schemes to privatize what little remains in its trust fund, that it may not be possible to save it. Sure it's a shame, but cutting bait now in favor of new ideas to provide for retired workers—forcing employers to provide portable fixed-benefit pensions or dedicating a percent of GDP into a national 401(k)—would surely attract Generation X voters convinced that they were never going to see a dime from Social Security anyway. Let the Republicans be blamed for killing the old system while taking credit for the new one.

Republicans want Democrats to stay on the defensive. Admitting that "the Republican Party is adrift domestically" and that "the accomplishments of the 20th century" were "mostly Democratic," David Brooks wants Republicans to appear as if they "progressively promote change, while Democrats remain the churlish defenders of the status quo." He suggests that Republicans use the banner of "reform" to bastardize Democratic programs. "Entitlement reform, tax reform, more welfare reform, education reform, immigration reform, tort reform and on and on." I say: let them. We have new territory to conquer.

Liberals can also steal the Republicans' idea-repackaging tactic. During the eighties, Democrats flirted with referring to expenditures on their favorite social programs as "investments." Just when this sales pitch was starting to catch on, they dropped it. There's that liberal problem again: no follow-through.

The ideal strategy, of course, is coming up with ideas that really *are* new. Solving problems that everyone has always ignored, the kind of systemic pains in the ass that we discussed in chapter 3, guarantees victory. More important for liberal idealists, real solutions to big problems make life better. That's what liberalism is all about.

REWORKING THE MEDIA

Republicans are master manipulators of the mass media. As someone identified with the Left—a fact that I find telling and amusing, considering how conservative I would be considered in just about any other country—I see firsthand how staggeringly differently liberals are treated from conservatives. More than anything else, liberals are simply ignored. Right-wing pundits like Bill O'Reilly and Ann Coulter have a home at their own television network, Fox News, and its pale imitator MSNBC, where they are invited to expound their retrograde views on the breaking news of the day. There's nothing like that on the opposite side of the political spectrum; even less widely disseminated "liberal" broadcasters like PBS and NPR tend to use panels composed of two hard-right Republican analysts with one centrist Democrat. Radio and print are the same; there just isn't a mainstream venue where prominent lefties—people as far to the left as Rush Limbaugh is to the right—appear with any degree of frequency.

Don't believe me? When is the last time you saw leftie stars like Noam Chomsky, Howard Zinn, or Ralph Nader appear in a national media forum? It happens from time to time, but it's infrequent. And they don't get primetime billing when they do.

"You'd have to be deaf, dumb and blind to believe that liberals get more generous coverage [than conservatives]," Eric Alterman wrote in the *Nation.* "In the press itself there is no liberal equivalent to nakedly biased news sources like Fox News, the *Wall Street Journal* editorial pages, the

Washington Times, the *New York Post*, Rush Limbaugh, Matt Drudge and *The McLaughlin Group*, which dictate punditocracy discourse and cable schmoozathons." Alterman's beef is with what he perceives as the right-wing bias of the media and its effect on the general public. Perhaps more pernicious, and certainly less discussed, is its effect on liberals and their fellow travelers.

If you're a liberal Democrat, to read the paper, listen to the radio, or watch TV is to feel, even if you enjoy a staggering amount of self-confidence in your opinions, alone. Here's a pernicious example that I came across while I was working on this book. "Republicans and Democrats have different memories of the 2000 presidential debates," wrote Nathan Carleton in the Duke University college newspaper. Aha, I thought. Finally: someone hip to the baffling national disconnect in perception about that event. Too bad he's a college kid, but whatever—some of the best political writing in America appears in the college press. Nathan went on: "The former remember Governor George W. Bush sticking to his guns against three different Al Gores—one pompous, one heavily sedated and one maniacal—and showing skeptical Americans that he was quick on his feet and knowledgeable about foreign policy. Democrats, on the other hand, are still angry with the media for their pre-debate coverage. They believe that people like Bill Dunman of *Business Week* severely affected public opinion by gushingly billing Gore as a 'masterful' debater. Because Gore's skills were so hyped up, many claim, viewers gave the overwhelmed Bush a handicap and saw the debates as victories for him simply because they weren't blowouts."

Um, no. *Hell* no. No one I've talked to about the 2000 debates has ever mentioned Bill Dunman or "overhyped expectations" about Gore. Most Democrats watched the debates and thought that Gore won hands down. As these things go, it was a pretty easy call to make. Bush looked confused, goofy, and intellectually challenged. Gore came off as sardonic, in control of himself and the stage (I couldn't stop laughing when he walked right up to Bush and loomed over him ominously, making Bush flinch), and had mastered the issues being discussed. Reading Carleton made me wonder, like Winston Smith in Orwell's *1984*, whether I could trust my own memory. I was positive that Bush had lost all three debates. Yet even a writer who concedes the existence of a disconnect between liberals and conservatives doesn't acknowledge the real reasons for the perception gap. Did the

Republican voters who thought Gore made an ass of himself see the same version of the debates as I did?

TV news is even more Orwellian. The MSNBC cable news station aired promotional ads for their own network during December 2003. Along with a few innocuous "questions" its viewers would supposedly like to see answered, MSNBC's ad claimed, was this one: "Will Bush win Florida again?" What brilliant propaganda. It is, after all, far from a given that Bush won Florida in 2000. To the contrary, the controversy over Florida ranks with the single-bullet theory of the JFK assassination as an issue that no one expects to see resolved anytime soon. "Again," indeed. Has Oceania always been at war, as the Party claims, with Eastasia? I could have sworn, really I could, that it used to be Eurasia.

Another example occurred when Democratic presidential candidate Howard Dean was repeatedly accused of "missteps" or of "talking off the cuff" by supposedly nonpartisan journalists. What had Dean said? America, he remarked after the capture of Saddam Hussein by U.S. forces occupying Iraq, is "no safer today than the day the planes struck the World Trade Center." Then, when asked whether he thought Osama bin Laden would or should be found guilty in a trial, he replied: "I've resisted pronouncing a sentence before guilt is found," Dean said in the interview. "I have this old-fashioned notion that even with people like Osama, who is very likely to be found guilty, we should do our best not to, in positions of executive power, not to prejudge jury trials."

Dean's statements seemed reasonable enough. Given that the Department of Homeland Security raised America's alert status and that the Federal Aviation Administration refused permission to land to half a dozen European jets headed for the States during the subsequent 2003 year-end holiday season, it was fair to say that Saddam's capture hadn't made America any safer. And of course Osama would be considered innocent before being found guilty in a court of law. That's still the American legal system, isn't it?

The Republican and small-c-conservative-dominated news media creates a feeling among liberals that they're alienated from the national community. It's impossible to quantify the effect of never seeing your points of view expressed by mainstream pundits and talking heads, or never seeing your favorite writers or comedians get a fair shake. It hurts Democrats in terms of direct political support, but the long-term effect of institutional marginalization is more pernicious: it causes liberals to opt out entirely of the small-d democratic system. A similar phenomenon of alienation afflicts ethnic minorities: when black faces appear on TV, they're usually hanging above an orange prison jumpsuit at an arraignment or getting shot to save the lives of their white policeman partners. African-Americans rarely see themselves describing the news, as the subject of (good) news or making fun of the news. As far as the body politic is concerned, they might as well not exist. Blacks and other minorities are the Invisible Man. They get the message and they tune out as a result. If and when mainstream society—white society—wants to say something to them, it'll be too late.

Liberalism, though the basis for the standards that dominate mass media in America, has been similarly marginalized in print and on the airwaves. Constantly derided as "out of the mainstream" or "out of touch" by conservative talking heads who live in million-dollar condominium apartments on Fifth Avenue, they turn to NPR, the BBC, and online versions of British newspapers for their news fix. Study after study proves that Democrats are less likely to vote than Republicans. "It's all about message," says Frank Luntz, the Republican pollster who wrote the "Contract with America." "You look for a message that gets your voters to the polls on Election Day. But it has to be well thought out, because you don't want to stir up your opponent's voters. You want them to stay home." From a Republican standpoint, it's best that Democratic voters never see their own opinions validated by respected opinion-mongers.

Marginalization of liberals is killing democracy. It's the moral responsibility of wealthy liberals to fund a left-wing version of Fox News, a left-wing Clear Channel Communications, and a left-wing Gannett newspaper chain. Until millionaire Democrats like Barbra Streisand, Alec Baldwin, and Walter Cronkite rise to the occasion and put their money where their mouths are, mainstream Democrats shouldn't give them or their books, films, or recordings the time of day. Seed money from wealthy Democrats could be supplemented by selling shares in new media companies to ideologically sympathetic voters. Like the war bonds sold during the two World Wars, an appeal should be made to patriotic Americans to take back the country from the right-wing nuts, with a tacit understanding that their investment may or may never be paid back, depending on whether the venture has a chance of becoming profitable.

PURGING THE ONE IN EVERY CROWD

Democrats must also root out the enemies in their midst with the same intensity of mercilessness as is exhibited on the other side.

For my money the biggest obstacle to left-of-center groups getting organized and girding for battle with the conservatives is the idiot who won't shut up. Every meeting of liberals has one: the one fool who takes the progress out of progressivism by making sure that nothing gets done. He—it's usually, though not always, a he—launches into some long-winded, irrelevant, pointless tirade that destroys the energy and momentum of the gathering, effectively reducing everyone present to a frustrated, seething ball of resentment. Everyone else wants to shout: "Shut the fuck up!" but no one does. To be progressive, after all, is to be tolerant. Polite. Understanding.

Fuck that.

Politeness and deference and reasonableness have gotten us into one hell of a mess. Liberals are damned near paralyzed by tolerating all the kooks, nuts, and half-wits who curse them with their presence every time they see that we're meeting somewhere to plan something. It's time to eject these idiots so the rest of us, the sane ones, can get down to serious business.

Of course, this is easier than it sounds. During the question-and-answer portion following one of my speeches recently, one guy—he seemed nice enough, but he was just rambling on and on, not making much sense, not saying anything that anyone wanted to hear, that's for sure—became my event's One Wanker. Until he stood up to deliver his diatribe on God knows what, the group, which comprised some 275 people trying to brainstorm about ways to demonstrate opposition to the Bush administration, had been electrified. My speech had gone well, the questions and answers had been intelligent, and useful tactics were being discussed. Now, as Wanker droned on and on, stringing together nouns and verbs in phrases that were grammatically correct but otherwise nonsensical, each passing second was sucking the vitality out of the room faster than American jobs fleeing overseas. Something had to be done, and as the person in charge I knew that I was the only person who could do something about it. "Okay, thanks, sit down, that's enough," I said just loudly enough to be heard over him. I'd been too nice. He kept talking. I pulled the mike close. "SHUT. UP." He looked up. "NOW," I said.

There was an audible gasp. But I had *seemed* like such a nice guy a few seconds earlier! My politics were just right! I thought Bush was a bad person, cared about the planet, and wanted to see rapists locked up for life.

Wasn't I, as a leftie, tolerant of this asshole's right to bore the living shit out of 275 human beings for 275 or 550 or 825 person-minutes? And yet, here I was, telling a person, the fruit of God's loins, to be quiet so us sane and articulate people could get some goddamned work done. As things turned out, shutting down Wanker was the right thing to do. The conversation soon returned to its previous level of spirited exchange about tactics and ideology. No doubt a few of the people in the room left the gathering convinced that I was a jerk, but when you're fighting for a cause, the cause comes before your reputation as a stand-up guy.

The wanker in your midst won't always be the slightly smelly dude at the planning committee meeting for the antiwar rally. He may be an it. It may be widely disseminated media outlets like the *New Republic, Slate.com,* and *SpinSanity.com*, conservative outfits that assume a liberal cloak that allows them to express ideas at odds with even the most flexible definition of the word. It might be a congressperson who uses the Democratic party label to get elected but after winning merely takes up a seat that a *real* liberal should have gotten instead—and consistently votes with the Right on the big issues when it matters most. Whether the wanker in question is a nationally renowned politician or some local asshole who won't shut up, we need to suss them out, denounce them, and chuck them out before they can do much damage to our cause.

THE POWER OF RELENTLESSNESS

We have many enemies. The trick is to choose the targets of our wrath carefully and to attack them, like a sniper, with laser-like accuracy and relentlessness. The Right is extremely adept at this practice; I know this from having been a target of a Bushist censorship campaign.

I draw two hundred cartoons a year. Unsurprisingly one becomes the subject of national controversy from time to time. About six months after September 11, I drew one such cartoon called "terror widows." That piece, which lampooned the way that September 11 widows like Lisa Beamer (whose husband cried "let's roll," supposedly leading the charge to attack his plane's hijackers before their flight crashed in Pennsylvania) and Ted Olsen (the Republican solicitor general, whose conservative TV commentator wife Barbara had died on the jet that hit the Pentagon) had cynically exploited their spouses' deaths for personal profit or to promote their personal, religious, or political agenda, appeared on a Thursday. Although a few of my regular readers wrote to say they found "terror widows" to be a bit harsher than my usual stuff, there wasn't much reaction.

Four days later, the following Tuesday, all hell broke loose. The *New York Times* and *Washington Post* dropped the piece from their websites (its "subject matter was inappropriate," said a *Times* spokesman), media interview requests kept my phone ringing night and day, and New York City police officers filled up my answering machine with threats of death and bodily harm. (My caller ID box identified their precincts and phone extensions. Some of New York's Finest helpfully left their names and ranks on my voicemail.) When the dust cleared a few days later—after I'd gone on CNN, MSNBC, and Fox News's *O'Reilly Factor* to explain myself—I reconstructed how and why the controversy had erupted *four days after* the cartoon's publication.

There are anywhere from a few hundred to a couple of thousand right-wing "warbloggers," political fanatics who post comments and links about current events to their Internet websites. (Noting that these cyberwarriors support the Bush wars against Afghanistan and Iraq from the comfort of their suburban dens, leftie wags mock these people as "chickenbloggers.") Few Americans have heard of warblogger "stars" like James Lileks or Andrew Sullivan, and their websites are so drearily predictable that that's unlikely to change soon. If Bush shot Cheney in a drunken rage involving a dominatrix, castor oil, and a syphilitic mongoose, these guys would come up with some argument to defend him. The power of the warbloggers stems from their ability to share information and coordinate mass e-mail attacks against unsuspecting victims. Once one of these goons spotted "terror widows"—I suppose I should be flattered that right-wingers take the time to follow my work—and interlinked to my cartoon's URL and each other's sites with amazing speed, urging each other to e-mail the *Times* and *Post* to demand that they take down my "outrageous" cartoon. They also sent out an e-mail listing contact e-mails for my employers, including my book publisher, to webmasters who run Republican and likeminded right-wing sites. They asked them to write to the addresses to express their "outrage" and urge that I be fired, blackballed, arrested, killed, etc.

It was hard to keep track of exact figures, but my best estimate is that roughly twenty-four hundred people actually sent out such e-mails, each to ten recipients. While this blizzard of digitized hate speech didn't succeed in getting me fired—in keeping with the dictum that all publicity is good publicity, it actually raised my profile and caused me to pick up several new clients—it did convince the nation's two most important newspapers to censor the cartoon in question. (Only the most Web-savvy editors are sufficiently erudite to distinguish a genuine reader e-mail from one generated by a concerted mass censorship campaign. Twenty-four hundred e-mails seems like a high number, but not when they come from all over the world. They're less impressive still when you consider that few if any of them come from individuals who subscribe to the newspaper to which they're writing.) Even after "terror widows," warbloggers continued to harass the *Times*. Two years later, Times Digital caved in, dropping my cartoons and deleting their archives.

Every Republican/Bush supporter/Christian conservative sees himself or herself as a soldier in an army, an activist in a movement. They join the PTA to spread the Gospel, create weblogs to spread the word to their immediate family and friends, and interlink in order to form a Borg-like "hive mind" that acts as a far stronger force than the sum of its constituent parts. Most warbloggers are acne-scarred teenagers or middle-aged white men living in the middle of nowhere, with no life and nothing better to do than to work themselves into a lather over the way some cartoonist splattered India ink across a piece of Bristol board. I have yet to read a single right-wing blog that broke the format's standard operating procedure: link to news story or opinion article by/about/in favor of liberal politician/pundit/miscellaneous assorted figure and pour on hateful derision. "Ted Rall is a vile little creep." "Rall is a Commy [sic] asshole." "I won't rest until he faces a federal grand jury." And my personal fave: "Ted Rall is a smarmy, sick little scumbucket, a carping pinheaded suckweasel, a loathsome flea-infested gnat-brained maniac, a clueless amoral sloth-witted nutjob, a cranky bug-faced communist zombie, a loathsome viper of journalistic terrorism, a deranged drooling demon-cow of conspiratorial Chomskyite insanity with the intellect of pocket lint." Wow.

Big words from small men. You can't read a Republican blog without feeling a little shock at the awesome amount of effort they pour into websites that are each read by an average of fifty people planetwide. Some of these pathetic souls post new links more than once an *hour*; it isn't uncommon to see posting times listed from the middle of the night. These people get up every day and pour themselves into these things. They draw from their inexhaustible supply of sexually frustrated anger, which they disseminate online, at family dinners, over drinks with friends and in letters to the editor. (One wonders why they're so furious. Am I missing something? Aren't *their* guys in charge of all three branches of government?) So angry, and so devoted are they to their righteous crusade to eradicate liberalism from the planet, they arrange for other people to fill in for them when they're sick or on vacation.

Sadly, the Left has nothing to match the warbloggers' relentlessness and cohesion. Liberal bloggers are more likely to consider both sides, see validity in opposing points of view and assume a reasonable tone when addressing people and positions with which they disagree. Launching e-mail smear campaigns against a right-wing columnist or cartoonist whose words or pictures annoyed them would never occur to them. For one thing, liberals rarely get angry or remain angry for long when they do. "We're not real haters," Democratic consultant Bob Shrum says. Fortunately for America, the Bush administration is helping to change that.

The band Funkadelic urged: "Free your mind and your ass will follow." Much of this book has been devoted to suggesting what top leaders should do to make the Democratic Party and American liberalism more viable from the top down. But nothing the leading lights of liberalism can do will have any practical effect unless we, as individual progressives, spend every waking hour plotting and scheming, working to spread our message over dinner and drinks and even breakfast to anyone and everyone willing to hear it. We've got to become proselytizers fueled by the same caffeinated energy and unstoppable glee that we see in those who would load us into cattle cars if they got the chance. If you let a day pass without writing a letter to the editor, starting a blog, or painting some progressive graffiti somewhere, you're part of the vast right-wing conspiracy. Apathy kills. So does slouching into a comfy chair and giving up hope. Slap an environmentally friendly bumpersticker on an SUV, argue with a neighbor, call into a talk show. Do something that matters. *Be fucking relentless.*

When you stop, when you get tired, when you give up, they win.

A MANIFESTO FOR A NEW AMERICA

About a third of Americans believe in ghosts (34 percent) and an equal number in UFOs (34 percent), and about a quarter accept things like astrology (29 percent), reincarnation (25 percent) and witches (24 percent). Women are more likely than men to believe in almost all topics asked about in the poll, including 12 percentage points more likely to believe in miracles and eight points more likely to trust there is a heaven. The one significant exception is UFOs, with 39 percent of men compared to 30 percent of women saying they accept the existence of unidentified flying objects. Young people are much more likely than older Americans to believe in both hell and the devil. An 86 percent majority of adults between the ages of 18 to 34 believe in hell, but that drops to 68 percent for those over age 70. Similarly, 79 percent of young people believe in the devil compared to 67 percent of the over-70 age group. Republicans are more likely than Democrats to say they believe in God (by eight percentage points), in heaven (by 10 points), in hell (by 15 points), and considerably more likely to believe in the devil (by 17 points). Democrats are more likely than Republicans to say they believe in reincarnation (by 14 percentage points), in astrology (by 14 points), in ghosts (by eight points) and UFOs (by five points).

—Fox News/Opinion Dynamics poll, December 2003

At this time in our history there's an interesting internal ideological inconsistency afflicting American voters. At the same time that self-identified affiliation with a specific political party is ebbing, even while the ranks of self-declared independents are growing and fewer people than ever are exercising their right to vote, the United States is more politically polarized than at any time since the 1960s. Politics matter more than ever, yet people are voting less. The main reasons for this apparent contradiction: George W. Bush's personality, the way he came to power, and the policies of his administration.

An August 2003 poll by the *Washington Post* tells the story of a deeply divided people: a staggering 80 percent of Democrats disagree with Bush's handling of the economy while an equally high 77 percent of Republicans approve. Seventy-six percent of Democrats dislike his budget priorities; 71 percent of Republicans think they're just peachy. The occupation of Iraq, Bush's highest-profile foreign policy project to date, inspires a similar diametric split: two-thirds of Democrats say we should get our troops out of the Middle East immediately, while 86 percent of Republicans think there's no need to change gears. The same poll showed that eight out of ten Democrats would vote for whomever ended up capturing their party's nomination—they'd support a turnip over Bush—whereas nine out of ten Republicans planned to support Bush, whose nomination was already assured. Independents may have cast the deciding votes in previous elections, but not this time: indies split 43 to 39 percent in favor of Bush, a statistical dead heat.

Party affiliation still matters, thanks largely to the fact that the two-party system is the one thing both parties agree most upon. In addition, a replacement hasn't appeared on the horizon. But both major parties have so muddied their ideological waters during the past few decades, whether they're welfare-reforming liberals or compassionate conservatives, that they're encouraging apathy and destroying their own, in Madison Avenue lingo, brand loyalty. Republicans pretend to support a balanced budget amendment yet it's Republican presidents—Reagan and Bush #43—who ran up the largest budget deficits in history. Democrats claim that they want to defend workers against rapacious corporate employers, yet the most recent Democratic president expended his precious political capital on free trade agreements—NAFTA, GATT, the WTO—all opposed by labor because they cost American jobs. "New Democrats" coalescing around the banner of the Democratic Leadership Council borrowed pages from traditional GOP platform planks on welfare reform and a strong defense. Neoconservative Republicans, whose ideological roots are an odd blend of Cold War paranoia, post-1960s disillusionment, and an interest in Israel so obsessive that they want its tactics used by the United States, led Bush to two "preemptive" wars and unprecedented government interference in the private lives of individuals: acts that contravene his father's classic conservatism.

The results of this rhetorical mish-mash are an electorate with reduced loyalty to either party and lower voter turnout. At the height of mushy post-Newt-pre-Monica Clintonism in 1996, a period of relative ideological calm, 46 percent of respondents to a Medill News Service poll described themselves as independents. Democrats accounted for 24 percent, and Republicans for 17 percent, of respondents. Even among those willing to count themselves as loyalists to one of the two big parties, more than a fourth said that they didn't discern a substantial difference between the two. "Parties in the past would provide a focus for people who don't pay enough attention to politics. They gave them choices," commented Walter Dean Burnham, author of *Elections and Democratic Institutions: The Current Crisis in American Politics.* "Now they are part of an expensive, candidate-driven system to which a large part of the electorate can't relate."

There's another, simpler explanation for our simultaneously politicized and politically apathetic citizenry. We have strong opinions but we doubt that voting is a meaningful way to express them, much less an effective means of seeing them translated into law.

Other theories abound. Burham also blames reduced party relevance on the replacement of old-fashioned door-to-door canvassing with TV advertising. University of Iowa political science professor Arthur Miller (not the playwright) says that candidates hurt their parties by marketing themselves as outsider-reformers at odds with the organizations that endorse them: "[Candidates] go out there and say, 'My party is the worst thing there is. But elect me and I'll change everything.' These politicians are largely to blame for the depressed voter turnout." Party-bashing wins one year's election for one man by cannibalizing the future of the same party's next slate of candidates. Clinton achieved electoral success by distancing himself from "big government" Democrats. Now the Democratic Party has to address criticism from its own leaders as well as the Republicans.

Before Bush came along, it was hard for Americans to tell the two parties apart. Odds are that this perception, part of a long-term trend, will resume after Bush leaves office and his polarizing politics have worn off. In a sense, therefore, the present crises of domestic and foreign policy present both parties with an unusual opportunity to address this underlying structural dilemma. Both parties still have their faults, but it's easier to tell them apart.

Despite the parties' attempts at creating ideological confusion among voters, Americans are hard-wired with shorthand summaries of Democrats and Republicans stand for. Democrats are for "ordinary people." They fight poverty, care about the environment, and favor equal rights for women, ethnic minorities, and gay people. Republicans support business, fiscal responsibility, privacy rights, and want to create an environment hospitable to the entrepreneurship that drives capitalism and, by extension, freedom and democracy.

Some of these perceptions are true, others not. Whatever—voters rely on spin since they can't know the truth.

In some respects, party politics reflects trends of widening political and cultural schisms in the population as a whole, which creates an even bigger challenge for those seeking to create a new paradigm. Authors John Judis and Ruy Teixeira argue that, as Timothy Noah summarized for *Slate.com*, George McGovern's 1972 failed presidential bid set the stage for our current situation. The South Dakota liberal, they say, alienated traditionally Democratic working-class white males but "laid the foundation for a 'progressive centrist' Democratic coalition of the future: working women, minorities, highly skilled professionals, people who live in university communities that have now evolved into new-economy 'ideopolises.' While the McGovern coalition has ballooned . . . an important slice of the Reagan coalition—evangelical Christians—has leveled off or even started to shrink." Indeed, Democrats are more likely than Republicans to be female, live in an urban area, and belong to an ethnic minority. Since these are growing population segments, that's good for liberals. Unfortunately, they are also more likely to be older than thirty and earn under $30,000 per year. Income disparity is causing this population segment to increase in size, but a party by and for poor people has trouble collecting campaign contributions. And while the pool of elderly voters is temporarily increasing, that won't always be the case. In the long run it's better to trend young than old.

Both parties, in other words, are looking for love in all the wrong places. They're so busy poaching supporters among those whose basic ideals contradict their party platform that they risk losing their souls. Democrats are wallowing in the dead end of identity politics, bluntly targeting minority and feminist rage against every white male in the country when it's only some white guys, most of them dead and gone, who were responsible for keeping them down. Marx is dead but class is still destiny; you have infinitely more in common with someone who earns the same income than you do with someone whose skin tint happens to match yours. Demographic trends may eventually bring more voters into the liberal fold, but these new acquisitions won't stay loyal unless the Left is able to credibly present itself as a dynamic force for positive change. For Republicans, sucking up to America's Taliban (Christian fundamentalists) forces them to espouse government intrusion into people's personal lives— for instance, supporting anti-sodomy laws that led to the prosecution of a *straight* Texas couple having anal sex observed by a peeping Tom—that goes against everything conservatism stands for. The urge to keep the feds out of your bedroom, after all, is one of the most attractive aspects of Republicanism. The GOP is slitting its own throat by kowtowing to its rightist fringe.

We've examined some of the reasons why liberals have lost key battles in recent years and suggested new tactics that would help them reverse that trend. Now it's time to present ideas worth fighting for. The centerpiece of a new progressive strategy should be an appeal to self-interest. We must launch an ongoing campaign to convince ordinary Americans that they should vote Democratic—not because it's morally right or good for society, but because it's good for them as well as their country. Most Americans should vote liberal because they *are* liberal.

A common truism states that relationships require a 50-50 effort. Both sides have to meet each other half way. However, it actually takes a lot more than that to keep a friend or lover—each party must give 100 percent. Without an overlap of good will, there's too much risk of some stupid mis-understanding creating a gap in trust that ultimately leads to a total breach. If anything, the relationship between a voter and a candidate (or party) is even more lopsided. A person or political party vying for a citizen's support must expend 99 percent of the effort in the "relationship." The only thing society asks of a voter is to drag his lazy ass off his sofa to go cast a vote. (And even that puny effort isn't mandated by law in the U.S., as it is elsewhere.) Politicians who complain about voter apathy are onto something, but disin-terest in the two-party system is a symptom of problems with the process. Asking people to vote is pointless. If the system is healthy they will.

It's up to politicians to make themselves, and the electoral system, so incredibly interesting and relevant and essential that people are compelled to want to participate. People watch television because they like it, not because it's an obligation. Similarly, as much as activists want to make voter participation a mandatory chore of citizenship, the American people will continue to vote in low numbers until a charismatic politician touting an irresistible platform of ideas stimulates them to act differently.

The following section is devoted to the task of creating a viable political platform for America's new majority party.

Ideological consistency holds special appeal in our uncertain world. At a time when Americans worry that their planes will be hijacked and their buses will be bombed, as employment security becomes a thing of the past, as the divorce rate hovers around 50 percent and kidnap victims turn up dead in rivers and fields, as religious leaders are caught sexually molesting children, when a German man receives hundreds of responses to an Internet posting asking for volunteers to be killed and eaten, a political party that declares consistent, bedrock principles in an effort to mitigate the worst effects of modern society, will enjoy broad appeal.

An ideologically consistent party—a reformed Democratic Party—would promote policies that draw from the three main strains of American politics:

- Liberalism's *compassionate* devotion to helping people who need help and protecting the weak from being exploited by the strong, a mission that sometimes requires new laws;
- Conservativism's *prudent* interest in protecting our nation from those who mean it harm, resisting unnecessary change and saving money from the good times for a rainy day;
- Libertarianism's obsessive defense of *personal freedom* as expressed via absolute adherence to the Bill of Rights, and getting government out of our lives as much as possible.

These are the most universally appealing components of America's three dominant ideologies. Conversely, few people buy into any of these three strains wholesale. Liberal indulgence to lazy complainers, conservative selling out to corporations, and wacky libertarian arguments that roads would pave themselves if the government stopped collecting taxes are ideological orphans. No one really believes that "compassionate" conservative businessmen give a damn about anyone but themselves, no one agrees with old school liberals that it's okay for layabouts to bask under their sun lamps while collecting checks from the government, and no one believes, as libertarians assert, that if we unbuild it they will come.

If you consider political issues from a long-term perspective, these three "greatest hits of U.S. political thinking" don't contradict each other at all. Old-school liberals oppose balanced budget laws because they prefer to reserve the right to run up deficit spending for social programs that they like. However, borrowing now to help people who are suffering today hurts the economy down the road. Because debt has to be repaid many times over with compound interest, deficit spending for social programs creates even more misery later on, at a time when required budgetary frugality will block any consideration of social welfare spending.

True fiscal conservatism, ironically, makes it easier for government to afford programs that help the poor—but only when paired with the liberal compassion that drives such spending in the first place. Prudent management of government budgets provides the funds we need to make people's lives better.

Old-school lefties ridicule libertarian-style constitutional purism, but in so doing they give reactionaries ammunition to call them hypocrites. Picking which parts of the Bill of Rights to support or reject—because they abhor gun violence, liberals defend free speech but not the Second Amendment right to bear arms—provides an opening to rightists who want to take away other freedoms one at a time. Nothing short of complete unreserved support of the entire Bill of Rights and Constitution allows liberals to protect the values they cherish, the ideas that they believe define America. Libertarians promulgate some silly ideas about taxes, but liberals should embrace/borrow/steal their take on the Constitution: for libertarians as for most Americans, individual freedom always trumps the good of society as a whole. Liberals, who understand the importance of minority rights, should adopt that aspect of libertarianism in their platform.

True liberals, if they were honest with themselves and the country, would eschew political correctness. Republicans score propaganda points against the Left on affirmative action because racial quotas are patently discriminatory and hypocritical. They *are* quotas, not "preferences." Democrats cannot defend their assertion that everyone deserves equal rights and opportunities while pushing a "reverse racist" policy that *denies* equal rights and opportunities to a class of people. Either all Americans are equal or we're not. There can be no exceptions. The equality principle must also apply to speech. Liberals should defend the right to utter racist and other offensive forms of speech with the same ferocity as they would a pro-Palestinian or Marxist professor's right to share his views with his students. The First Amendment doesn't pick sides and neither should we.

Once you distill these seemingly disparate ethical strains—drawn from political schools of thought that traditionally refuse to acknowledge one another as valid—what remains is a common-sense-based philosophy that suits the vast majority of Americans. Truck drivers and ballet dancers and cartoonists and checkout clerks don't consult their copies of the Democratic, Republican, Green, or Libertarian party platforms in order to determine how to feel about an issue. They think what they think, period. More often than not, what they think falls into the aforementioned blend of liberal compassion, conservative prudence, and the libertarian love of personal freedom. The Democratic and Republican parties try to blur those lines—and their ideological blending works temporarily. According to *Time*, "nearly two-thirds of the public, including 42 percent of Democrats, consider [George W. Bush] the compassionate man he claims to be." The perception that Bush has liberal qualities has helped the Republican Party. But don't be fooled: most people know that "compassionate conservatism" is no more than a slogan. Liberals have built up infinitely more credibility in this arena.

At this point, Democrats are better poised than any existing major political organization to pull off a successful transformation into America's long-term majority party. First, Democrats are down and out and they know it. Defeat sparks introspection, and liberals are more open than usual to changing their approach to get back into the game. Second, the right-ward swing of the Republican Party under George W. Bush has breathed new life into the left-wing base of American liberalism. Polarization feeds radicalism; radicalization creates energy. Third, self-identified conservatives—who account for a third of the electorate—don't all vote Republican. Only half do. Many old-school conservatives are dismayed by the current GOP leadership's abandonment of traditional conservative principles, particularly on deficit spending, free trade, and empire-building abroad. If classic conservatives were convinced that "big spenders" and politically correct types were no longer in charge, they could be persuaded to join a revamped Democratic Party. Compared to the Republican, Green, and Libertarian parties, the current Democratic platform requires fewer alterations to create a consistent list of stances that appeals to this proposed majority coalition. A few nips here, a few tucks there, and a new liberalism that lifts the best parts of conservatism and libertarianism, one that appeals to nearly every American, could be cobbled together.

That said, the Republicans could surprise me. They have before. Some current GOP initiatives, such as the party's drive to attract more minority voters, might inspire it to cut loose its vile southern-right wing—the virulent racists they won by opposing civil rights in the sixties. In some respects Republicans are better poised than Democrats to bring in the libertarians; were they to adopt the libertarians' staunch defense of personal liberties, a more open-minded GOP could become the majority party not merely by vote, but by population and temperament. It doesn't matter to me whether the Democrats or Republicans or some other outfit becomes the party dedicated to defending American common sense; I'll happily support whichever one gets there first. I am, however, a realist. Right now, as things currently stand—I know, that's a big caveat—the Democrats offer the shortest path to realizing this laudable goal.

American politics can't be revolutionized from the top down, argues Texas populist Jim Hightower. In an interview with the *Progressive*, Hightower says: "You don't build a movement by running for president. It's got to be built by good organizing at the grassroots level around issues, like privacy, like NAFTA and the WTO, like the USA-Patriot Act. And then running people for mayor, state rep, then moving up to Congress. I think we are eight-to-twelve years away from electing a president." Is he right? I don't know. Our history offers examples of change coming from the masses as well as individual leaders.

I do know this:

Without good candidates, effective fundraising, smarter tactics, and renewed long-term dedication to improving our country, a coherent platform will go nowhere. It is nevertheless essential to craft a list of positions for that smarter, richer, more sharply focused party to sell. Even the best advertising campaign falls flat without a good product to promote. Here's a platform worth fighting for, reflective of the thinking of most of the people of the United States, and worthy of us as a nation:

OUR NEEDS

Our nation is the wealthiest society in the history of mankind. At no other time has a community of human beings lived together that enjoyed as auspicious a combination of natural resources, an educated and skilled workforce, and strategic dominance over the rest of mankind. It is inexcusable that, in a land of so much plenty, poverty forces some citizens to go without shelter, medical care, education, retirement benefits, and the other essential needs of life. We recognize that it is our moral obligation, as well as in the long-term best interest of our country, for the well-off to provide these basic rights to those who happen to be less fortunate.

A full-time job should pay a full-time salary. Beth Shulman's book *The Betrayal of Work: How Low-Wage Jobs Fail 30 Million Americans* documents how 30 million people working full-time jobs that pay less than $8.70 an hour (the relevant rate during the late nineties)—fall beneath the federal government's official poverty line. Anyone who works full-time deserves to be paid wages that permits him or her to rent a basic dwelling, drive a modest car, and watch a movie now and then. To make this happen, the minimum wage must be increased to levels that exceed the poverty rate and increased at a rate proportional to the rate of inflation.

Working hard entitles you to a worry-free retirement. The Social Security System created during the 1930s, originally envisioned as a mere supplement to employer-funded retirement plans that are all but non-existent today, is teetering on the edge of bankruptcy due to mismanagement and demographic shifts. Already the Social Security retirement age is scheduled to rise to the age of sixty-nine in the year 2028. All hard-working Americans deserve the right to a carefree retirement after having worked for many years. We will create a full-fledged federalized retirement system funded through an employer tax that will be prudently invested in order to guarantee a post-retirement income comparable to what each employee earned during his or her working career, up to a reasonable limit. We expect wealthy American workers to rely on themselves, rather than the government, after they retire.

Everyone has the right to the best possible education. The best jobs require college degrees; accordingly, a decent education should be available to anyone willing to devote herself to her studies. This process must begin with primary and secondary public schools, which currently suffer from an unfair disparity between those located in poor municipalities and those in wealthy enclaves. Federalizing the financing of these schools would eliminate this unequal treatment of our children and create a consistent, national curriculum. When urban and suburban schools enjoy equal funding, affirmative action for college admissions becomes unnecessary. Similarly, our system of for-profit private four-year universities has outlived its usefulness at a time when a four-year degree has become as essential to obtain work as a high school degree was two generations ago. These colleges and universities must be made financially accessible to every student who qualifies to attend one, regardless of their ability to pay. This can be accomplished by bringing these private institutions under government control or by funding tuition through direct grants. The student loan system, which reduces our best and brightest young men and women into indentured servants after graduation, must be eliminated and current outstanding loans forgiven.

No American should be homeless. A 1998 UNICEF report estimates that three-quarters of a million Americans sleep outdoors every night. This is wrong. We must build high-quality temporary shelters and permanent low-income housing in every city and town to provide housing for dispossessed people; the mentally disabled should be cared for in separate facilities where their special needs can be addressed. Whereas liberals of the twentieth century defended the "right" of the homeless to sleep outdoors if they so preferred, we deny this "privilege" and urge the police to forcibly deliver these citizens to appropriate housing facilities. Ordinary citizens should enjoy the ability to walk the streets of their cities without being accosted by aggressive panhandlers.

No American should be denied medical care. Forty-four million Americans have no health insurance whatsoever. "When one of every seven of Americans lacks even the most basic coverage, it's time for some creative problem-solving," says Kate Sullivan of the U.S. Chamber of Commerce. We agree. When one also considers the estimated 40 million people considered "underinsured," the state of medical care in the United States is a national disgrace. The ability to be treated by a competent doctor of your choosing is not a privilege. It is a basic right. We will nationalize the nation's medical care system, including its rapacious for-profit hospitals, pharmaceutical companies, and HMOs, and transform them from profit centers into facilities devoted to the public health. The health insurance business, which exists solely to generate shareholder earnings, will be abolished.

We have the right to collective bargaining. Union membership has fallen from 35 percent during the 1950s to 13 percent today. AFL-CIO President John Sweeney blames bosses: "Employers engage in every tactic imaginable to block workers' freedom to form a union." But you can hardly blame companies for preferring not to deal with unions. The profit incentive drives corporations to reduce labor costs by any means necessary. And past tales of union corruption, such as the many scandals that tarnished the reputation of the Teamsters, have caused countless workers to distrust organized labor. The fact nevertheless remains that 87 percent of American workers do not enjoy the power to withhold their labor from their employers by striking for an increase in wages or other improvements in their conditions of employment. The imbalance in the free market between labor and management has contributed to a downward slide of real wages over recent decades. Laws that make it difficult for unions to organize, such as a federal rule that permits employers to force their workers to attend anti-union meetings, should be struck down. The Taft-Hartley Labor Act of 1947, passed at the start of the Red Scare, bans secondary strikes—an essential tool for workers throughout the world—and permits the U.S. attorney general to obtain an eighty-day injunction in cases where a judge can be convinced that a threatened strike "imperiled the national health or safety." What President Harry Truman called "a slave labor act" should be abolished.

Those who rule us should live like us. We favor a law to limit the salaries, benefits, and vacation time alloted members of the House of Representatives and Senate, the president and vice president of the United States, and other top government officials to the minimum wage, worst benefit package, and stingiest vacation allotment offered to the least fortunate full-time worker in the United States. Only by experiencing the problems of our least well-off citizens will Congress begin to understand the struggle of average Americans survive from week to week. We hope that self-interest will succeed where duty failed by encouraging our legislators to seek creative long-term solutions to the difficulties of their constituents.

OUR FREEDOMS

There has been an unfortunate tendency by ideologues of the Left and Right to treat the sacred rights enshrined by our Constitution and its Bill of Rights like a Chinese menu: fully embracing some rights while rejecting those that don't agree with their narrow ideologies. We believe that you are either American or you are not; the essence of being American means agreeing to defend our constitutional rights in their entirety. At a time when some citizens are smearing their fellows with the brush of treason, the definition of an American is a simple one: someone who defends the fundamental legal structure of the United States, which rests upon its Constitution and Bill of Rights. Should there come a time when one or more of the provisions of our Constitution needs to be amended, this should be done carefully, with due consideration, and should never concern relatively trivial matters like permitting prayer in public schools, gay marriage, or a ban on the burning of the American flag.

Americans have the right to own guns. Unlike those who defend some sections of the Constitution while unraveling those they don't like, we defend the Second Amendment right to bear arms. We agree that gun owners are an important defense against tyranny as well as a last-ditch force for national defense. The government enjoys the right, however, to license the issuance of firearms to ensure that they are not owned by those unqualified to use them in a safe manner. No one would suggest that government should not license the drivers of automobiles. The same goes for deadly weapons.

We are all equal. Ethnic minorities and other groups of Americans have suffered, and continue to suffer from, systematic discrimination in education, employment opportunities, housing, and more subtle forms of bias. While these injustices are deplorable, and we strive to eliminate them at once, it is not possible, or moral, to right these wrongs—historical or present tense—by hurting groups like white men who are perceived to enjoy a social advantage. All too often, affirmative action has been indistinguishable from quotas. It's a blunt instrument that admits the daughter of a wealthy African-American judge ahead of the son of a poor white coal miner, a convenient way for racists to spread the lie that minorities can't achieve on their own merits, and a post facto remedy to problems created earlier, often in failing inner-city public schools. We must federalize funding and centralize control of the nation's public schools while eliminating programs like school vouchers that transfer needed public tax dollars to private for-profit and religious schools. If groups that benefit from affirmative action programs enjoy the opportunity to attend well-funded, fully staffed public schools as children, they will not require shaving points off the average GPAs and SAT scores needed for college admissions and good jobs. Since this reform switch will take at least a generation to fully implement, affirmative action should be phased out over time to maximize the chances of women, blacks, and others to achieve the American dream.

Whether or not to abort a child is a terrible decision to be made solely by its mother. A 2000 survey by the *Los Angeles Times* shows that while 57 percent of Americans consider abortion to be murder, two-thirds believe that this decision should be left to a woman and her physician. "Americans, in terms of their own code of morality, may view abortion as murder and may be comfortable with it being illegal, but most Americans don't want to impose that on other people," says Susan Carroll of the Center for American Women and Politics at Rutgers University. That conflict is natural; from a biological standpoint abortion is the killing of an unborn baby. At the same time, many women who are unable or unwilling to care for offspring should have the option of, essentially, legally murdering their child. We encourage men and women to take every precaution to avoid unwanted pregnancy, while recognizing the sad fact that abortions will inevitably take place. Women should continue to enjoy the right to control their bodies and their role in the reproductive process, but we will not go along with those who ask for state financing for abortion, nor with those who describe the procedure as a harmless form of birth control. Abortion should be readily available. It should not be an easy decision.

Gays and lesbians are our brothers and sisters. We do not approve of homosexuality. We're not required to; like the moon and the stars, gays *are*. Neither do we disapprove. We accept gays and lesbians, and embrace them as our fellow citizens and human beings. The fact that gays account for anywhere from 5 to 10 percent of our population does not make them abnormal; it merely makes them members of a minority. Minority rights are enshrined in our Constitution and so we extend the right to all Americans to do whatever they would like in their bedrooms. Gays should enjoy the right to serve in the armed forces as openly and proudly as their heterosexual counterparts, as well as the right to lead their lives free of harassment or violence. While we do not endorse special "hate crime" legislation—every life is equally precious, no more and no less—we understand that what goes on between consenting adults in the privacy of their homes is nobody's business but their own. The argument that legalizing gay marriage would diminish the value of straight marriage falls upon deaf ears for this reason; whether the couple next door is same- or opposite-sex no more affects the success of your own union than seeing that couple suffer a devastating divorce. Americans should reach out to their neighbors to offer help, not to tell them how to live.

Children are human beings. "What about the children?" has become a standard cry in discussions about any number of issues, a cliché so hackneyed that it has become a recurring joke in the animated television series *The Simpsons*. We talk a good game when it comes to protecting children—typically this involves censorship of libraries and the World Wide Web—but we're falling down on the job when it comes to their basic needs. It's time that our Constitution provides full, unequivocal civil rights to American citizens under the age of eighteen. While certain privileges, such as the right to vote, drive an automobile, consume alcohol, and serve in the armed forces may be restricted based on age, a Children's Rights Amendment should codify a child with demonstrated mental and emotional competence with the unalienable right to, for example, choose which parent to live with in the event of his parents' divorce or obtain an abortion without parental consent. Separate wage structures for children, such as the sub-minimum "training wage" established by a number of states, should be prohibited. Children should be granted the ability to defend their rights in the civil court system.

Trashing our freedoms does not protect us from those who wish us harm. Less than a year after September 11, 64 percent of Americans told an ABC News-*Washington Post* poll that they endorsed giving the FBI authority to monitor libraries, churches, and the Internet in order to protect us from possible future terrorist attacks. In time of crisis it is always tempting to sacrifice individual rights to government agencies, but history proves that this is a bad trade-off: those rights are hard to get back after the threat has passed. Moreover, sacrificing freedom rarely helps fight the perceived enemy. The September 11 attacks led to the passage of the USA-Patriot Act, which allows federal agents to search our homes and monitor our communications without obtaining a warrant. The subsequent invasion of Afghanistan preceded the opening of a concentration camp to hold Afghan prisoners of war at Guantánamo Bay, Cuba, where hundreds of men are held in appalling conditions. (They are not charged with a crime, permitted to see a lawyer, or to leave their fenced cages more than the thirty minutes per week allotted for their weekly shower.) To paraphrase a remark that was thrown around a lot in late 2001, if we abandon our basic values as Americans, then the terrorists truly have won. America's concentration camp in Gitmo is a terrorist victory. The USA-Patriot Act must be repealed. Guantánamo Bay must be closed and its prisoners released or brought to trial. Firm and decisive action must be brought to bear on those who seek to harm innocent American civilians, but that does not require, or justify, depriving those same innocents of the freedoms for which so many have given their lives.

The right to seek redress in a court of law shall not be abridged. In a recent debate in the Ohio state senate, a representative argued that litigation had gotten out of control. Citing statistics that indicate that the cost of the tort system (civil cases brought against a defendant in the hope of collecting monetary damages) had increased 14.3 percent during a period when general economic growth had only gone up by 2.6 percent, he claimed that the average Ohio taxpayer was indirectly bearing an annual cost of $721 because of greedy lawyers and their clients. If civil litigation is increasing relative to the overall size of the economy, however, it's because consumers and citizens increasingly have nowhere else to turn to seek redress for wrongdoing. Deregulation has allowed businesses to shrug off customer complaints. Federal agencies have been ordered to stop enforcing existing rules and regulations. Even the Better Business Bureau no longer accepts reports of shady business practices. Those who advocate limiting damage awards would cut off the last recourse many Americans have in order to seek redress for having been wronged. Helpless people would become even more vulnerable to rapacious corporations. The best way to reduce the expense of litigation is for potential defendants to engage in honest dealings with potential plaintiffs and for government to rigorously enforce existing rules and to impose new ones where needed. Draconian tort reform attacks on *individual* lawsuits, such as a proposed plan to limit the amount a woman could collect for a botched mastectomy to $250,000 (while there are no proposals to limit awards to one corporation that sues another), are anathema to the American system of justice.

Government should stay out of the God business. We concur with the traditional reading of the "establishment clause" of the U.S. Constitution, which has been interpreted by legal scholars for two centuries as implying that the United States is by definition a secular nation. We submit that freedom of religion necessitates the freedom *not* to believe and that any faith that relies on bullying others into submission to the dictates of the pulpit is doomed sooner rather than later. Regardless of whether or not belief in a higher being is desirable, however, it is both distasteful and inappropriate for government to involve itself in any respect with matters of religiosity. When a politician like George W. Bush names the "philosopher-thinker" he most identifies with as "Christ, because he changed my heart," and his attorney general says that in America "we have no king but Jesus," they debase Christianity and insult millions of citizens who reject their beliefs. Accordingly, the motto "In God We Trust" should be removed from U.S. currency and public buildings. Presidents and other political leaders should refrain from referencing their religious affiliations or sprinkling their speech with such lines as "God bless America." Private parochial and religious schools must never benefit, directly or indirectly, from government tax revenues—school voucher schemes that do so should not be countenanced. We do not ask for freedom *from* religion in public life. We ask public figures to refrain from discussing religion. In America, faith is a strictly personal matter.

Voting is a privilege. A 1997 poll by the National Constitution Center found that half of all Americans did not know that there are 100 U.S. senators. One quarter didn't know what the First Amendment says. Forty percent could not say that there are three branches of government, much less identify them. People who do not possess at least a rudimentary knowledge about our system of government and current events should not be permitted to cast votes that determine our nation's fate. We would not allow untrained pilots to fly airplanes, yet the consequences of uniformed voting are far more dire than a mere plane crash. Americans seeking to cast votes should be required to answer a few simple questions, such as the ability to identify their state capital and one of their U.S. senators.

OUR SAFETY

Judges should decide punishment. Half the states hobble criminal court judges with a rigid "three strikes" sentencing guideline that requires defendants convicted of a third serious felony—these include murder, rape, arson, robbery, kidnapping, even burglary—to be sent to prison for the rest of their lives with no chance for parole. As Charles Fannan writes in *Friction* magazine about California's 1994 "three strikes" initiative, "Perhaps the most egregious consequences of this measure are the draconian sentences that are given to many third-strikers. One hapless victim of this harsh law received a 25-year-to-life sentence for stealing a package of meat worth $5.62. Another man received a life term for shoplifting a pack of cigarettes, and another unlucky third-striker was given a 30-year-to-life sentence for stealing a video recorder and a coin collection. Punishment was appropriate in all of these cases, but these sentences were grossly excessive. These examples of judicial absurdity are not exceptions to the rule, many third-strikers are serving life sentences because they were convicted of petty offenses punishable under the three strikes law." Fortunately states like Washington, first in the country to pass a "three strikes" law, are liberalizing their criminal codes by, for instance, reducing sentences for drug offenses and dedicating money for drug treatment. Washington expects to *save* $45 million a year by releasing low-risk offenders. "Look at the people who are behind these [new] laws," points out Joseph Lehman, secretary of the Washington State Department of Corrections. "They are not all advocates of a liberal philosophy." Judges want, need, and deserve the right to use their own discretion to separate dangerous predators from small-time crooks and dole out punishment accordingly. While it is true that some judges will prove excessively harsh or lenient in their sentencing, schemes like "three strikes" do even more damage by eliminating the opportunity for a human being to consider the fate of convicted persons using basic common sense. Judges and juries should have full judicial discretion.

Murdering murderers debases all of us. All of the usual arguments in favor of capital punishment have been thoroughly debunked. Death penalty litigation is frequently more expensive than lifetime incarceration. States with active death chambers rarely see the frequently vaunted "deterrent effect" of reduced crime crates. We do not dispute that those who kill and rape deserve to die. We believe, however, that the state should set an example based on law and ethics, and that murdering murderers reduces the executioner to the moral depravity of the condemned. The United States should join the ranks of the overwhelming majority of the world's industrialized nations that have banned the death penalty. Life in prison is punishment enough, and permits guilty mistaken verdicts to be overturned before it's too late.

Let our people go. Two million people, a greater per capita prison population than that of any other industrialized nation, are now incarcerated in the United States. The overwhelming majority of these men and women are serving time for minor drug offenses: possessing or selling small quantities of marijuana, cocaine, or prescription pills. In 2002 the United States spent a staggering $46 billion—one-eighth of the federal budget deficit— to keep these prisoners behind bars. While we condemn the use of illegal drugs and believe that more should be done to prevent their dissemination, these sentences are pointless and excessive. People convicted of minor drug offenses should be sentenced to substantial fines, rehabilitation treatment, and community service. For example, Karen Shook, a mother of three children, was sentenced to twenty to forty years in Michigan state prison for conspiracy to sell 2.5 ounces of cocaine. It was her first offense. (Fortunately, she was freed when the state liberalized its drug laws.) "There is a smarter way to deal with criminals, rather than just being tough on them and putting them away for the rest of their lives," argues John Vratil, chairman of Kansas's State Senate judiciary committee. "Even those people who favor being tough on crime don't want to find the money to build more prisons and go back on their pledge of 'no new taxes'," notes Vratil, a Republican. Kansas is moving in the right direction, having mandated treatment for first-time drug offenders. That will reduce the state's inmate population from nine thousand to seventy-six hundred a year. Similar reforms should be enacted nationwide.

We are judged by how we treat those whom we condemn. If a society is judged by the way it treats those it most dislikes, we are not doing well. American prison inmates, trapped out of sight of television cameras, have been subjected to the whims of "get tough on crime" political demagogues who eliminate their rights and privileges in order to curry favor with angry voters during election years. The average prisoner works thirty-five hours a week for slave wages—twelve cents to one dollar per hour. He or she is deprived of such basic medical care as the right to see a dentist. To visit a prison is to come face to face with nineteenth-century America; this is wrong. Recidivism will always be a problem in the criminal justice system, but first offenders and other people genuinely interested in rehabilitation must be given a second chance to change their lives after they finish serving their time. After prisoners are released, they should not have to disclose their past to prospective employers. Initiatives like Megan's Law, which require convicted child molesters to register with local police and notify their new neighbors of their presence, make it impossible for these men to start afresh. (These are cynical attempts to foist law enforcement responsibilities onto hapless civilians while appearing to be "tough on crime." If authorities are truly concerned that a prisoner continues to represent a threat to their community, he should be kept in custody rather than released.) Being deprived of one's freedom, as anyone who has done time can attest, is punishment enough. Torture in the form of inadequate medical care, abuse in the form of exploitation, and harassment in the form of post-release strictures have no place in a civilized society.

White-collar crime deserves real time. A man who steals millions of dollars via embezzlement or fraud should be treated at least as harshly as one who steals a hundred bucks from someone in a dark alley. Corporate criminals should face jail time without special privileges for their supposed social status.

OUR SECURITY

Declaring war is not the decision of one man. No president should dispatch substantial numbers of troops overseas without the explicit consent of the United States Congress as documented by a formal declaration of war—an instrument that has not been handed down since 1941. (Not coincidently, World War II was the last conflict that enjoyed broad support from the American public.) War is the gravest matter in which a nation-state can engage. It must never be entered into lightly. Policies of preemption, as proven by our failure to find supposed weapons of mass destruction in Iraq, are a recipe for disaster. The United States should assume a defensive military posture, being prepared and willing to defend itself aggressively if attacked while taking care not to provoke such attacks. It should not engage in wars of expansion, aggression, or neocolonialism, nor should it support such wars by proxy, as it did in Afghanistan during the Soviet occupation. War should be the last resort of a civilized nation.

A strong military is fundamental to our security. Our troops are woefully underpaid—thousands of full-time soldiers qualify for food stamps and other forms of welfare—and housed in substandard homes on military bases. Attracting high-quality servicemen to an all-volunteer army requires higher than average salaries and benefits, and we must be willing to make the sacrifices necessary to ensure that high remuneration. The greatest threats to our national security are overextension of the American empire and resulting economic insecurity. We have seen these perils in our wars in Afghanistan and Iraq, where more than two-thirds of active duty military troops are bogged down with no end in sight, at an extraordinary expense of at least $100 billion per annum. Empire-building will bankrupt us. We must put an end to the current practice governing defense appropriations, wherein contactors are awarded a set amount of money and asked what they can produce for that sum, and replace it with competitive bidding. Building weapons systems purely for deterrent effect, as we did during the Cold War, is a waste of money that accelerates arms proliferation. We must ensure that our troops are the best paid, best equipped, and best trained in the world—and we can do it for a fraction of the current defense budget, which is projected to account for more than 70 percent of all federal spending by 2005.

Foreign aid must be revamped or eliminated. A University of Maryland Program on International Policy Attitudes (PIPA) poll taken shortly after September 11 found that "The American public continues to show strong support for giving foreign aid in principle. Nearly eight in ten (79 percent) agreed that 'the United States should be willing to share at least a small portion of its wealth with those in the world who are in great need.'" Americans would be shocked to learn that their nation contributes a mere one percent of gross domestic product to foreign aid—the least of any industrialized nation. It's not enough, yet it's also too much when one considers where the money is going. Of $3.8 billion allocated by Congress for "foreign aid" for the 2001 fiscal year, $2.1 billion took the form of military assistance and $600 million in economic subsidies to Israel. Egypt received $1.3 billion in weapons and $615 million for social programs. Jordan and Colombia (for drug interdiction) bring up the rear; the remaining few hundred million bucks were divvied up among 140 nations. When American citizens visualize "foreign aid," they imagine bags of grain stamped "Gift of the American people" being dropped to starving Africans. They're certainly not thinking of F-16s and other high-tech weapons to be used by Middle Eastern leaders to assassinate their political opponents. Congress should designate the term "foreign aid" to mean aid for food, medicine, infrastructure, and other strictly peaceful purposes—not arms. Military aid to other nations should be eliminated entirely; our alliances should be limited to mutual-defense treaties that guarantee each other's territorial integrity. Taking sides in disputes that do not concern us should never rise to the level of funneling weaponry to one side over the other.

If others hate us, it's our duty to convince them not to. A June 2003 BBC poll of the citizens of eleven nations shows that the United States is one of the most despised nations in the world. According to the BBC: "Asked who is the more dangerous to world peace and stability, the United States was rated higher than Al Qaeda by respondents in both Jordan (71 percent) and Indonesia (66 percent). America was also rated more dangerous than two countries considered as 'rogue states' by Washington. It was rated more dangerous than Iran, by people in Jordan, Indonesia, Russia, South Korea and Brazil, and more dangerous than Syria by respondents all the countries, except for Australia, Israel and the United States." Interestingly, people in these nations hate our policies a lot more than they hate us: "Attitudes towards America as a whole, however, were a lot more favorable, with 50 percent expressing fairly or very favorable views, as opposed to 40 percent of unfavorable views." As the world's sole remaining superpower, it is tempting to dismiss the views of citizens from nations unable to challenge our economic and military prowess as emanating from the jealous and ignorant. We must remember, however, that historical cycles dictate that we will not always be the world's richest nation—and that our children and grandchildren will be held to account for the actions we take today. Therefore, we must assume a less aggressive and arrogant posture in dealing with the international community. We must scrupulously respect the right of other countries to conduct their affairs however they deem appropriate, including respect for ideologies and economic systems with which we may not agree. In return we demand that same right of self-determination for ourselves. We pledge that we will no longer interfere in foreign elections or demand "regime change" abroad. Although we reserve the right to disagree with international bodies, we will listen carefully, and join in when we can whenever the world moves to take action on a matter of international import, such as the Kyoto Protocol to reduce the emission of greenhouse gases. While we will never again commit our military forces to aggressive wars of the Panama, Gulf War, and Iraq war varieties, we will not hesitate to intervene, in conjunction with international bodies, to end spiraling genocide of the variety that occurred in Bosnia and Rwanda during the 1990s.

We can stop illegal drugs if we want. Despite the Soviet Union's thousands of miles-long borders with the marijuana- and opium-producing nations of Central and South Asia, it was virtually impossible during communist times to purchase illegal narcotics in Russia. Nowadays pot—available on any street and in any high school in the United States for a few dollars—is scarce and expensive in Japan. The Soviet and Japanese governments didn't have to jail millions or run cheesy anti-drug ads on TV to keep their societies drug-free—they relied on strict border controls. Here in the United States, we have been brainwashed by tired propaganda claiming that our long borders with Canada and Mexico cannot be defended. Consider, however, that during the 1970s, a period of widespread narcotics addiction in the U.S., it was virtually impossible to purchase a bottle of banned Russian vodka. Today it's all but impossible, despite high demand, to obtain Cohiba cigars made in communist Cuba. The reason for this bizarre incongruity is obvious: our borders are guarded by officials who deliberately look the other way as cocaine, heroin, and other dangerous narcotics are imported for distribution on American streets. We must renew our commitment to safeguarding the American people by rigorously screening our borders for these shipments, both by hiring highly paid professional border patrolpersons and by prosecuting those found guilty of allowing drugs to pass through, either by corruption or incompetence. Furthermore, we must not fight the "war on drugs" overseas. U.S. DEA programs supporting the right-wing government of Colombia, for example, are little more than a lame pretext for propping up an unpopular regime. They rarely have the desired effect of reducing the importation of drugs, and they create resentment among those oppressed by the regimes we prop up.

Trade sanctions hurt innocent people, not dictators. For more than forty years the United States has imposed trade sanctions in order to encourage the Cuban people to rise up and overthrow Fidel Castro. (In a 2003 vote of the U.N. General Assembly on the anti-Cuban blockade, 179 nations voted to end sanctions. Only three—the United States, Israel, and the Marshall Islands—voted in favor.) For more than ten years we did the same thing in Iraq, hoping against hope that hungry and angry Iraqis would depose Saddam Hussein. Now we're imposing similar sanctions on the military dictatorship of Myanmar, the former British colony of Burma. We slapped eighty-five new economic sanctions on foreign countries between 1996 and 2001 alone! The practical effect of trade sanctions, often and ironically imposed by the same folks who promote unfettered free trade because it's supposed to encourage dictatorships to transition to democracy, is to alienate and harden the resolve of regimes whose policies we are trying to affect. "Instead of giving us time, instead of giving us encouragement and a pat on the back, [Western countries] are always coming with threats, like sanctions and more sanctions," remarked Colonel Hla Min of the Burmese SLORC junta. Trade sanctions don't work because we don't live in a united world. Nations outside of the sphere of alliances of the sanctions-imposing countries tend to see sanctions as opportunities. "We are not worried about U.S. and European sanctions, as trade with India, China and Thailand is already good," asserts Burmese ambassador to the U.N. Dr. Kyaw Win. The real victims of Burmese trade sanctions are the thirty to forty thousand young women estimated by the State Department to have lost their jobs. (Department spokesman Richard Boucher says: "We do believe that some of those young women have gone into the sex trade.") In Burma, 44 percent of children suffer from malnourishment. An estimated 750,000 Iraqi children died of hunger and lack of adequate medical care due to 1990s U.S. sanctions—yet trade didn't end. France, Russia, and other nations continued to do business with Saddam Hussein. As a point of principle, and in recognition of historical precedent, we reject the use of trade sanctions targeted at civilian populations in order to effect changes in personnel or policy abroad.

We respect the international community. The United Nations was our idea, is headquartered in New York and is the successor to the League of Nations, the brainchild of U.S. president Woodrow Wilson. Those who say that we should get out of the U.N. or stop paying our dues are, therefore, un-American. Though it is an intrinsically imperfect and flawed institution, we affirm our desire and interest to take an active role in the U.N. because the world would be an even more dangerous place without it. We should no longer reject or refuse to adhere to U.N. resolutions on a piecemeal basis; for example, we should call on our ally Israel to enforce Resolution 242, which calls for complete withdrawal from the occupied Palestinian territories.

The energy crisis never ended. It shouldn't require repeating that U.S. dependency on foreign oil reserves puts our economic and military security at risk. Although the U.S. accounts for just five percent of the world's population, it consumes a quarter of its oil—and produces a quarter of its air pollution. It's high time for the U.S. to get serious about cleaner sources of power, including solar, hybrid, wind, hydroelectric, and nuclear. The federal government should incent private industry to convert to cleaner forms of energy, and set deadlines for the automakers to increase fuel efficiency and begin producing non-gasoline-consuming vehicles in significant numbers. The U.S. must dedicate itself to creating subway, light rail, and bus systems in all major cities and a high-speed rail system similar to those found in Europe, Japan, and other industrialized nations.

Veterans should want for nothing. No one who risks his or her life to defend the United States should lack of the basic necessities of life after serving honorably. Our current system of VA hospitals is a disgrace; veteran's benefits are shamefully low. We must make the following commitment to our men and women in uniform: no matter what happens, your countrymen will always be there for you the way you were there for us when it counted.

OUR FUTURE

Government must balance its budget. As long as it permits adequate flexibility in the event of an economic downturn or other national emergency, we support a balanced budget amendment to the Constitution. We do, however, pledge to balance the fed-eral budget when we are in power and to encourage leaders from other parties to do so when we are not. A balanced budget could currently be achieved by returning to the progressive system of taxation in place during the economic boom of the late 1950s, wherein the maximum tax rate for those who earned more than $1 million per year was 90 percent. Those who receive society's greatest privileges should pay the highest proportion of the costs. There is also considerable waste in a wide variety of spending programs ranging from welfare to Social Security to defense; these must be eliminated in the interest of eliminating the punitive cost of interest on the national debt.

We must help people who are suffering but avoid rewarding laziness. The purpose of welfare is to give people who are unable to work the help they need during difficult times. In some cases, such as those who suffer from medical conditions that prevent them from holding a job, assistance must be made on a permanent basis. In most other cases, welfare—whether in the form of food stamps, aid to dependent children, unemployment benefits, or housing assistance—should be generous but temporary. Able-bodied individuals who refuse work when it becomes available should not be eligible for taxpayer-funded assistance. Those who abuse our national generosity via fraud should be vigorously prosecuted. On the other hand, if a person becomes un- or underemployed through no fault of their own, it is the responsibility of those of us who are better off to provide the help that will forestall their fall into wholesale poverty. We must strive to create an ideal world in which anyone who wants to work enjoys that opportunity; until that ideal is achieved, welfare programs help prevent temporary periods of downward mobility from becoming permanent.

Public funds cannot be used for private purposes. With the exception of matters of important national security such as the need to subsidize the expenses of developing alternative energy resources, government should not funnel aid to business directly or indirectly. If government finds it necessary to help an important corporate concern, as it did by bailing out Chrysler during the seventies, the company's future profits should be repaid to the treasury. Free markets must be regulated, not funded. Furthermore, subsidizing one company or a genre of businesses has the practical effect of choosing sides. At its worst, this could stifle the development of promising new lines of entrepreneurship; at best it's tremendously unfair. States and municipalities should not compete against each other, as industrial development agencies now do by abating taxes, building roads, and waiving regulations, in order to secure new business. The business of America is people, not business.

The environment is humanity's #1 priority. Lester Brown put it best: "When we ask the question 'Do we have enough time?' or 'How much time do we have?' we have to be specific—how much time for what? Do we have enough time to save the Aral Sea? No, it's dead. Can we save India's rain forests? Probably not, they may have reached the point of no return. Can we save the glaciers in Glacier National Park? Probably not. Half of them are gone already and the other half are projected to disappear within the next thirty years. Can we reverse the environmental trends that are slowly undermining the global economy before we face economic decline and collapse of the sort that was experienced by earlier civilizations? I think so, I think we can. But we don't have a lot of time." Should we allow air, water, and ecosystem to become fouled, nothing else will matter. Safeguarding the environment will always be our top national security, bar none. When conflicts arise between the environment and business, between the environment and jobs, and between the environment and profits, the safety and sanctity of the global and national environment must take precedence.

Capitalism dies when government permits monopolies. It has long been recognized that one of the most unfortunate side effects of capitalism is the tendency of capital to accrue in increasing amounts to the benefit of a smaller and smaller elite group of individuals and corporations. Paradoxically, monopolies stifle the competitive instinct that drives the engine of capitalism; when one company becomes too dominant in its field it becomes prohibitive for challengers, no matter how smart or driven, to take them on. The current deregulatory climate that began during the Reagan-Bush years and continued under Clinton and Bush II has led to an alarming number of mergers and supermergers. Ironically companies like AOL Time Warner, which dominates a wide range of businesses from Internet access to popular music, have reduced the profits of the entities they superceded. The current practice of rubberstamping applications for mergers should be halted; wherever doubt occurs, a merger should not be approved. Companies like Microsoft, which have engaged in ethical lapses and outright malfeasance, should be broken up and/or nationalized both to punish their executives and to create increased and diversified competition. The business of America is people, not business—and the government must assiduously safeguard the interest of its citizens over the quest of big business for short-term profits.

The United States should admit more legal, and fewer illegal, immigrants. According to the Immigration and Naturalization Service, about three hundred thousand illegal immigrants slip into the United States every year. More than 7 million people, 70 percent of them from Mexico, currently live in the United States illegally. Because they're constantly on the run and afraid of the authorities, these people cannot become a part of their community. They move often, causing their children to change schools frequently or to not attend at all. They often don't pay taxes, they're not subject to the military draft and, because they're desperate for work, they take jobs that pay substandard wages, driving down the value of labor across the board. They're exploited by employers in sweatshops and the agricultural sector, and they reduce average salaries and thus economic growth. Guarding national borders is perhaps the single most important function of the modern nation-state; insecure or porous borders put the lie to the idea that a country exists at all. In the past, the government has turned a blind eye to illegal immigration because so many well-connected businesses rely on illegals for cheap labor. This must cease. Those who hire illegal workers should be subjected to fines and jail time and their companies should be seized by the federal government. Borders must be secured to prevent these people from entering; when caught they should be deported. It should be impossible for an illegal immigrant to earn a living in the United States. At the same time, this harsh new policy on illegal immigration must be tempered with a common sense approach to deal with the recent past: those people who are already here, who were encouraged to come here with a wink and nudge and have already laid down roots, should be offered full amnesty and a chance at citizenship if they agree to take language and culture classes about the nation in which they now reside. Furthermore, a strong border-protection policy must be coupled with increased *legal* immigration. In 1998, only 660,477 immigrants were legally admitted to the United States—about one-quarter of one percent of our total population. At this rate, we will only increase our population by 25 percent by the year 2100. That's an absurdly low rate. We are a nation of immigrants—every American, including the American Indians, originally came from somewhere else. Legal immigration should be dramatically increased to allow those with special skills and the willingness to work hard to make our nation wealthier in all the ways that count.

There is no such thing as free trade. The trouble with unregulated free trade is that it throws the balance between labor and management out of whack. Companies may open a factory anywhere in the world in order to take advantage of low wages; a shoe company, for example, would probably find that the $20 per month average salary in Kazakhstan more than compensates for the high cost of shipping the assembled product to consumers in Western countries. Employees, on the other hand, are not free to seek the highest salaries. If the steel mill in your hometown in eastern Ohio closes down, you can't hop on a plane to search for a higher-paying job in Saudi Arabia. While you might obtain a visa, you probably won't score a work permit and you certainly won't be allowed to stay permanently. And even if you possess some special skill that induces the House of Saud to make an exception in your case, the cultural shock—not to mention missing your friends and family—make it unlikely that you're going to pack up and head for the desert. This flexibility gap between labor and capital is the fundamental flaw of free trade; until and unless our world moves to a unified government and economic system, globalization will drive down wages and environmental protections for the benefit of a few short-sighted corporate executives. Nonetheless, it is undeniable that there are goods that cannot be obtained in our country and that trade between nations is essential for many industries to thrive. We should not encourage the importation of goods except for those that cannot be produced here in the United States. Products that can, and are, made here—like cars and major appliances—should either be prohibited or subjected to high tariffs in order to, yes, protect our workers from predatory pricing structures based on the gap in incomes between American and third world workers. Previous free trade agreements, like NAFTA and GATT, that have cost the United States hundreds of thousands of jobs, should be rescinded.

Wage attrition must end. The average real weekly wages of production and nonsupervisory workers fell from $315 (in 1992 dollars) in 1973 to $264 in 1989. The 1990s economic boom brought this figure up to $271 in 1999, but that was still less than 1962. It has fallen since then. All throughout that period, American workers were becoming more productive—but the fruits of that increased productivity have gone to people other than those doing the work. Corporate profits have zoomed up as the disparity of income between rich and poor has widened. To ensure that the blessings of our nation are shared more fairly, every American worker should be guaranteed an annual wage increase equal to or greater than the corresponding increase in the consumer price index.

Rich people should pay higher taxes than poor people. The purpose of income taxes is two-fold: to raise revenues for government and to redistribute wealth. A decades-long trend has led to a stupefying division between rich and poor, one that nearly approaches third world standards: five percent of Americans own more than 60 percent of all the nation's wealth. At least four million households suffer from hunger; Bill Gates is personally worth $40 billion. (His personal net worth exceeds the annual gross domestic product of all but the top fourth of the world's richest nations.) The government should tax the income and assets of people like Gates and use the proceeds to fund projects that benefit all of us. A fair tax system looks like a baseball game: fans who get to sit in the box pay hundreds of dollars for the privilege; "bleacher creatures" pay a few bucks. Similarly, wealthy individuals and businesses should be taxed nearly to death. We scoff at the old argument that high taxes discourage hard work; to the contrary, human initiative is often its own reward. Moreover, keeping 10 percent of $1 million is better than keeping 90 percent of $10,000. A progressive tax system should be restored and expanded. Regressive taxes, such as the Social Security withholding tax that doesn't apply to six- and seven-figureincomes, should be readjusted.

295 WAKE UP, YOU'RE LIBERAL

U.S. corporations should serve American interests. A company that incorporates its headquarters overseas, whether to avoid paying U.S. taxes or for other reasons, should be treated as a foreign entity for the purpose of tariffs and taxation. Government agencies should not offer contracts to foreign companies unless no American companies are available to do the same work. The officers of American corporations are burdened with an awesome responsibility; they are charged with the economic well-being of the American people. Thus they should not be permitted to pay themselves extravagant salaries. (A 1980s-era proposal by the Securities and Exchange Commission to limit CEO salaries to 20 times that of a company's lowest-paid worker seems like a good place to start.) Executives who indulge in fraudulent bookkeeping or other forms of malfeasance should expect to face substantial jail time for their crimes. Corporations that harm the public interest in any respect, whether by harming the environment or laying off workers in time of profitability, should expect to be subjected to government-led "regime change."

While remaining true to our basic ideals of fairness, equality, and justice, we pledge to constantly remain open to new ways of thinking, identifying emerging problems to be addressed, and, most importantly, never being satisfied with the status quo. We will never settle for second best, so-so, or just good enough. We are Americans. We can be, and we can do, anything.

EPILOGUE

You owe your friends the best advice you can give them. They deserve the truth, they swear that they want it, and yet—they so rarely take it.

The optimist in me drove me to write this book, but now that it's in your hands the little realist in the back of my skull keeps snarking that all my effort was just a waste of time. Indeed, the Left maybe too demoralized, the Right too strong, and the nation too far gone to save from authoritarianism at home and overexpansion leading to bankruptcy abroad. I don't expect the Democrats to study up and start kicking ass any time soon, nor do I believe that many progressive organizations have what it takes to get serious about their worthy goals. The culture of wimpiness may be so ingrained into the liberal mindset that its ideals are doomed, as right-wingers claim, to the ash heap of history. Would I bet money that liberals will follow my advice? A little. Not my life savings or anything.

The myriad problems with past liberal strategies and attitudes have deep roots and conservatives currently enjoy enormous advantages. Inertia—forward, backward, or stationary—is hard to change. The great physicist Isaac Newton's First Law of Motion states that an object at rest tends to stay at rest, and an object in motion tends to stay in motion, with the same speed and in the same direction unless acted upon by an outside force. Liberals need to take direction from the inside out. It won't be easy.

Things usually become worse before they get better. We Americans like to believe that progress is the natural state of history and politics, but to lift another analogy from the natural world, the Second Law of Thermodynamics dictates that the tendency of things to fall apart may be more relevant to our times than Newton's First Law. The more we involve ourselves in bedraggled hellholes like Afghanistan and Iraq, after all, the more their historical and social entropy, their anarchy and tribalism, seem to rub off on us. It may be that neither the United States nor its patriotic citizens have suffered enough to motivate them to become serious about changing course.

Because I know the New York subway system better than most people—I was obsessed with underground railroads when I first came here—friends sometimes call me for advice about navigating the city beneath the concrete. During the bad old 1980s, when the trains were still covered with graffiti and street crime was out of control, a friend asked me whether I thought she should travel to a particular subway station in Brooklyn late at night. Hell no, I advised. Take a cab. Her proposed destination, a warren of dark tunnels rendered dodgy by the scaffolded dead ends of an endless reconstruction project, had been the scene of a recent fatal stabbing.

A few days later, she called me to let me know that she'd been mugged at the station in question—after she'd promised me that she wouldn't go there. A guy had pulled a knife on her. Fortunately, he ran off with her purse without using it. It could have been worse.

"But I *told* you not to go to that dump!" I said, relieved but annoyed that she hadn't followed my advice. "Why did you bother to ask me in the first place?"

There was a pause on the line. "I had already decided to go when I called you," she confessed. "I wanted you to make me feel better about it."

Liberals may or may not have already determined where they want to go in the years ahead, but they desperately need advice—whether they know it or not. Here's mine. If people pick up a few points here and there, that would be more than I have any right to expect. If they choose to continue the same old tired tactics that have led to disaster after disaster over the last few decades, if they ignore good counsel, they, we, and I may lose everything we hold dear. No matter what happens, though, I've said my piece. If we meet in a bomb shelter years from today, eating dead rats and water biscuits out of rusty tin cans as dust shakes from the ceiling, I hope you won't blame me.

—New York City, March 2004

SELECT BIBLIOGRAPHY

ABORTION

Bush, George W. "President Bush Signs Partial Abortion Ban Act of 2003." The Ronald Reagan Building, November 5, 2003, <http://www.whitehouse.gov/news/releases/2003/11/20031105-1.html>

Stolberg, Sheryl Gay. "Abortion Vote Leaves Many in the Senate Conflicted." *New York Times*, October 23, 2003.

———. "Bill Barring Abortion Procedure Drew on Backing From Many Friends of Roe v. Wade." *New York Times*, October 23, 2003.

ARMS TRADE

Shanker, Thom. "U.S. Remains Leader in Global Arms Sales, Report Says." *New York Times*, September 25, 2003.

BUSH ADMINISTRATION

Boaz, David. "The Bush Betrayal." *Washington Post*, November 30, 2003, <http://www.cato.org/research/articles/boaz-031130.html>

Calabresi, Massimo. "Colin Powell: Planning for an Exit." *Time*, August 31, 2002, <http://www.time.com/time/nation/article/0,8599,346150,00.html>

Dickerson, John F. and Karen Tumulty. "Love Him, Hate Him President." *Time*, December 1, 2003, <http://www.time.com/time/archive/preview/from_covers/0,10987,1101031201-548789,00.html>

Lilleston, Randy. "Making the presidency his own: After shaky start, Bush gains public approval" CNN, <http://edition.cnn.com/SPECIALS/2001/bush.100/stories/overview.html>

CLINTON ADMINISTRATION

Blumenthal, Sidney. *The Clinton Wars.* New York: Farrar Straus & Giroux, 2003.

Dionne Jr., E .J. and Robert Kuttner. "Did Clinton Succeed or Fail?" *American Prospect*, August 28, 2000, <http://www.prospect.org/print-friendly/print/V11/19/dionne-e.html>

Fleschner, Malcolm. "Lead Time." *SellingPower.com*, <http://www.sellingpower.com/article/leadtime.asp>

Reich, Robert B. *Locked in the Cabinet.* New York: Vintage Books, 1998.

Woellert, Lorraine. "Bill Clinton Is Gone . . . And So Is the Buzz." *Business Week*. May 13, 2002, <http://www.businessweek.com/magazine/content/02_19/b3782102.htm>

CONSERVATISM

Eland, Ivan. "Newt's Defense Gift: Georgia on My Mind." Cato Institute, November 24, 1997, <http://www.cato.org/dailys/11-24-97.html>

Fukuyama, Francis. *The End of History and the Last Man.* New York: Avon Books, 1993.

Rentschler, William. "Barry Goldwater: Icon of Political Integrity." *USA Today Magazine*, March 2000.

Thies, Clifford F. "Barry Goldwater 1909–1998." Republican Liberty Caucus, <http://www.republicanliberty.org/comment/ct_99-02.htm>

CORPORATIONS

Burns, Scott. "The Big Dogs Eat Fois Gras: Fortune and The Great CEO Pay Heist." *Dallas Morning News*, July 8, 2001, <http://www.dallasnews.com/business/scottburns/columns/archives/2001/010708SU.htm>

CBS News. "The Ethics of Business." July 8–9, 2002, <http://www.cbsnews.com/htdocs/c2k/bizback.pdf>

Johnston, David Cay. "U.S. Corporations Are Using Bermuda to Slash Tax Bills." *New York Times*, February 18, 2002.

Nace, Ted. *Gangs of America: The Rise of Corporate Power and the Disabling of Democracy.* Berrett-Koehler, 2003.

CRIME AND PUNISHMENT

Butterfield, Fox. "States Review Prison Policies," *New York Times,* November 11, 2003.

Fannan, Charles. "The Insanity of the Three Strikes and You're Out Law." *Friction*, January 30, 2002, <http://www.frictionmagazine.com/politik/current_events/three_strikes.asp>

Sarat, Austin. *When the State Kills: Capital Punishment and the American Condition.* Princeton University Press, 2001.

DEMOCRATIC PARTY

Bai, Matt. "Notion Building." *New York Times Magazine*, October 12, 2003.

BBC. "US airline sued over Concorde crash." September 27, 2000, <http://news.bbc.co.uk/1/low/world/europe/944654.stm>

Burke, Amy. "Party Decline: A Primer." *American Prospect*, May 1, 1998.

Bury, Chris. "The Clinton Years." *Frontline*. PBS , January 16, 2001, <http://www.pbs.org/wgbh/pages/frontline/shows/clinton/etc/script.html>

CBS News. "Clinton Offers Rx For Ailing Democrats." December 3, 2002, <http://www.cbsnews.com/stories/2002/12/04/politics/main531768.shtml>

Clymer, Adam. "Democrats Seek Focus And More Money, Too." *New York Times*, May 26, 2003.

Conason, Joe. "Democrats have only themselves to blame." *Salon.com*, November 6, 2002, <http://www.salon.com/politics/conason/2002/11/06/bush/>

From, Al. "Bush's no moderate—he's to the right of Reagan." *Christian Science Monitor*, April 26, 2001, <http://search.csmonitor.com/durable/2001/04/26/fp11s2-csm.shtml>

Greenberg, Anna. "Do Real Men Vote Democratic?" *American Prospect*, October 23, 2000, <http://www.prospect.org/print-friendly/print/V11/22/greenberg-a.html>

Hightower, Jim. Interview. *Progressive*, November 2003, <http:// www.progressive.org/nov03/intv1103.html>

Judis, John B. and Texeira Judis. *The Emerging Democratic Majority.* New York: Scribner Books, 2002.

Kristof, Nicholas D. "The Left Dumbs Down." *New York Times*, November 5, 2002.

Miller, Zell. "How Democrats Lost the South." *Washington Times*, November 3, 2003, <http://www.washtimes.com/national/20031103-123326-5341r.htm>

Morris, L. R. "Jimmy Carter's Ruling Class." *Harper's*, October 1977.

Nagourney, Adam. "Centrist Democrats Warn party Not to Present Itself as 'Far Left.'" *New York Times*, July 29, 2003.

Noah, Timothy. "Democrats 36,000, Part 2." *Slate.com*, November 12, 2002, <http://slate.msn.com/id/2073887/>

Schumer, Fran. "A Paddle for the Mainstream." *New York Times*, November 12, 2003.

Weisberg, Jacob. "Big-Tent Democrats." *Slate.com*, October 31, 1997, <http://slate.msn.com/id/2290/>

EDUCATION

Burd, Stephen. "Bush's Next Target?" *Chronicle of Higher Education*, July 11, 2003, <http://www.utwatch.org/oldnews/chron_bush_7_11_03.html>

Columbia Record. "Report Finds Overcrowding in New York City Schools at Crisis Level." February 17, 1995, <http://www.columbia.edu/cu/record/archives/vol20/vol20_iss17/record2017.31.html>

Kennedy, Denis. "The Case for Reforming Public Education." *Democratic Underground*, April 14, 2001, <http://www.democraticunderground.com/articles/01/04/010414_education.html>

Lewin, Tamar. "4 Highest-Paid University Presidents Top $800,000 a Year." *New York Times*, November 10, 2003.

Mazelis, Fred. "New York City schools crisis continues." World Socialist Web Site, <http://www.wsws.org/articles/1999/may1999/nyc-m24.shtml>

Morin, Richard. "College Degree: Key to the American Dream?" *Washington Post*, May 8, 2000, <http://www.washingtonpost.com/wp-srv/politics/polls/wat/archive/wat050800.htm>

National Center for Education Statistics. "Homeschooling in the United States: 1999," <http://nces.ed.gov/pubs2001/Homeschool/>

Public Agenda. "Great Expectations: How the Public and Parents—White, African American and Hispanic—View Higher Education." *Public Agenda*, <http://www.publicagenda.org/specials/highered/highered.htm>

Winter, Greg. "Public College Tuition Rose 14% in '03, Survey Finds." *New York Times*, October 22, 2003.

ENVIRONMENT

Lobjakas, Ahto. "Environmentalist Predicts Economic Collapse If Trends Continue." Radio Free Europe/Radio Liberty, December 2002, <http://www.rferl.org/nca/features/2002/02/19022002101548.asp>

FREE TRADE

Axtman, Kris. "NAFTA's shop-floor impact." *Christian Science Monitor*, November 4, 2003, <http://www.csmonitor.com/2003/1104/p01s01-usec.html >

Faux, Jeff. "NAFTA at Seven." Economic Policy Institute, April 2001, <http://www.epinet.org/content.cfm/briefingpapers_nafta01_index>

MacArthur, John R.,*The Selling of Free Trade*. Hill & Wang, 2000.

Program on International Policy Attitudes. "International Trade: International Labor Standards," <http://www.americans-world.org/digest/global_issues/intertrade/laborstandards.cfm>

GAYS AND LESBIANS

Robertson, Pat. "Isn't My Happiness Most Important to God?" *700 Club*, Christian Broadcasting Network, December 20, 2003, <http://www.cbn.com/700club/askpat/BIO_101703.asp>

Robertson, Pat and Jerry Falwell. "Agents of Intolerance? Quotes from Pat and Jerry." *TomPaine.com*, March 2, 2000, <http://www.tompaine.com/feature2.cfm/ID/2820>

Seelye, Katharine Q. and Janet Elder. "Strong Support is Found for Ban on Gay Marriage," *New York Times*, December 21, 2003, A1.

GOVERNMENT SPENDING

Bartlett, Bruce R. "The President's Budget Request for Fiscal Year 2004." Senate and House Democratic Policy Committees Joint Hearing, February 7, 2003, <http://democrats.senate.gov/dpc/hearings/hearing2/Bartlett.pdf>

HEALTHCARE

Bernstein, Michael J. "Polls show public concern about health care slipping." *AM News*, September 2, 2002, <http://www.ama-assn.org/amednews/2002/09/02/gvsc0902.htm>

Peltz, Perri and Kara Thomas. "Hospital emergency rooms see patient population explosion," CNN, July 14, 2000, <http://www.cnn.com/2000/HEALTH/07/14/emergency.room/>

Reuters. "Health care fears top concern for Americans: poll." March 7, 2003.

United States Chamber of Commerce. "U.S. Chamber Calls News of 41.2 Million Uninsured Americans 'A Disgrace'—Urges Action to Create More Employer Options on Health Plans." September 27, 2002, <http://www.uschamber.com/press/releases/2002/september/02-159.htm>

Wilson, Pancheta. *Inside the HMO: America's Healthcare in Crisis.* Bernleigh Enterprise, 1999.

IMMIGRATION

United States Department of Justice, Immigration and Naturalization Service. "Legal Immigration, Fiscal Year 1998," <http://uscis.gov/graphics/publicaffairs/newsrels/98Legal.pdf>

IRAN-CONTRA SCANDAL

Kornbluh, Peter, Malcolm Byrne, and Theodore Draper, Editors. *The Iran-Contra Scandal: The Declassified History (The National Security Archive Document).* New York: New Press, 1993.

Walsh, Lawrence E., *Firewall: The Iran-Contra Conspiracy and Cover-Up* (New York: W.W. Norton & Company, 1998)

Webb, Gary and Maxine Waters. *Dark Alliance: The CIA, the Contras, and the Crack Cocaine Explosion.* New York: Seven Stories Press, 1999.

THE LEFT

Dowie, Mark. "The young inherit the Sierra Club." *Salon.com*, May 28, 1996, <http://www.salon.com/news/news960528.html>

Gain, Heather. "Hate Speech Continues Despite Calls for Compassion." *National NOW Times*, National Organization for Women, 2001, <http://www.now.org/nnt/special-2001/hatespeech.html>

Garofalo, Janeane. Interview with Howard Kurtz. "Reliable Sources," CNN, January 26, 2003, <http://www.cnn.com/TRANSCRIPTS/0301/26/rs.00.html>

Weinstein, James. *The Long Detour: The History and Future of the American Left.* New York: Westview Press, 2003.

Wilkie, Dana. "U.S. Anti-War Movement Based in the Mainstream." *San Diego Union-Tribune*, February 14, 2003, <http://advancement.sdsu.edu/marcomm/news/clips/Archive/Feb2003/021403/021403antiwar.htm>

LIBERALISM

Digital History. "The Struggle for Women's Suffrage," <http://www.digitalhistory.uh.edu/database/article_display.cfm?HHID=258>

Jordan, Barbara. "Who Then Will Speak for the Common Good?" Keynote Address to the Democratic National Convention, July 12, 1976, <http://www.kiosk2000.com/DCOnline/Legacies.htm>

Keillor, Garrison. "You Say Potato. . . . " *Time*, April 22, 1996.

Lehman, Herbert H. "The Triumph of Liberalism." Address at Columbia University, April 9, 1958, <http://www.columbia.edu/cu/lweb/indiv/lehsuite/liberalism/liberalism1.html>

Li, Minqi. "After Neoliberalism." *Monthly Review*, January 2004, 21.

Time. "Jimmy Carter: Person of the Year." January 3, 1977, <http://www.time.com/time/personoftheyear/archive/stories/1976.html>

Tipton, David. "Liberalism falling from American favor." *Daily Beacon*, (University of Tennessee) August 29, 1995.

MEDIA BIAS

Alterman, Eric. *What Liberal Media? The Truth About Bias and the News*. New York: Basic Books, 2003.

———. "The Vandals *Repeat* Did Not Take the Handles." *Nation*, June 18, 2001, <http://www.commondreams.org/views01/0601-05.htm>

Bevilacqua, Joe. "Liberalize the Media." *TomPaine.com*, July 3, 2003, <http://www.tompaine.com/feature2.cfm/ID/8248>

Conason, Joe. *Big Lies: The Right-Wing Propaganda Machine and How It Distorts the Truth*. New York: Thomas Dunne Books, 2003.

Cook, John. "Democratic activist buys liberal-radio firm." *Chicago Tribune*, November 19, 2003, <http://www.makethemaccountable.org/articles/AnShell_sold/AnShell_sold.htm>

Edny, Hazel Trice. "Media Cleans Up Strom Thurmond's Racist Quote." *Baltimore Times*, January 2, 2003, <http://www.btimes.com/news/Article/Article.asp?NewsID=2692&sID=3>

Tumulty, Karen. "Will We See Gore TV?" *Time*, June 18, 2003, <http://www.time.com/time/nation/article/0,8599,459345,00.html>

Volden, Jon. "Bush gets what he wants." "Your Views," *Bremerton (Washington) Sun*, February 24, 2003, <http://www.thesunlink.com/redesign/2003-02-24/opinion/82633.shtml>

NEOFASCISM

Allen, William Sheridan. *The Nazi Seizure of Power: The Experience of a Single German Town 1922–1945*. New York: Orchard Books, 1984.
Keyes, Alan. "The Fix Is In?" *WorldNetDaily.com*, April 7, 2001, <http://www.declaration.net/articles/keyes-fix-in.asp>
Sullivan, Andrew. "Fifth Column Watch." *Daily Dish*, November 15, 2003, <http://www.andrewsullivan.com/index.php?dish_inc=archives/2003_11_0 9_dish_archive.html#106870294027804545>

POLITICAL TACTICS

Associated Press, "Bush pleaded guilty to drunken driving in 1976." November 3, 2000, <http://newstribune.com/stories/110300/wor_1103000043.asp>
————. "Patricia Ireland Dismissed As YWCA Chief," October 20, 2003, <http:// http://www.fortwayne.com/mld/journalgazette/news/nation/7062980.htm>
BBC,. "Democrats accused of 'dirty tricks.'" November 3, 2000, <http://news.bbc.co.uk/1/hi/world/americas/1005914.stm>
Bumiller, Elisabeth. "Keepers of Bush Image Lift Stagecraft to New Heights." *New York Times*, May 16, 2003.
Bumiller, Elisabeth and Alison Mitchell. "Bush and His Aides Accuse Democrats of Second-Guessing." *New York Times,* May 18, 2002.
CNN. "Democrats pound GOP campaign ad." November 23, 2003, <http://www.cnn.com/2003/ALLPOLITICS/11/23/eleco4.prez.democrats.g op.ad/>
Corn, David. *The Lies of George W. Bush: Mastering the Politics of Deception* New York: Crown Books, 2003.
Ho, Rodney. "CBS won't show 'Reagans' series, moves it to cable." *Atlanta Journal-Constitution*, November 5, 2003.
Holman, Kwame. Political Wrap Background. *NewsHour with Jim Lehrer*. March 1, 2002, <http://www.pbs.org/newshour/bb/political_wrap/jan-juneo2/wrap_3-1a.html>
Jamieson, Kathleen Hall. *Dirty Politics: Deception, Distraction, and Democracy*. Oxford Press, 1993.
Kutler, Stanley. *Abuse of Power: The New Nixon Tapes*. New York: Touchstone Books, 1998.
Lopez, Steve. "Lone ranger." CNN, December 9, 1999, <http://www.cnn.com/ALLPOLITICS/time/1999/12/06/mccain2.html>
Meyer, Dick. "Tom Daschle, Potemkin Villain." CBS News, March 7, 2002, <http://www.cbsnews.com/stories/2002/03/07/opinion/main503212.shtml >

Morris, Dick. *Behind the Oval Office*. New York: Renaissance Books, 1998.

———. *The New Prince*. New York: Renaissance Books, 2000.

———. *Power Plays*. New York: Regan Books, 2002.

Nagourney, Adam and Sheryl Gay Stolberg. "Impolitic, Maybe, but in Character," *New York Times*, April 25, 2003.

Nichols, John. "Apathy, Inc.: Republicans aim to drive down voter turnout." *Progressive*, October 1998.

O'Neill, Brian. "Must-see TV with a political twist." *Pittsburgh Post-Gazette*, October 23, 2000, <http://www.post-gazette.com/columnists/20001023brian-column1.asp>

Perry, John L. "Up the Alp Without a Foothold." *NewsMax.com*, January 31, 2002, <http://www.newsmax.com/commentarchive.shtml?a=2002/1/31/060932>

Ratcliffe, R. G. and Karen Masterson. "DeLay admits to role in hunting for Democrats: DPS focus of 'potentially criminal' action." *Houston Chronicle*, May 23, 2003, <http://www.chron.com/cs/CDA/ssistory.mpl/topstory/1921866>

Shenon, Philip. "U.S. Moves to Block Money For Troops Held in '91 War." *New York Times*, November 10, 2003.

POVERTY

Kusmer, Ken. "Groups working to rehabilitate homeless veterans: Vets are more likely than average to be homeless." *Ocala (Florida) Star Banner*, November 9, 2003

Landes, David S. *The Wealth and Poverty of Nations*. New York: W.W. Norton & Company, 1999.

O'Flaherty, Brendan. *Making Room: The Economics of Homelessness*. Boston: Harvard University Press, 1998.

REPUBLICAN PARTY

Allen, Mike. "Bush Faces Sustained Dissension on the Right: 'A Sense of Disappointment Is Spreading.'" *Washington Post*, April 22, 2002, A01, <http://www.washingtonpost.com/ac2/wp-dyn/A25616-2002Apr21?language=printer>

Allen, Mike and Kathy Sawyer. "Return to Moon May Be on Agenda." *Washington Post*, December 5, 2003, A01, <http://www.washingtonpost.com/wp-dyn/articles/A36960-2003Dec4.html>

Barnes, Fred. "The (Finally) Emerging Republican Majority." *Weekly Standard*, October 27, 2003, <http://www.weeklystandard.com/Content/Public/Articles/000/000/003/259yvdec.asp>

Barrett, Jennifer. "Newsweek Poll: A Growing Dissatisfaction." *Newsweek*, October 11, 2003, <http://msnbc.msn.com/Default.aspx?id=3158214&p1=0>

Clymer, Adam. "Buoyed By Resurgence, G.O.P. Strives For An Era Of Dominance." *New York Times*, May 25, 2003.

CNN. "Strom Thurmond dead at 100." December 17, 2003, <http://www.cnn.com/2003/ALLPOLITICS/06/26/thurmond.obit/>

Coulter, Ann. *Slander: Liberal Lies About the American Right.* New York: Crown Books, 2002.

———. *Treason: Liberal Treachery from the Cold War to the War on Terrorism.* New York: Crown Books, 2003.

Goeringer, Conrad. "Dobson Says He'll Bolt From Republican Party." *AANews*, February 13, 1998, <http://www.positiveatheism.org/writ/abimalac.htm>

Lum, Matt. "Texas Delegates Protest Gay Representative: Log Cabins and Republicans Present United Front." *Texas Triangle*, <http://www.txtriangle.com/archive/843/statenews.htm>

Moore, James. *Bush's Brain: How Karl Rove Made George W. Bush Presidential.* New York: John Wiley & Sons, 2003.

Nyhan, Brendan. "Bully Brigade." *Salon.com*, March 5, 2002, <http://www.totalobscurity.com/mind/news/bully-brigade.htm>

Weiser, Carl. "GOP lawmakers' next job: sell the president's policies." Gannett News Service, <http://www.gannettonline.com/gns/bush/state2.html>

SOCIAL SECURITY

Morin, Richard. "Americans Tired of Guessing Social Security's Future." *Washington Post*, May 31, 1999, <http://www.washingtonpost.com/wp-srv/politics/polls/wat/archive/wat053199.htm>

TAXES

ABC News. "Evaluating the IRS: Agency's Image Improves as Audit Rate Declines." ABC News, April 15, 2002, <http://abcnews.go.com/sections/business/Tax2002/taxes_poll_020415.html>

ABC News. "Tax Debate: Bush Tries to Sell Tax Cuts, But Not Everyone's Buying." April 24, 2003, <http://abcnews.go.com/sections/business/WorldNewsTonight/taxcutdebate_030424.html>

Bumiller, Elisabeth. "Bush Makes Tax Cut Pitch to Ohioans." *New York Times*, April 25, 2003.

Firestone, David. "With Tax Cut Bill Passed, Republicans Call for More." *New York Times*, May 24, 2003.

Newsmax.com. "Bush Unveils $670 Billion Plan for Economic Stimulus." January 8, 2003, <http://www.newsmax.com/archives/articles/2003/1/7/175052.shtml>

Krugman, Paul. *The Great Unraveling: Losing Our Way in the New Century.* New York: W.W. Norton & Co., 2003

Peterson, Peter G. *Testimony Before the House Financial Services Committee.* The Concord Coalition, April 30, 2003, <http://www.concordcoalition.org/federal_budget/030430petersontestimonyexecsummary.htm>

2000 ELECTION

Abramowitz, Alben W. "Indecision 2000." *Emory Magazine,* Winter 2001, <http://www.emory.edu/EMORY_MAGAZINE/winter2001/indecision.html>

Associated Press. "Broward County finishes recount." November 25, 2000, <http://quest.cjonline.com/stories/112500/gen_1125004909.shtml>

Baker, James. Interview with Jim Lehrer. *NewsHour with Jim Lehrer,* PBS, November 10, 2000, <http://www.pbs.org/newshour/bb/election/july-dec00/florida_11-10.html>

Barstow, David and Don Van Natta Jr. "Bush focus: Get in overseas votes," *New York Times,* July 15, 2001.

Burgess, Lisa. "IG says military procedures weren't reason why ballots weren't counted." *Stars and Stripes,* June 23, 2001, <http://ww2.pstripes.osd.mil/01/jun01/ed062301u.html>

Campbell, Duncan. "Greens' growing strength threatens to let Bush steal it." *Guardian,* June 28, 2000, <http://www.guardian.co.uk/US_election_race/Story/0,2763,337255,00.html>

CNN. "Bush files fifth suit over absentee ballots." November 26, 2000, <http://www.cnn.com/2000/ALLPOLITICS/stories/11/26/absentee.ballots/ >

———. "Gore loses Miami-Dade appeal; Palm Beach can count 'dimples.'" November 22, 2000, <http://www.cnn.com/2000/ALLPOLITICS/stories/11/22/recount.wrap/>

Fox News. "Gore Criticizes Media for Turning Its Collective Back on Him, Democrats." November 28, 2002, <http://www.foxnews.com/story/0,2933,71633,00.html>

Gibbs, Nancy. "Reversal of Fortune." *Time,* November 20, 2000, <http://www.time.com/time/pacific/magazine/20001120/cover1.html>

Holman, Kwame. "Florida Recount." *NewsHour with Jim Lehrer,* November 27, 2000, <http://www.pbs.org/newshour/bb/election/july-dec00/fl_11-27.html>

Kamen, Al. "Pedaling the 124-Year Cycle," *Washington Post,* December 4, 2000, A25, <http://www.washingtonpost.com/ac2/wp-dyn?pagename=article&node=&contentId=A20070-2000Dec3&notFound=true>

———. "Texas Eye Replanting Lawn." *Washington Post,* December 6, 2000, p. A33, <http://www.washingtonpost.com/ac2/wp-dyn?pagename=article&node=politics/fedpage/columns/intheloop&contentId=A30170-2000Dec5&notFound=true>

Kane, Gary. "If clearly marked 'over-votes' had counted." *Palm Beach Post*, November 12, 2001, <http://www.palmbeachpost.com/news/content/news/overvotes.html>

Kulish, Nicholas and Jim VandeHei. "Election 2000 GOP Protest in Miami-Dade Is a Well-Organized Effort: Bush Campaign Pays Tab For Aides From Capitol Hill Flown in for Rallies." *Wall Street Journal*, November 27, 2000.

Lantigua, John. "Miami's rent-a-riot ." *Salon.com*, <http://dir.salon.com/politics/feature/2000/11/28/miami/index.html>

Nieves, Evelyn. "A Party Crasher's Lone Regret: That He Didn't Get More Votes." *New York Times*, February 18, 2001.

Schechter, Joel. "A Cabinet Post For Nader?," *San Francisco Examiner*, October 9, 2000.

Schmidt, Susan. "GOP Officials Complain About Military Vote Challenges." *Washington Post*, November 19, 2000, A23, <http://www.washingtonpost.com/wp-srv/onpolitics/elections/numbers19.htm>

United States Code, Title 28 (Judiciary and Judicial Procedure, Part IV (Jurisdiction and Venue, Chapter 85 (District Courts; Jurisdiction), Section 1344—Election Disputes), <http://caselaw.lp.findlaw.com/casecode/uscodes/28/parts/iv/chapters/85/sections/section_1344.html>

University of California at Santa Barbara. "Text: Gore Speech on His Florida Challenge," *Election 2000, The Florida Papers*, November 27, 2000, <http://www.presidency.ucsb.edu/docs/florida2000/gore11-27.php>

USA Today, "Chronology of the Florida Recount," May 10, 2001, <http://www.usatoday.com/news/washington/2001-05-10-recountchrono.htm>

VandeHei, Jim. "Democratic Hopefuls Bash Bush in Florida." *Washington Post*, December 7, 2003, A05, <http://www.washingtonpost.com/ac2/wp-dyn/A41917-2003Dec6?language=printer>

Wasserman, Harvey. "The Unelected President." *Columbus Alive*, January 18–24, 2001.

2004 ELECTION

Brooks, David, "Running on Reform," *The New York Times*, January 3, 2004, A15.

Bumiller, Elisabeth, "A Quick California Campaign Swing Adds to Bush's Coffers," *The New York Times*, June 27, 2003.

Hazen, Don, "It's Still the Economy, Stupid," *Alternet.org*, May 16, 2003, <http://www.alternet.org/story.html?StoryID=15917>

Ivins, Molly, "Howard Dean's a Winner," Creators Syndicate, December 20, 2003, <http://www.democrats.us/editorial/ivins120503.shtml>

Milbank, Dana. "In GOP Ratings Game, Dean Runs 2nd to Nobody." *Washington Post*, November 30, 2003, A04, <http://www.washingtonpost.com/ac2/wp-dyn?pagename=article&node=&contentId=A22009-2003Nov29&not Found=true>

Nagourney, Adam. "Worried Democrats See Daunting '04 Hurdles." *New York Times*, August 31, 2003.

Quinnipiac University, "Unnamed Democrat Edges Bush In '04, Quinnipiac University National Poll Finds; Most Americans Are Not Satisfied With Life Today." March 6, 2003, <http://www.quinnipiac.edu/x5010.xml>

Rosenbaum, David E. "Bush Plays It Fast, With Hard Money." *New York Times*, June 29, 2003.

Stevenson, Richard W. "Bush Spending for '04 Tops Any Rival's." *New York Times*, October 22, 2003.

TRADE SANCTIONS

Jagan, Larry. "Do sanctions against Burma work?" BBC News, June 20, 2003, <http://newsvote.bbc.co.uk/mpapps/pagetools/print/news.bbc.co.uk/2/hi/asia-pacific/3006908.stm>

VOTER ATTITUDES

Blanton, Dana. "More Believe In God Than Heaven." Fox News, October 16, 2003, <http://www.foxnews.com/story/0,2933,99945,00.html>

Broder, David S. "Partisan gap is at a high, poll finds," *Washington Post*, November 8, 2003, <http://msnbc.msn.com/id/3403658/>

Dionne Jr., E. J. *Why Americans Hate Politics.* New York: Simon & Schuster, 1992.

Gitlin, Todd. "Aristocracy of the dropouts: Republicans will prevail as long as nonvoters rule America." *Salon.com*, November 3, 1998, <http://www.salon.com/news/1998/11/cov_03news.html>

Hostettler, John. "We Love the Constitution . . . Whatever it Says." October 22, 1997, <http://www.house.gov/hostettler/Issues/Hostettler-issues-1997-10-22-constitution-knowledge.htm>

Institute for Global Ethics. "Poll Shows Voters Want Greater Civility, Ethical Behavior in Campaigns," December 15, 1999, <http://www.globalethics.org/news/cvs.html>

Jackson, Derrick Z. "America is More Divided Than Ever." *Boston Globe*, November 12, 2003, <http://www.commondreams.org/views03/1112-01.htm>

McEvers, Kelly. "Iowa party affiliation on the downturn," Medill News Service, <http://www.yvoteonline.org/noshows1996_poll_partyia.shtml>

Morin, Richard. "The Artful Dodgers." *Washington Post*, June 22, 1998, <http://www.washingtonpost.com/wp-srv/politics/polls/wat/archive/wato62298.htm>

Morris, David, Telis Demos, and Gary Langer. "Party Parity." ABC News, November 4, 2003, <http://abcnews.go.com/sections/us/Politics/poll_party_allegiance031104.html>

Shenk, David. *Data Smog: Surviving the Information Glut*. San Francisco: Harper Publishing, 1998.

Thompson, Ann. "Feeling Safer Now Than Four Years Ago," *Chronwatch.com*, September 22, 2003, <http://www.chronwatch.com/content/content Display.asp?aid=4306>

WAR AGAINST IRAQ

ABC News. "The Plan: Were Neo-Conservatives' 1998 Memos a Blueprint for Iraq War?" *Nightline*, March 10, 2003, <http://abcnews.go.com/sections/nightline/DailyNews/pnac_030310.html>

Abrams, Elliott, et al. *Open Letter to President Clinton*. Project for the New American Century, January 26, 1998, <http://www.newamericancentury.org/iraqclintonletter.htm>

Andrews, Edmund L. and Susan Sachs. "Iraq's Slide Into Lawlessness Squanders Good Will for U.S." *New York Times*, May 18, 2003.

BBC. "In quotes: Iraq WMD report reaction," October 3, 2003, <http://news.bbc.co.uk/2/hi/middle_east/3161032.stm>

———. "Poll suggests world hostile to US," June 16, 2003, <http://news.bbc.co.uk/2/hi/americas/2994924.stm>

———. "US team finds no Iraq WMD," October 3, 2003, <http://news.bbc.co.uk/1/hi/world/middle_east/3157246.stm>

Bush, George W. "Bush endorses Iraq protests," Interview with Sir David Frost, BBC News, November 16, 2003, <http://news.bbc.co.uk/1/hi/programmes/breakfast_with_frost/3274787.stm>

CBS News. "War With Iraq: Americans In No Hurry." October 7, 2002, <http://www.cbsnews.com/stories/2002/10/06/opinion/polls/printable524496.shtml>

Dionne Jr., E. J. "In Search of a War Rationale." *Washington Post*, August 16, 2002, page A25, <http://www.washingtonpost.com/ac2/wp-dyn/A24446-2002Aug15?language=printer>

Fisk, Robert. "Saddam Statue Scene Staged." *Independent* (UK), April 11, 2003, <http://www.twf.org/News/Y2003/0411-Statue.html>

Fox News. "Democrat Lawmakers Defend Iraq Visit." October 3, 2002, <http://www.foxnews.com/story/0,2933,64657,00.html>

McDonough, Challiss. "Iraq Correspondent Report." Voice of America, December 13, 2003, <http://www.globalsecurity.org/military/library/news/2003/12/mil-031213-32e724a1.htm>

McManus, Doyle. "U.S. Future in Iraq a Growing Concern." *Los Angeles Times*, November 21, 2003, <http://www.latimes.com/news/custom/timespoll/la-na-iraqpoll21nov21,1,7443843.story?coll=la-news-times_poll>

Noah, Timothy. "Gaslighting the press about nation-building . . . again." *Slate.com*, February 28, 2003, <http://slate.msn.com/id/2079496/>

Risen, James and Judith Miller. "No Illicit Arms Found in Iraq, U.S. Inspector Tells Congress." *New York Times*, October 3, 2003.

Sanger, David E. "A reckoning for Bush over Iraq weapons claims." *New York Times*, October 4, 2003.

Woodward, Bob. *Bush at War.* New York: Simon & Schuster, 2002.

WAR ON TERROR

BBC. "US defends Guantanamo policy." October 10, 2003, <http://news.bbc.co.uk/1/low/world/americas/3182346.stm>

Bush, George W. "Remarks by the President at the 20th Anniversary of the National Endowment for Democracy." United States Chamber of Commerce, Washington, D.C., November 6, 2003, <http://www.whitehouse.gov/news/releases/2003/11/20031106-2.html>

Donovan, Jeffrey. "U.S. State Department Releases Human Rights Report Criticizing New Allies." *EurasiaNet.org*, March 6, 2002, <http://www.eurasianet.org/departments/rights/articles/eav030602.shtml>

Falk, Pamela. "Why Care About Guantánamo?" CBS News, July 3, 2003, <http://www.cbsnews.com/stories/2003/07/03/opinion/printable561712.shtml>

Falk, Richard A. *The Great Terror War.* Olive Branch Press, 2002.

———. "Why International Law Matters." *Nation*, March 10, 2003.

Ferguson, Niall. *Empire: The Rise and Demise of the British World Order and the Lessons for Global Power.* New York: Basic Books, 2003.

Greenway, H. D. S. "Will the US one day regret its post-9/11 excesses?" *Boston Globe*, October 17, 2003, <http://www.boston.com/news/globe/editorial_opinion/oped/articles/2003/10/17/will_the_us_one_day_regret_its_post_911_excesses/>

Gwyn, Richard. "An Image of U.S. Lawlessness (A Canadian's View)." *Toronto Star*, November 30, 2003.

Hartmann, Thom. "How An Earlier 'Patriot Act' Law Brought Down A President." *CommonDreams.org*, June 16, 2003, <http://www.commondreams.org/views03/0616-03.htm>

Johnson, Chalmers. *The Sorrows of Empire.* New York: Henry Holt and Company, 2004.

Kirkland, Michael. "High court to hear Guantánamo challenges." United Press International, *Washington Times*, November 10, 2003, <http://washingtontimes.com/upi-breaking/20031110-102010-9141r.htm>

Ledeen, Michael A."Nothing to lose but their chains." *Spectator*, November 22, 2003, <http://www.spectator.co.uk/article.php3?table=old&section=current&issue=2003-11-22&id=3755 >

Ledeen, Michael A. *The War Against the Terror Masters.* New York: St. Martin's Press, 2003.

Lewis, Neil A. "Detainees From the Afghan War Remain in a Legal Limbo in Cuba." *New York Times*, April 24, 2003.

———. "Red Cross Criticizes Indefinite Detention In Guantánamo Bay." *New York Times*, October 10, 2003.

Montini, E. J. "An ex-POW can correct mistakes at Guantanamo." *Arizona Republic*, December 7, 2003, <http://www.azcentral.com/arizonarepublic/local/articles/1207montini07.html>

National Security Council. *The National Security Strategy of the United States of America.* The White House, September 17, 2002, <http://www.whitehouse.gov/nsc/nss.html>

Neiwert, David. "Tracking Fascism." *Cursor*, <http://www.cursor.org/stories/fascismiv.php>

Podesta, John. "USA Patriot Act: The Good, the Bad and the Sunset." *American Bar Association*, Winter 2002, <http://www.abanet.org/irr/hr/winter02/podesta.html>

Priniotakis, Manolis. "China's Designated Terrorists." *American Prospect*, October 19, 2001, <http://www.prospect.org/webfeatures/2001/10/priniotakis-m-10-19.html>

Sanger, David E. and Judith Miller, "Libya To Give Up Arms Programs, Bush Announces," *New York Times*, December 20, 2003, A1.

Sullivan, Andrew. "Flypaper: A Strategy Unfolds." September 6, 2003, <http://www.andrewsullivan.com/main_article.php?artnum=20030906>

Vidal, Gore. *Dreaming War.* New York: Thunder's Mouth Press, 2002.

WORK

Bovard, James. "How Fair Are the Fair Labor Standards?" Cato Institute, adapted from *Lost Rights: The Destruction of American Liberty.* New York: St. Martin's Press, 1994.

Brinson, Claudia Smith. "All work, no play." *The State*, June 10, 2003, <http://www.thestate.com/mld/thestate/living/columnists/6049680.htm>

Ehrenreich, Barbara. *Nickel and Dimed: On (Not) Getting By in America.* New York: Metropolitan Books, 2001.

Greenhouse, Steven. "Unions to Push to Make Organizing Easier." *New York Times*, August 31, 2003.

Hixson, Hal. "Seeds of Poverty & Forests of Wealth." *Clamor*, Issue 7, <http://www.clamormagazine.org/features/issue7_feature.html>

Kibbe, Matthew B.,"The Minimum Wage: Washington's Perennial Myth." Cato Institute, May 23, 1998, <http://www.cato.org/pubs/pas/pa106.html>

Merkle, Daniel. "Wage Hike Remains Popular." ABC News, October 6, 1999, <http://more.abcnews.go.com/sections/politics/DailyNews/poll991006.html>

Reich, Robert B. "A National Minimum Vacation." *American Prospect*, August 13, 2003, <http://www.prospect.org/webfeatures/2003/08/reich-r-08-13.html>

Robinson, Joe. *Work to Live: The Guide to Getting a Life*. New York: Perigree, 2003.

Schor, Juliet B. *The Overworked American: The Unexpected Decline of Leisure*. New York: Basic Books, 1993 Reprint Edition.

Shulman, Beth. *The Betrayal of Work: How Low-Wage Jobs Fail 30 Million Americans*. New York: New Press, 2003.

ACKNOWLEDGEMENTS

Thanks to Richard Nash of Soft Skull for a superb job as editor and his enthusiastic support of this book. Sarah Groff-Palermo applied her unparalleled knowledge and love of the English language as the best copy editor I've ever met. I bounced ideas off my friends Ted Keller, Randall Lane, and Cole Smithey. My wife, Judy, who served as a faithful unpaid editor, never complained while I squandered many weekends and part of our vacation in Italy making this book happen. Edith Holsinger, my teacher, mentor, and model Democrat when I was growing up, helped shaped my views of the two-party system and the role of liberalism in America. My mom, Yvonne Rall, whose fierce sense of right and wrong I've struggled to emulate, convinced me of the need for a book of this type. During the last few years of her long, interesting, and important life, my agent Toni Mendez encouraged this project as only she could. Toni, here's to you; I hope I did well.

Ted Rall grew up in Kettering, Ohio, and graduated from Columbia University with honors in history. He began working for local and national political campaigns during the mid-1970s, culminating with Walter Mondale's 1984 attempt to unseat President Reagan. He worked as a trader-trainee at Bear Stearns and as a loan officer for the Industrial Bank of Japan from 1985 to 1990.

During the 1990s, he became one of America's best-known editorial cartoonists and political writers. After working as a contributing editor and staff writer for *Might* and *P.O.V.* magazines, his work began running in *Time, Fortune, Esquire,* and *Newsweek* magazines, as well as such newspapers as the *New York Times, Los Angeles Times, San Francisco Chronicle, Chicago Tribune,* and *Village Voice.* He was a 1996 Pulitzer Prize finalist as well as the winner of the Robert F. Kennedy Journalism Award in both 1995 and 2000.

Rall's work is equally praised by its admirers and decried by detractors. The *Washington Post* called his award-winning graphic travelogue, *To Afghanistan and Back,* the best coverage by any American journalist about the U.S. war against the Taliban. Former Republican presidential candidate Alan Keyes has called for Rall to be jailed, censored, or possibly shot.

Rall lives in New York City.